James Andanson—Sygma

Soldiers of the People's Liberation Army on parade: No longer the fastest route to power, privilege and prestige

Hard Times for China's Army

While Mao Tse-tung was alive, a post in the Chinese People's Liberation Army was a fast route to power, prestige and privilege. No longer. Deng Xiaoping has trimmed the military's budget, weeded its ranks, reduced its perquisites and checked its political influence. And in contrast to the days when all China was instructed to "learn from the PLA," officers and men have been directed to "adjust" their thinking. "Those that have opinions or suggestions may submit them to the leadership," political commissar Wei Guoqing told a recent PLA conference. But, he added, "there must be no expression of opposition whatsoever in their actions."

Not surprisingly, army morale has plummeted. The troops are grumbling about Deng's policies, and officials admit that PLA enlistments have dropped off sharply. Much of the problem springs from cutbacks in benefits such as army home leave and elimination of the automatic bonuses army families in rural areas received when a son or husband joined the PLA.

Dissent: This year, China reduced the defense budget by $4.2 billion as part of the government's effort to erase its deficit. Military leaders find the cutbacks hard to accept. The army hierarchy worries that budget slashes will soon leave the PLA short of equipment. And PLA officers are concerned about law and order; by abandoning many Maoist tenets, they say, Deng

is paving the way for dissent and disunity. "We hope that the state increases by an appropriate amount the national-defense budget to speed up the process of modernizing our defense capability," said Gen. Yang Dezhi, Armed Forces Chief of Staff. "Of course," he added—somewhat enigmatically—"we cannot just sit and wait."

The Chinese press is full of pointed reminders that good soldiers follow Communist Party orders unswervingly. "If we fail

---

After years of riding high, the PLA now finds itself short of money, materiel— and political influence.

---

to do this, we might even blunder during war," Liberation Army Daily warned not long ago. The government has announced plans to require soldiers to swear a four-part oath of loyalty to the party leadership, and it has dusted off the cult of Lei Feng, a 1960s "soldier hero" who won fame for his selfless, obedient behavior—and for his willingness to darn his own socks. At the other extreme, the People's Daily took the unusual step of telling stories about a former

official—Mao's discredited Defense Minister, the late Lin Biao. According to the paper, Lin was a hopeless drug addict who could not kick the habit although Mao put his personal physician on the case. Finally, Lin led an abortive coup against Mao and died in disgrace. Deng, obviously, wants to avoid such troubles. To keep discipline tight, Deng recently installed a fellow reformist, 72-year-old Geng Biao, as China's new Defense Minister.

Given the primitive state of China's economy, Deng believes that the armed forces do not deserve priority over agricultural and industrial development. Yet as the 1979 Sino-Vietnamese war proved all too graphically, the PLA is in grave need of modernization. Troops with limited education must give way to men with higher skills; equipment designed decades ago must be replaced with weapons more suitable for the 1980s. By eliminating some of the PLA's privileges, Deng hopes to produce a leaner, more professional force. And by directing much of China's tight military budget toward research and development, he is aiming for some state-of-the-art weaponry a few years hence. "Relations between the military and the government are not as congenial as before," PLA Chief of Staff Yang Dezhi confessed recently. If Deng holds course, they could get even frostier.

FAY WILLEY with MELINDA LIU in Peking

THE CHINESE WAR MACHINE

A technical analysis of the strategy and weapons of the People's Republic of China

THE CHINESE WAR MACHINE

A technical analysis of the strategy and weapons of the People's Republic of China

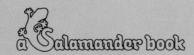

Published by Salamander Books Limited
LONDON

A SALAMANDER BOOK

Published by Salamander Books Ltd.,
Salamander House,
27 Old Gloucester Street,
London WC1N 3AF,
United Kingdom.

©Salamander Books Ltd. 1979

ISBN 0 86101 041 8

Distributed in the UK by New English Library Ltd.

Distributed in Australia/New Zealand by Summit Books, a division of
Paul Hamlyn Pty Ltd., Sydney, Australia.

All correspondence concerning the content of this volume should be
addressed to Salamander Books Ltd.

EDITOR'S ACKNOWLEDGMENTS

In the process of preparing this timely volume for publication I have been
fortunate in having received the help and advice of very many people and
organizations. It is not possible to mention them all here, but I do thank
them for their assistance.

It is with great sadness that I report the tragic death, early in 1979, of
Dr James E. Dornan, Jr., who gave me much inspiration and advice during
the early stages of planning this book. Dr Dornan was a recognized
authority on international relations, military strategy and Asian affairs. He
was much in demand as a speaker, lecturer and advisor, besides being the
author of some 60 articles and monographs and contributor to many
books and other publications dealing with international politics and
foreign policy; many of his studies were classified as secret. His work, his
energy and vitality, and his friendly, irrepressible wit and humour made a
lasting mark on individuals and institutions close to him and far outside
his native United States.

I am particularly grateful for all the efforts of, and support from Nigel de
Lee, of RMA Sandhurst, Colonel William V. Kennedy of the US Army War
College, Mr Fang Wen, Military, Naval and Air Attache of The People's
Republic of China at the Embassy in London, Mr Lu Yunxiang of Hsinhua
New China News Agency, the staff of the United States Naval Institute, the
US Library of Congress, the US Defense Intelligence Agency and other
United States Government organizations and agencies, David Miller,
Eugene Kolesnik and Ms Kate Spells.

Ray Bonds

CREDITS

Editor: Ray Bonds
Designer: Lloyd Martin

Drawings by Martin Alton (©Salamander Books Ltd.)
Maps by Richard Natkiel (©Salamander Books Ltd.)
Filmset by Modern Text Ltd., England.
Colour reproductions: Process Colour Centre Ltd., Tenreck Ltd. and
Colourcraftsmen Ltd.
Printed in Belgium by Henri Proost et Cie, Turnhout.

THE CONSULTANTS

Dr James E. Dornan, Jr. Before his death in 1979, Dr Dornan was Associate Professor and Chairman, Department of Politics, Catholic University of America, and Senior Political Science Scientist at the Strategic Studies Center of Stanford Research Institute International. He was a contributor to Salamander's previous titles, *The Soviet War Machine* and *The US War Machine* (for which he was also consultant).

Nigel de Lee is a Senior Lecturer in International Affairs at the Royal Military Academy, Sandhurst. He has an MA in War Studies from King's College, London University, and also attended the University of Leeds where he wrote History, including Chinese History.

THE AUTHORS

Bill Gunston is an internationally respected author on scientific and aviation subjects, having contributed to very many technical defence publications. Among his numerous books are the Salamander titles *The Illustrated Encyclopedia of the World's Modern Military Aircraft, The Encyclopedia of the World's Combat Aircraft* and *The Illustrated Encyclopedia of the World's Rockets and Missiles.* He is also co-author of Salamander's *Soviet Air Power,* and a contributor to their *The US War Machine* and *The Soviet War Machine.* He is former Technical Editor of *Flight International,* and is an assistant compiler of *Jane's All The World's Aircraft.*

Professor Harold C. Hinton is Professor of Political Science and International Affairs, The George Washington University, Washington, D.C. He has held consultantships with the US Department of State, the US Information Agency, the Rand Corporation, Stanford Research Institute and Research Analysis Corporation; he has had lectureships at numerous educational establishments, including the US Defense Intelligence School, the US National War College, and at Oxford University, and has been a speaker at many international conferences on arms control and international affairs (particularly Sino-Soviet and Sino-American relations). His many authoritative publications include *The Sino-Soviet Confrontation and the Future; Peking-Washington: China's Foreign Policy and the United States; and China's Turbulent Quest: An Analysis of China's Foreign Relations Since 1949.*

Colonel William V. Kennedy, Armor, US Army Reserve, has been a Strategic Research Analyst with the US Army War College Strategic Studies Institute since 1967, with Northeast Asia as his prime area of study. He has made several visits to Northeast Asia, concerned primarily with

aspects of the Sino-Soviet conflict. His military service has included active, National Guard and Reserve status continuously since 1946. He has served on active duty with the US Army in Japan and China, with the US Air Force Strategic Air Command in the United States and United Kingdom, among other assignments. He has had many articles on defence and international affairs published in authoritative technical journals.

Hugh Lyon, former Research Officer of the Shipbuilding Record Survey, London, is a founder-member of the Warships Society, and a contributor to many leading international defence periodicals. He contributed to the previous Salamander title, *The US War Machine* and is the author of their *The Encyclopedia of the World's Warships.*

Professor Harvey W. Nelsen is Associate Professor in the International Studies Program at the University of South Florida. He holds a doctorate in modern Chinese history from The George Washington University and has published numerous articles in the field of contemporary Chinese military affairs. He is the author of the excellent reference work, *The Chinese Military System: An Organizational Study of the Chinese People's Liberation Army* (Westview Press).

Bill Sweetman was a member of the editorial staff of the authoritative technical *Flight International* and has established an international reputation for his detailed, objective analyses of the Air Forces of the Communist powers. He is co-author of the Salamander titles, *Air Forces of the World* and *Soviet Air Power,* and has contributed technical articles on aviation subjects to several technical publications, including *Aeroplane Monthly* and *Middle East Economic Digest,* and has broadcast on BBC radio on a number of occasions.

CONTENTS

FOREWORD
by Brigadier Kenneth Hunt, OBE, MC.

Brigadier Hunt is Specialist Advisor to the Defence and External Affairs Sub-committee of the United Kingdom House of Commons, and is Director of the British Atlantic Committee. He was formerly a research associate and Deputy Director of the International Institute for Strategic Studies (IISS).

Power, said Chairman Mao, grows out of the barrel of a gun. The Chinese Red Army, the forerunner of the present People's Liberation Army (PLA), was built so that he could seize that power and with it establish the People's Republic of China. The PLA was thus not only present at the creation, it enabled it to happen. Politics and military activity were inseparable and so the PLA was involved in politics and became powerful. While now firmly subordinate to the Communist Party its influence remains strong. Teng Hsiao-ping, the Deputy Premier, is also Chief of Staff of the PLA and owes much to its protection for his return to power.

The PLA is, of course, huge, outnumbering even the Soviet forces. But numbers by themselves can be misleading. The weapons are old and on rudimentary scales, serviceable but of 1950s designs. The ground forces (the PLA includes army, navy and air force) are largely foot infantry. There is little armour or mechanization and logistics are minimal away from the railways. Aircraft are completely outmatched by those of the Soviet forces which face them, and indeed often by smaller neighbours as well. While the army may be adequate to some of its tasks, particularly in rugged or close country, the air force could hardly survive in modern combat. The navy is an inshore force, reliant largely on numbers.

It is said that generals always prepare to fight the last war. There may well be truth in that adage in China, where generals are much older than their Western counterparts, with experience going back to the Civil War of the 1930s and 1940s and to the Korean War. The equipment they have to work with, their command and control machinery, their communications, all fit the 1950s. In Korea in 1951 the Chinese forces suffered immense casualties using human wave tactics against United Nations fire power. That experience led to their being re-equipped with comparable Soviet-supplied weapons but training and tactics have hardly changed since then, while the armies of the rest of the world and particularly of the Soviet Union have moved on. The policy of self-reliance instituted after the break with the Soviet Union, and periodic political turmoil, imposed handicaps that cut the PLA off from modern military thought and weapons designs.

Just how good the PLA is now is hard to assess. Individual and small unit training seems good, within the limits set by old equipment. Men look impressively fit and motivated, and apparently content with their spartan life, which no doubt compares favourably with that of the countryside from which most of them come. Only part of their time is spent on military training—farming and political indoctrination taking up much of it. The recent war in Vietnam has told us very little. All the hard information we have is that Chinese forces reached a certain line. Whether they tried to go further and couldn't, whether they had difficulty in getting that far or in staying there, what casualties they suffered, what methods they used — none of these things is yet known. But the weaknesses inherent in their equipment limitations are clear enough and freely admitted by Chinese officers.

The strategy that has been adopted in the face of these weaknesses and for which much has been claimed, is that of People's War, coupled at the other extreme with the development of nuclear weapons. People's War is designed to take advantage of the vast size of the country and the rugged nature of much of it, and of the huge numbers not only of the PLA but of the militia that backs them. It is a strategy that would give ground, draw an invader in and then drown him in a sea of people. Nuclear weapons play no part in this but are there to deter nuclear attack by the Soviet Union.

It is, of course, the Soviet Union that is seen as the threat, as well it might be, given the size of the Soviet forces along the Chinese border. The task of the PLA is therefore to contain Soviet forces, but is People's War suitable for this? The answer is almost certainly not, since any Soviet threat would be not of deep invasion of China but of seizure of parts of it, Sinkiang and Manchuria most obviously. Sinkiang is not easily defensible and being sparsely populated does not lend itself to People's War tactics — there are no people to give support, no sea for the guerrilla fish to swim in, in Mao's words. Manchuria, important to China for its resources but to the Soviet Union as a potential buffer zone for her Eastern Siberian cities, is vulnerable to attack from two sides and could quickly be cut into two. A battle there could be dominated by Soviet armour and air power. People's War has no relevance in such circumstances.

The Chinese leadership is certainly aware of this and seeks to modernize the PLA to take account of it. The weapons the PLA presently has are those that China can build, not those that are needed, and so the policy of self-reliance is being abandoned and foreign military technology being sought. But the quantities involved are huge and the time it would take to modernize made much longer by the Chinese wish to buy the technology and build the weapons herself, mainly so as not to be dependent on outside sources again — the memory of dependence on the Soviet Union is a bitter one. While some weapons would be bought to fill immediate needs, re-equipment on any scale would take years to start and a decade to have significant effect. For the air force in particular a quantum jump in technology is involved, notably in the field of electronics. And the Soviet forces would naturally not be standing still all this time. The gap would be narrowed, not closed.

This book gives a great deal of information about all this that is not easily available elsewhere in such detail or so comprehensively. The chapter on history of the armed forces describes their origins, their formative experience and the politics that have also played a part in shaping them. There is discussion of organizations and equipments and an analysis of Chinese strategic thinking. The picture presented is a fascinating one, of forces about which the outside world knows all too little. What happens to them next depends on the course of internal political developments, probably no more predictable now than they have proved to be in the past. Yet there can be no real modernization of the forces or of the industry that must support them, unless there is a measure of internal stability. The Cultural Revolution disrupted education in schools and universities for some ten years, and that impediment must be overcome if new methods and new technologies are to take root. China is a very backward country. There is a heavy price for self-imposed isolation and upheaval still to be paid.

Some readers may not agree with the view expressed in this book that war between the Soviet Union and China is inevitable, though China herself seems to fear this. And some may not accept the thesis that Chinese nuclear weapons have no military value, that the deterrent is "a figment of Western imagination." There are some strong views expressed but they may lead the reader to question his own assumptions. There is information and analysis here that will enable him to reach his own judgments, however tentative they may be.

East Asia and the Pacific basin is a region of fast growing importance, political and economic. For a time after the Vietnam War it seemed that the broad lines of influence here had been set, but with a newly aggressive Vietnam and a Soviet Union seeking a place in Southeast Asia, things are fluid once again. In the policies of all the states in the area China looms large, her sheer, overhanging mass exercising fascination and her unpredictability causing concern. Chinese military power now seems set to grow, to measure itself against that of the Soviet Union and to have to live in a world in which even small powers can have access to advanced weapons. This book is an admirable guide to what that power now is and the problems the Chinese armed forces may have to face in the future.

Kenneth Hunt

Nigel de Lee

Senior Lecturer in International Affairs, Royal Military Academy, Sandhurst

Center ? in green: Mao Tse-Tung
Left, in white: Chou En-lai

Red Army troops on the march, led by the Communist Party, helped by the peasantry. The PLA is the first Army in China to achieve genuine and sustained popularity. Mao said that only an army firmly united to the people could be successful and politically reliable. Note that Mao is wearing the uniform of a regular soldier and carries a peasant's straw hat to emphasize this point. The uniform and arms of the troops show that the picture represents the Red Army during the Civil War of 1945-9. The peasants gave logistic support as porters, and some fought, with crude weapons such as spears. Young boys in the "Pioneers" acted as messengers and often carried swords. The absence of any weapons heavier than machine-guns is significant. Animals are still in extensive use.

The long tradition of peasant rebellion, foreign revolutionary ideas, the experience of invasion and the genius of Mao Tse-tung have moulded the character of the PLA. Today, developments in technology and the international balance of political and strategic relations are imposing changes on the Red Army of China. As always, conservatism and rigid ideology contend with pragmatism and new ideas, but the powerful will to survive and win remains constant.

1. *Sun Yat-sen, 1867-1925, founder of the Kuomintang, first President of China, philosopher and statesman. He is respected by the communists as a progressive, and his widow became a member of the Central Committee. Sun made the KMT a popular move-ment with an ideology based on three principles; democracy, nationalism, and Socio-economic reform. His death deprived the KMT of real political leadership. His principles, except for nationalism, were neglected and the KMT became corrupt, militarist, and oppressive.*
2. *Sun at a ceremony to mark the death of Lenin in 1924. Sun admired Soviet forms of organization and was happy to accept Russian advice and did, but rejected Bolshevik policy as inappropriate to Chinese needs and conditions.*
3. *Chinese soldiers at the time of the Sino-Japanese War of 1894-5. This war, fought for control of Korea, ended in a humiliating defeat for China and led to an expansion of Japanese influence in Manchuria. The Imperial*

Properly constituted states first appeared in China in the period of the Shang dynasty, 1450-1054 BC. Until 581 AD, the country alternated between periods of unity and periods of violent disorder. Meanwhile, two of the basic foundations of Imperial China, the Confucian ideology, and a strong civil service were developing. In 581 China was united by the Sui dynasty, and remained united until the collapse of the last dynasty, the Ch'ing, in 1911. Dynasties rose and fell, but the essential characteristics of Chinese civilization and government were unchanged. Foreign invaders and conquerors, the Mongols of the thirteenth century and the Manchus of the seventeenth, were absorbed and sinicized.

By the eighth century AD, Confucianism had become the official ideology of China. The country was ruled by a civil bureaucracy recruited from students of the Confucian classics. After Mencius' interpretation of Confucian writings was accepted as definitive in the twelfth century, the ideology developed no further. Confucian scholars and officials considered that the ideology, society and government of China had achieved perfection, so change could only be for the worse. The ideal of Confucian society was tranquillity. In consequence, Chinese society became deeply conservative. The political classes were suspicious of innovation or activism. They were hostile to commerce and military activity; merchants were regarded as parasites who profited from the work of others; soldiers were regarded as destroyers of life and wealth. The only decent occupations were administration, study and agriculture.

The authorities depended upon personal example, moral exhortation and voluntary cooperation, rather than upon law or force, to execute policy. The normal foreign policy was one of isolation. Foreigners were regarded as culturally inferior, and as possible sources of disturbance or ideological contamination. If possible they were to be kept out of China, controlled by bribes or contained by military force.

Despite the official policy, Chinese society changed gradually over the centuries; but because it was the exponent of conservatism and tranquillity, the bureaucracy was unable to adapt to the changes. An imperceptible inflation gradually impoverished the official classes, who were unable to increase their salaries as they were expected to set an example of frugality and self-restraint. In due course poverty gave rise to corruption and degeneracy amongst officials. Malpractice led to discontent amongst the peasantry and townsfolk, made evident by the activities of numerous secret societies and occasional local rebellions.

Massive rebellion, foreign aggression

By the beginning of the 19th century the bureaucracy was degenerate and discredited in many areas of China. The traditional form of government and society was proved inadequate when tested by new immediate and direct threats stemming from massive rebellion and foreign aggression. The great rebellions of the nineteenth century did enormous damage to the economic and political structure of the Chinese empire. The central government was impoverished and undermined. The treasury was emptied, and provincial warlords, leaders of the armies raised to suppress the T'ai P'ings and other rebels, emerged to challenge the power of the imperial authorities. The weakness and disunity were increased and exploited by foreign powers; in particular by Britain, France, the United States and Russia, and, later on, Japan. Between 1840 and 1860 Britain and France fought three wars against China. These wars settled questions of diplomatic status, legal jurisdiction, commerce, rights of entry to the interior of China, the position of missionaries, and the trade in opium. By 1860 Britain and France had broken the traditional Chinese foreign policy of isolationism. They had forced the Chinese to deal with foreign governments as equals, and to open up China to trade, missionaries, travellers and opium. They had also fatally weakened the authority of the Ch'ing government. Once Chinese weaknesses had been revealed, the Russians increased their diplomatic and military pressure on the landward frontiers of China, and exacted many territorial concessions. In the 1870s the Japanese began to bully China. They contested and even-

government was further weakened by its failure. A nationalist movement emerged based on hostility to the Japanese expansionism and to the Manchus for their incompetence. In this war many Chinese soldiers were armed with crossbows, pikes, swords, and other antique weapons.

4. *Ting Pi-wu, one of the founders of the Chinese Communist Party At the outset the party consisted mainly of intellectuals. Early attempts to emulate the Bolsheviks and recruit a mass membership from urban factory workers had little success.*

5. *Chu-Teh, 1886-1976, was born the son of a peasant. In his early life he served as an officer in the army of the warlord of Yunnan. Later he became a patriotic radical and joined the Communist Party. He and Mao and Ho Tung founded the Red Army in 1927. Eventually, as a Marshall of China, he commanded the largest army in the world. He remained as Commander-in-Chief of the PLA until he died in 1976.*

3

4

5

1. *Mao Tse-tung in 1927, a young revolutionary at an early stage in his career of violent struggle and political activism. He was born the son of a rich peasant in December 1893. In 1911 he took part in the Nationalist uprising in Changsha as a soldier. From 1913 until 1918 he attended teacher training college, where he showed a particular bent for history, geography, philosophy and politics. He became a socialist and a patriot, but appreciated the realpolitik of such statesmen as Bismarck. He was active in radical politics and journalism and involved in the patriotic resistance to foreign influence. In 1919 he was interested in anarchism, but in Spring 1920 he became an enthusiastic Marxist, and in July 1921 he was at the meeting which created the Chinese Communist Party. Mao at once set to work to attempt to politicise and organize industrial workers in Kiangsi, but was soon disillusioned. In 1923 fear of arrest forced him to flee and he went to Shanghai. In June Mao was elected to the Central Committee. He went back to*

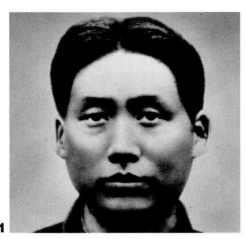

Hunan and began to organize the peasants. In 1926 he was made head of the Peasant Department of the Communist Party. He was convinced that the active support of the peasants was vital to the success of revolution in China. A Peasant Association was formed, led by Mao, and in 1926 it began to confiscate land. In 1927 he took part in the armed uprising at Nanchang, which was led by Chou En-lai (2). Mao led a force of peasants, miners, and defectors from warlord and KMT formations to support the revolt 3 On the failure of the uprising Mao gathered a force of 1,000 survivors at Sanwan under the banner of the 1st regiment of the 1st division of the 1st Workers and Peasants Army

4 A memorial hall in Nanchang marks the birthplace of the Red Army.

5. The remnants of the Red forces, pressed by enemy pursuit, fled into the wilderness of Ching-kangshan. Here Mao conducted experiments in civil-military relations to create a revolutionary base with the support of the rural population.

5

1. *Chou En-lai, colleague, critic and friend of Mao. He was born in 1899 to educated parents. He studied the classics in Peking and acquired a knowledge of modern subjects later in Japan. In 1919 he was involved in the patriotic May 4th Movement. While studying in* *Paris, 1920-1924 he set up the French branch of the Chinese Communist Party and recruited Chu Teh into the movement. Upon returning to China he joined the KMT and eventually he was Director of Political Training at the Whampoa Military Academy, the* *KMT officer training school. After Chiang's purge of communist members from the KMT In 1927 he became head of the Military Department of the CP Central Committee. He commanded the Red Forces in the unsuccessful "Autumn Harvest" uprising at* *Nanchang, then fled to Moscow where he studied revolutionary politics under Soviet guidance. Chou returned from the U.S.S.R. in time to go on the Long March. In the North Shensi Soviet he was a vigorous and able member of the ming elite. He was more*

tually eliminated Chinese control in Taiwan and Korea, and came into conflict with the Russians for a sphere of influence in Northeast China.

The Manchu government first responded to these foreign onslaughts by an attempt to return to the past, to revive and reinforce ancient ideas, practices and institutions. Science, nationalism and reformism were regarded as part of the degeneracy that had made China vulnerable to internal disorder and foreign pressure. When it became clear that such a reactionary policy could not succeed in strengthening China, the imperial authorities reluctantly planned certain constitutional, economic and military reforms. But they acted too late; during the last two decades of the nineteenth century the government, enfeebled and discredited by successful foreign intimidation, had lost control of the country. Most of China was ruled from day to day by warlords; provincial governors who were prepared to compromise with foreign powers and accept new and alien ideas if they could thereby increase their own wealth and military power. Meanwhile, nationalism expressed mainly in terms of xeno-

phobia, and reformism, became popular movements. The warlords ignored the Peking government; the nationalists and reformists planned to capture and transform it.

Empire overthrown: KMT faces warlords

In 1911 the Manchu government attempted to take direct control of the Chinese railway network. This attempt brought them into conflict with several cliques of warlords. On 10 October 1911 the Empire was overthrown by a *coup d'état* led by Yuan Shih-K'ai supported by a popular nationalist movement. At once China fell into political chaos. In Northern, Central and Western China cliques of warlords formed, each intriguing and struggling to increase it's own power. Some warlords, including Yuan Shih-K'ai aspired to unite China by force and found a new imperial dynasty. Others simply wanted to establish themselves in power over provinces or regions. All seemed to be selfish, unprincipled and disloyal. The inherent instability and

inefficiency of the warlords and their cliques, coupled with foreign intervention, prevented any of them from establishing an effective central government.

In Southern China a republic was proclaimed on the fall of the Manchus, and Dr Sun Yat-Sen, leader of the Kuomintang (KMT), was elected President. His intention was to reform and modernise China so as to produce a strong parliamentary democracy, free of foreign domination, with society based upon a stable mass of peasant proprietors. Attempts to cooperate with Yuan Shih-K'ai, and to influence his policy, failed because although Yuan believed that modernisation was necessary, he was hostile to the idea of democracy and was inclined to make concessions to the Japanese rather than lead resistance to them. The KMT leaders became convinced that they must destroy or subjugate the warlords by revolutionary violence before they could unite and reform China. In 1917 Sun Yat-Sen was impressed by the success of the Bolshevik revolution, and promptly adopted Bolshevik forms of organization and revolutionary methods. With Soviet advice, he formed a KMT Army to crush the warlords.

widely travelled and sophisticated than Mao, so better suited to handling delicate political and diplomatic negotiations.
2. In 1936 he flew from Yenan to Sian to persuade the KMT leaders not to launch an attack on the Soviet. He was successful and managed to induce Chiang Kai-shek to agree to the formation of a new United Front against the Japanese. Chou remained in the political and military élite group until he died. As premier of the People's Republic he survived the storms of the Great Leap Forward, 1956-9 and the Great Proletarian Cultural Revolution of 1965-9. After 1971 he was regarded as the natural successor to Mao and his death in 1976 before Mao, called the succession into question.
3. Mao in North Shensi, wearing the uniform of a regular soldier of the Red Army. By the time the Soviet in North Shensi had been established Mao was in undisputed control of the Communist Party and, through the doctrine "politics come first", in control of the Red Army.

3

1. *Chu Teh at the end of the Long March to North Shensi. On arrival he and Mao laboured to reorganize the Red Army into a force fit to resist expected attacks by KMT, warlord, and Japanese troops.*
2. *The best trained and equipped*

soldiers of the Soviet, like the men of the 15th corps, were formed into some 7 divisions and given the task of defending the base area. Other troops were sent out into the countryside beyond the Soviet to operate on an irregular basis and to train peasant recruits.

3. *The Long March had, and still has, great impact on the Red Army. Between 1934 and 1936 Red Soldiers from a number of Soviets in Southern and Central China moved thousands of miles across some of the most desolate and inhospitable terrain in China.*

They crossed rivers, mountain ranges and swamps in the face of enemy action, thirst, starvation, and a punitive shortage of boots. Many died on the way. By natural selection those who got to North Shensi were tough, resolute and dedicated. The March ensured the

The Communist Party of China (CPC) was formed in July 1921 by a dozen radical intellectuals inspired by patriotic and marxist ideas. The party was very small and had no military strength. On advice from Moscow, the communists formed a United Front with the KMT in 1923. Their policy was to support the progressive bourgeoisie of the KMT against the reactionary feudal warlords. At the same time they would recruit within the KMT, and infiltrate its governing bodies, so as to move its policy to the left. The communists were allowed to join the KMT as individual members, and within the left wing their cause prospered. But in 1925 and 1926 the position of the communists and the United Front were undermined, first by the death of Sun Yat-Sen in March 1925, and then by Chiang K'ai-Shek's successful military coup to seize power within the KMT in March 1926. Chiang was more suspicious and intolerant of the communists than Sun had been.

Chiang's purge on the KMT communists

In July 1926 the KMT Army, some 100,000 strong, commenced the Northern Expedition, a strategic offensive intended to destroy the central and northern warlords and unite China by force. As the KMT Army advanced, the communists were active in the rear areas, organizing the peasantry. They spread marxist ideas and gained popularity by attacks on landlords and moneylenders. By the Spring of 1927 Chiang was exasperated by the political activities of the communists and decided that they must be purged from the KMT. The left wing of the KMT, overawed by Chiang's military strength, abandoned their communist allies. In July 1927 Chiang inaugurated a reign of terror against communists within the KMT. Some were killed, others expelled from the KMT, still more forced to resign from the CPC. The strength of the CPC was quickly reduced from 50,000 to 25,000.

In response the Communist Central Committee ordered a series of urban uprisings. One of these took place at Nanch'ang, and it was during this uprising that the embryo of the

People's Liberation Army (PLA) was formed. The communist forces in Nanch'ang consisted of three elements; the "Ironsides", some 50,000 Cantonese of the KMT 4th Corps of whom a third were communists who carried some of their comrades with them; the city garrison of Whampoa cadets, led by their commander, Chu Teh; and a collection of KMT deserters, striking coalminers from Hanyang, and peasants, led by Mao Tse-Tung. Chu Teh proclaimed the formation of the Red Army, and the communists seized Nanch'ang.

The communists failed to attract support from the population of Nanch'ang, and as superior enemy forces approached, were forced to retreat. Hostile forces kept them on the

move until some 4,000 survivors reached Ching-Kang-Shan, an area of heavily wooded broken country. Here the Reds absorbed into their ranks a number of local bandits, and organized the surrounding countryside on a Soviet system. While at Ching-Kang-Shan, Mao devised and tested some of his distinctive theories of civil-military relations, tactics and strategy. He concluded that enthusiastic support from the peasantry was absolutely essential to the survival of the Red Army and the Communisty Party. Only an inspired and indoctrinated peasantry could supply the necessary food, shelter, manpower and intelligence. Such support could only be obtained as a result of intensive political work, carried out by the Red Army as well as by the Civil

Communisty Party. Political and military activities became inextricably interdependent: soldiers were political workers, and political organizers prepared the way for successful military operations. The basic principle that all military action depended upon political direction for success, and that consequently soldiers must submit to political control, was firmly established by a conference at Kut'ien in 1929. This conference was held as the Red Army marched from Ching-Kang-Shan, rendered untenable by an enemy blockade, to South Kiangsi where it halted and organized a new soviet base area.

In 1930 the CPC was split by controversies over questions of ideology and strategy. Mao believed that the communists must concentrate their efforts on

the countryside. They must win the loyalty of the peasants by helping them to free themselves from the domination of their landlords and rural usurers. The landlords' militia should be crushed, and then rents, prices and interest rates forcibly reduced. Eventually landlords should be dispossessed. Having indoctrinated and organized the peasantry, the communists must then wage a war of attrition, based on guerrilla operations and political warfare, to reduce all enemies, native and foreign, to surrender or destruction. Conventional military operations were impossible due to the poverty of resources available; and experience in 1927 had proved that attempts to seize cities by uprising would be costly and futile. The Central Committee, unduly

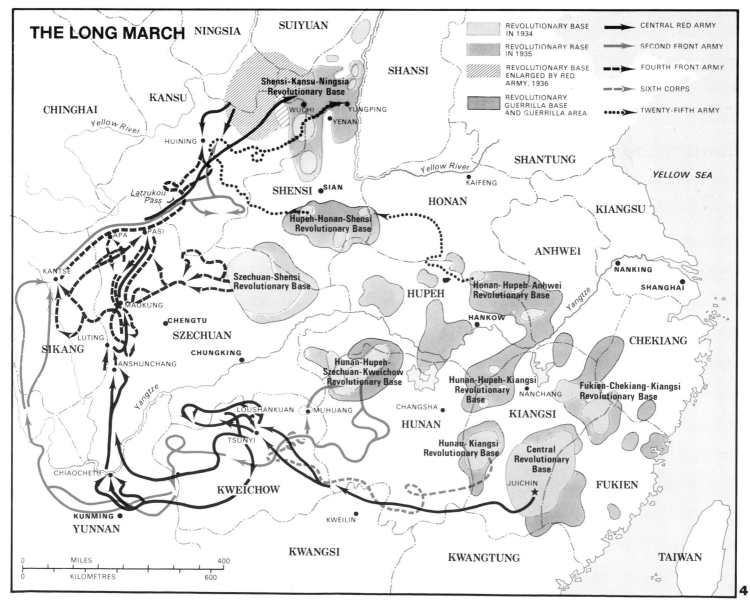

1. *Red Cavalry advance in column of threes through a mountain defile during the Anti-Japanese War, 1937-1945. Cavalry were the most mobile troops available to the communists because they lacked motor transport and the railway network was largely under Japanese or KMT control.*

2. *Peasants under the direction of the Red Army wreck a railway. The railways were the main strategic lines of communication in China at the time of the Anti-Japanese War. In 1940. in the first phase of the "100 Regiments" Campaign, the Red Army mobilised huge numbers of peasants to disrupt Japanese communications by the physical destruction of main roads, railways and canals.*

3. *Old Japanese aircraft on a raid over China. The Japanese used air attack not only to support ground forces in operations against enemy troops, but also to spread terror and panic amongst civilians in the rear areas of the Chinese armies. As few cities were protected by proper AA defence*

or air raid precautions these attacks had a devastating and disruptive effect.

4. Red Army regular troops were trained to make maximum use of all means of concealment and deception in order to achieve surprise in the attack. Their favourite tactic was the hit-and-run ambush. When engaged in towns or villages they showed a great degree of ingenuity in using hard cover, improvized fieldworks and tunnels, as these soldiers are.

5. Men of a Peasant Self-Defence Corps on the march with a motley array of old, captured and home-made weapons. The main role of these men after the 100-Regiments Campaign was to train for the future and to give intelligence, food, water, labour, and shelter to Red Army units and guerrillas. But they also spread the communist doctrine and sometimes made attacks on soft targets such as the landlords' forces or local KMT militia. In 1945 the purpose of these corps was fulfilled. Within a few weeks they provided enough men to double the size of the Red Army.

3

4

5

1. US Marine riot squad in Shanghai in 1938. Japanese aggression against China in 1937 quickly led to great turbulence. Chinese patriots struck back at the Japanese by boycotting Japanese goods, attacks on Japanese property, and popular demonstra- tions which often turned into riots. There were violent disorders in Shanghai, which threatened the security of the International settle- ment, and American troops were deployed in order to protect US property. By now many Americans were sympathetic to China. They saw the Chinese as the innocent victims of insatiable and brutal Japanese aggression. The line of policy pursued by the USA was based on the "open door" principle. This was that all powers should be allowed equal access to China for trading, and that no power should attempt to take political control of China or establish an exclusive sphere of influence. The arrival of Japanese troops in Shanghai in 1937 raised the level of tension between Japan and the USA, and was one of the reasons for the American policy of

dependent on inappropriate Russian advice, and out of touch with reality, still put its faith in the urban working classes, and ordered another round of urban uprisings. As in 1927, all these were miserable failures. Those who disagreed with the Maoist view were largely discredited, and many were actually killed. The uprisings did not seriously weaken the KMT, but they did draw the attention of Chiang to the menace in the rear. In 1928 Chiang reached Peking, but was unable to advance into Manchuria due to threats of Japanese intervention. The Japanese were determined to secure their invest- ments and special position in Northeast China, and were prepared to use force to do so. Chiang did not feel strong enough to fight them. However, his forces were strong enough to attack the communists with confidence, and in 1930 the KMT policy was to secure the rear areas before attempting to stem or reverse the tide of Japanese aggression.

Starting in Autumn 1930 KMT forces launched a series of five "extermina- tion campaigns" against Red Army soviet base areas. The communist forces employed conventional defensive- operations, guerrilla operations and psychological warfare against the KMT. All these methods brought a measure of success. A number of small soviet areas were swiftly overrun and vanished, but the major ones held out for several years. The Red forces launched a number of successful limited counter-attacks, including a well organized spoiling offensive in 1932. These successes extended the life of the soviets and provided the Red forces with most of their military stores. When under overwhelming pressure the Red forces resorted to guerrilla warfare to escape annihilation and maintain local tactical initiative against dispersed enemy forces. Propa- ganda and subversion played upon the weaknesses of the KMT Army, which had been forced to absorb many war- lord contingents, contained many rival factions, and which was demoralised by increasing Japanese activity in the North. In 1931 a whole brigade defected from the KMT Army to the communists, and in 1932 the KMT 28th Route Army changed sides en bloc.

However, the Reds were gradually worn down by the relentless pressure applied to them by enemy forces superior in equipment and numbers. In October 1933 Chiang, advised by the German General von Seeckt, launched the fifth Extermination Campaign against the South Kiangsi Soviet. Strong columns cleared the area of the soviet segment by segment, each advance being consolidated by lines of entrenchments reinforced by mobile reserves of cavalry, armoured cars, armoured trains and aircraft. Motorised patrols along newly constructed roads, protected by blockhouses, steadily reduced the area in which the communists could operate freely. The communists were deprived of food and room to manoeuvre. When pressed, they could no longer resort to "tactics of avoidance".

Late in 1934 the communists in South Kiangsi broke out of their besieged position and, pursued by the enemy, set off to find another base area. This

economic sanctions against Japan. American sanctions eventually made the Japanese extend their efforts into Southeast Asia in search of strategic materials, and so brought them into direct conflict with other western powers — notably, the Netherlands, Britain, France, as well as the United States.

2. The Red Army in Northern China near the end of the Anti-Japanese War. After 1941 the Red Army, safely ensconced in North Shensi, prepared for civil war against the KMT. On the defeat of Japan in 1945 the Red Army called up peasant reserves, put guerrillas into regular formations, and commenced operations to seize Manchuria and contest control of North and Central China. By swift action they gained the initiative.

was the beginning of the Long March, a strategic retreat to North Shensi. Red forces from the Hsiang-O-Hsi soviet in West Hunan and West Hupei, and the Oyuwan soviet in the Ta Pieh Shan also took part. Three columns of Red troops traversed 6 to 8,000 miles of the most difficult terrain in China, constantly attacked by KMT, warlord and tribal forces, further reduced by extremes of climate and starvation. Some 120,000 set out on the Long March, of whom only 20,000 or so survived.

Reorganization of the Red Army

But although it was costly, the Long March achieved its main purpose: the communist party and the Red Army survived. In Autumn 1935 the Reds began to construct a new base in North Shensi. The Red Army was reorganized; seven "divisions" were formed on a regular basis (although not so equipped), and held within the soviet for purposes of defence. Political teams and guerrilla forces were sent out into the countryside beyond to subvert the authority of the KMT and organize and train the peasants for guerrilla war.

Meanwhile Chiang assembled and deployed his forces so as to surround the North Shensi soviet and prepared for his sixth Extermination Campaign. This attack was not made because of Japanese aggression and skilful propaganda by the communists, who proposed a new United Front against foreign invaders. The KMT commanders whose forces had encircled North Shensi were reluctant to commit their troops to an offensive in Shensi while the Japanese were pressing on the suburbs of Peking. Late in 1936 Chiang arrived in Sian to ensure that the sixth Extermination Campaign went forward as ordered. He was kidnapped by his own subordinates and held prisoner until, partly due to the persuasive talents of Chou En Lai, he agreed to a new United Front against the Japanese.

As a result the Red Army was in theory incorporated into the KMT Army. The troops in North Shensi were reorganised into three divisions and designated the 28th KMT Route Army. In 1938 a communist division on the south bank of the Yangtze was designated the KMT New 4th Route Army. These arrangements temporarily secured the Reds from attack by KMT forces without imposing upon them any enforceable military obligations. Eventually the KMT, infuriated by the refusal of the communists to obey orders to attack the Japanese in full strength, broke up the United Front by an attack on the New 4th Route Army in Spring 1941. But by that stage the KMT forces had been pushed south by the Japanese Army whose objective was to conquer all areas of China of economic value, and the KMT could not attack the North Shensi soviet.

The policy of the communists in the period 1937-45 was broadly to survive by avoiding major operations and carry on political work amongst the rural population in preparation for the future. However they did make some spectacular attacks on the Japanese,

1. The Japanese surrender. Allied troops on parade in the Tien An Men in Peking in August 1945 to mark the formal capitulation of Japanese forces in China to the KMT. Although the KMT government was recognized by the Allies, including the USSR, as the legitimate government of China, many Japanese garrisons were forced to give up their arms to the Red Army. Chiang Kai-shek was confident of American support to help him win the coming Civil War, but the US was war-weary and disillusioned by Chiang's inactivity in the war with Japan. They were alienated when the KMT rejected their schemes for a coalition government with the Reds, outraged when the KMT suppressed the Democratic League, a movement to promote social democracy. While the Red Army moved into Manchuria and the USSR supplied it with captured Japanese armaments, US support for Chiang was half-hearted. By the time the US had decided that the Reds in China must be stopped, it was too late to take effective action.

2. *Red infantry storm the walls of Chinchow in 1946. Such assaults were usually made by successive massed waves of infantry after extended preparation by blockade, starvation, propaganda and bombardment. In this case close support is provided by a* light machine-gun group. Assaults were often made in severe weather to catch out the garrison.
3. *Red infantry advance past an American-made truck and field-gun. During the Civil War of 1945-9 the Reds were still short of all sorts of heavy and* sophisticated kit. They could manufacture small arms, and simple weapons such as mines. Mao said that the PLA must use the KMT forces as its quarter-master, and a great deal of equipment, much of it originally from the US, was taken and used by the Reds. Some of it is still in use in the PLA today!
4. *Mao on the road to victory. After the foundation of the North Shensi Soviet, Mao became the undisputed political and military leader of the Chinese Communist movement.*

4

1. *Communist assault troops, with support from light tanks, move into the industrial quarter of a city. These tanks were probably captured from the Japanese, like much of the artillery, and manned by Japanese or KMT prisoners under supervision. The Red Army* was still very short of specialist troops. It did not become competent in the use of tanks and artillery until the Korean War.
2. *Mao and Chu Teh, the Party and the Army planning operations. The Chinese Communists have always held* that in practice there can be no distinction between political and military activity, but that in the event of a conflict of interests, political considerations must take precedence. During the Civil War the rule was easily enforced because all the senior Communist leaders had had great military and political experience. Later on, military and civil functions diverged, and there were some sharp conflicts in the 1950s and 1960s as a result.
3. *Chiang Kai-shek, the Methodist Generalissimo, leader of the KMT*

and keep up constant guerrilla resistance, in order to assume the mantle of patriotic resistance and make their propaganda more effective. In September 1937 Lin Piao led the 115th Division in a highly successful ambush of a Japanese mechanised column at Ping Sing Pass from which the Red forces gained great credit and their first major haul of heavy equipment, in particular field guns and wireless sets, most of which was useless because the Red forces were not trained to use it.

In summer 1940 the communists mobilised a million soldiers and huge numbers of peasants for their only full scale offensive against the Japanese—the "Hundred Regiments" Campaign. In the first phase the Reds disrupted enemy lines of communication by the physical destruction of roads, railways and canals, work carried out with pick and shovel by peasants and soldiers. In the second phase Red soldiers attacked isolated Japanese garrisons. Phase one was successful, phase two much less so, and enemy retribution was terrible and effective.

From summer 1941 until summer 1942 the Japanese subjected Northern China to the "Three All" Campaign, based upon the principles "kill all, destroy all, burn all". The campaign struck directly at the intelligence and administrative base of the Red Army by measures designed to control, terrorise and subject the peasantry. The Japanese did not seek Red troops; they destroyed surplus food and shelter, and so deprived the peasantry of the means of giving logistic support to the Reds. They controlled movement to stop the flow of vital intelligence and recruits, and set up networks of collaborators to counter the communist political organization. This campaign did great damage to the communists, and they attempted no further major effort against the Japanese. Until 1945 they concentrated upon preparation for the future when the Japanese would some day be gone. There was a reversion to basic political work and basic training of peasant Self Defence Corps reinforcements for the Red Army of the future.

The long years of patient preparation and restraint bore fruit in 1945 at the end of World War II. As soon as the Japanese had surrendered to the Allies in August, the communists made ready for civil war. The beaten Japanese troops were stripped of weapons, equipment and clothing by Red Soldiers. Trained peasant reserves were called up and embodied in regular units, to increase the size of the 8th Route Army from 400,000 to 800,000 and the New 4th Route Army from 80,000 to 110,000. The regular formations were organized in five field armies, each deployed in a self-supporting theatre of operations; 1st Field Army in the North-west;2nd Field Army in the Centre and South-West; 3rd Field Army in the South-East; 4th Field Army, which was created new in 1945, in Manchuria; and 5th Field Army in the North. Early in the civil war the communists sent 4th Field Army to seize Manchuria, the main industrial base area of China. The 4th Field Army thus occupied the area of China most desirable to the KMT regime, and made contact with Russian forces who handed over vast quantities of war material taken from the Japanese. The 2nd and 3rd Field Armies obstructed the advance of the KMT Armies from the south-west by ambush and by damaging the means of communication.

The KMT forces eventually reached Manchuria, some by sea and air with American help, and took possession of the cities. But the KMT had become weary, demoralised, degenerate and disunited after years of fighting, followed by defeat, dependence on the USA, and inactivity. The KMT armies could occupy the cities, but the communists were in control of the surrounding countryside. Gradually the Red forces isolated the cities by persistent guerrilla attacks, and cut off the flow of intelligence and food. Eventually some cities were so beset

and chief opponent of Mao, arrives in Taipei after the defeat of his army in 1945. He was born in 1887, the son of a peasant, and received military education in Paoting and Tokyo. In Japan he became a Nationalist and a disciple of Sun Yat-sen, to whom

he was related by marriage. In 1924 he was a founder member and the first President of the Whampoa Academy. He trained the newly founded KMT Army to unify China by force. He was less tolerant of Communists than Sun, and after 1925 became

suspicious of Communist intrigues in the movement. In 1926 he seized power by a coup, and in Summer 1927 ordered a savage purge of Reds from the KMT. In the meantime, from 1926 on the KMT Army was advancing North. In 1928 Chiang's forces

reached Peking and he was elected President of China. But his political judgement did not match his military skill.
After defeat in the Civil War Chiang fled to Taiwan where he ruled under American protection until his death in 1975.

that they could be supplied and reinforced only by heavily escorted convoys, which were often ambushed. Attempts to provide resupply by air were ruinously expensive and inadequate. By the summer of 1947 KMT morale was broken, and the cities began to fall, one by one; usually to a crude system of bombardment followed by concentric assault by waves of massed infantry after a long preparation of blockade and subversion. As the cities fell, the KMT became fatalist and defeatist. Many KMT units defected to join the Red Army, along with many KMT soldiers prematurely demobilized in 1945 and 1946. The Reds began to shift from guerrilla to regular operations.

In the November 1948 the decisive battle of the civil war was fought in the region of Suchow. It took the form of a huge strategic ambush of the best of the KMT mechanised formations, and **2** their annihilation broke the KMT Army's strength and will to fight. In January 1949 the Peking-Tientsin pocket was taken by the communists, and KMT resistance collapsed. Advancing south, Red forces crossed the Yangtze virtually unopposed in April 1949. Chiang fled to Taiwan, and the communist forces, renamed as the People's Liberation Army (PLA) in July 1946 mopped up enemy remnants in the south and west.

Foundation of the People's Republic

On 1 October 1949 the Chinese People's Republic was proclaimed, and the PLA became a national army, an institution of state, while retaining its character as the military instrument of political revolution. New responsibilities were superimposed upon old ones. The PLA had to eliminate organized resistance to the new regime, attempt to re-establish the ancient frontiers of China, defend the country against external attack, and reinforce, and in some areas constitute, the machinery of civil government.

An early attempt to "complete the revolution" by finishing off Chiang was unsuccessful. Attempted seaborne assaults on Quemoy and Matsu by 3rd **3** Field Army failed with great loss of life,

1. Peking falls to the Red Army, January 1949. After a long blockade and several abortive attempts at relief, the Peking – Tientsin pocket surrendered, thus sounding the death-knell of the KMT government. The Red forces entered Peking, greeted with a mixture of enthusiasm and relief by the people. The KMT armies fled south, abandoning one natural position after another in a rapid and progressive collapse of morale.

2. October 1949: Chu Teh announces the creation of the Chinese People's Republic in a special Order of the Day. At this point the PLA became a national army with new duties and responsibilities, such as defence of the frontiers; but it also retained all its old functions as the armed wing of the revolutionary move- ment, dedicated to national resurgence and the social transformation of China.

3. Mao proclaims the foundation of the People's Republic from the Tien An Men in Peking. At this time Mao looked forward to a rapid advance for communist and

anti-colonialist ideas throughout the world. He was confident that China and the USSR combined would prove unbeatable in the imminent global struggle with capitalism and imperialism. These sanguine expectations were quickly disappointed, and helped to embitter relations between China and Russia.

4. Red soldiers occupy the roof of Chiang's palace in Nanking, the KMT capital. The PLA crossed the Yangtse unopposed and took the city in hot pursuit of retreating KMT trops. Chiang hastily gathered his best two divisions and quit the Mainland, never to return.

5. Mao reviews PLA armoured forces at Peking in 1949. Mao was always dubious as to the value of heavy weapons such as tanks. He preferred to rely upon human factors rather than material ones to defeat the enemy, as expressed in his slogan, "men over weapons". He also believed that an army of simple conscripts with small arms would be much more loyal to the revolution than highly trained professional soldiers.

4

5

1. *Mao reads a newspaper report of the fall of Nanking. Mao believed that propaganda and the management of information are vital to victory in a People's War. In North Shensi the Soviet ran a very active press, and the Party worked hard to bring literacy to the People and Army. Mao said, "An Army without culture is a dull-witted army, and a dull-witted army cannot defeat the enemy."*
2. *Hed soldiers cross the Yalu to fight the UN Forces in Korea. These "Chinese People's Volunteers" were all drawn from the ranks of 5th Field Army. Their first offensive, to clear UN forces away from the border, was a great success due to the effective use of night movement to achieve surprise. But, once the UN forces had recovered from the shock of Chinese intervention, they were able to use superior firepower to good effect.*
3. *American B-29s over Korea give a devastating answer to the hordes of riflemen sent into battle by the PLA. Initially, Chinese troops in the Korean peninsula had no defence at all against UN*

1

and plans for an attack on Taiwan itself were frustrated by the deployment of American naval forces in the Straits.

The PLA was more successful in regard to re-establishing Chinese authority in Tibet. In summer 1950 some seven divisions from 2nd and 1st Field Armies moved in and forced the Dalai Lama, the religious and political ruler of Tibet, to submit.

Later in 1950 the PLA was thrown on the defensive by the perceived threat to the security of Manchuria and Northern China generated by the intervention of United Nations forces in Korea. As UN forces drew closer to the Chinese frontier with North Korea in Autumn 1950, no fewer than 300,000 "Chinese People's Volunteers", mainly units of 4th Field Army, crossed the Yalu River and lay in wait for them. The Chinese counter-attack was initially successful, although casualties were heavy. In Spring 1951 the Chinese advance was halted by United Nations fire-power. The Chinese commanders

2

air attacks. Later, they acquired jet interceptors from the Soviet Union. They were never able to mount a bombing offensive of their own against UN forces.
4. Chinese infantry move across a stricken field in Korea. After the huge losses of the mobile phase

of the war, caused by the effects of modern firepower on "human waves" of infantry in the attack, the PLA dug in and adapted to trench warfare, the negation of Maoist tactics. They sought to maintain the offensive spirit by vigorous patrols, raids, and infiltration. The

soldiers soon showed a natural talent for these small-scale operations. Meanwhile the PLA obtained tanks, artillery and aircraft from the Soviet Union. They also acquired Soviet training, organization and habits. These new characteristics disturbed

Mao, who worked to undermine Soviet practice in the PLA. The resultant conflicts led to the sacking of P'eng Te-huai, Minister of Defence, in 1959, and his replacement by Lin Piao. Lin revived political education in the PLA and banished Soviet practices.

were soon taught some bitter lessons in Korea as they met properly organized and fully equipped modern forces for the first time. They discovered that they could not rely upon the local peasantry for logistic support, as they had in China. They were also unable to manoeuvre freely to avoid combat on unfavourable terms as they were constrained to fight a linear defensive war on a narrow front. There was little opportunity here for the "tactics of avoidance".

Commanders became convinced that to survive they must match the fire power of the UN forces. As a result the PLA became dependant upon the Soviet Union for equipment, weapons, supplies and concomitant training and doctrine. Soviet influence became very strong, and by 1953 the PLA was organized and trained along Soviet lines, although lacking Soviet scales of equipment. The adoption of Soviet procedures and the emergence of the PLA as a potentially professional Army

1. *Civilian victims of the war in Korea. During their advance South the North Korean forces took many civilian political prisoners. When forced to retreat they massacred large numbers of these unfortunates. Some were shot; others, like these in the* picture, *were herded into caves, walled-up, and left to suffocate.*
2. *Stubborn landlord elements executed by Peasant Militia. In the immediate aftermath of the Civil War there were ruthless purges of rich peasants, comprador-capitalists and collaborators.*

Those who did not take flight in time were tried by revolutionary tribunals and usually condemned to death.
3. *KMT troops escape to Taiwan. KMT soldiers load ammunition abroad an American LST before embarking for sanctuary. Of those* left behind, some were killed, others were given long terms of "reform through labour" before they were rehabilitated. The KMT forces on Taiwan, re-equipped by the US were a continuous threat to the security of Mainland China for twenty years. Artillery

1

2

3

bombardments from Quemoy and Matsu, espionage and commando raids mounted from Taiwan maintained KMT claims to be the one legitimate government of China.

4. Young members of the Militia parade in Peking in October 1959 to celebrate the tenth anniversary of the People's Republic. During the "Great Leap Forward" the Militia was increased to some 200 million and its importance restored. Mao wanted to re-integrate the PLA into the masses under the slogan "everyone a soldier, every soldier a peasant and worker".

5. Two of the "Gang of Four", Chiang Ching (Mao's wife) and Chang Ch'un-chiao, attend the Party Congress in 1973. After Mao's death the "Gang of Four" managed to seize power in Peking, but were deposed by Hua Kuo-feng and Teng Hsiao-p'ing with support from senior PLA commanders. Their fate is not known.

6. Mao's last resting place. After his death Mao was embalmed and put into a crystal coffin. The coffin rests in a marble mausoleum in Tien An Men square in Peking.

4

5

6

1. Under the Chinese constitution, the chairman of the Chinese Communist Party (Hua Kuo-feng) is commander in chief of the armed forces, through a concurrent appointment as chairman of the Central Military Commission of the Central Committee, Chinese Communist Party.

2. The High Command of the PLA, a system which controls the Navy and Air Force as well as the Army. The Central Military Commission is an organ of the Communist Party, and the General Political Department is staffed entirely with Party members.

The Local Forces have a separate chain of command to the Main Force Corps, a measure to dilute the power of the military command structure. The General Staff reports direct to the Military Commission. The Second Artillery is the Chinese Nuclear Force. In the event of war the Main

Force Commanders at Regional level would probably be allowed freedom of action as independent theatre commanders. Commanders of Military Districts would use Local Regular Forces to support the Main Forces, call up the militia for logistic service, and embody Select Militia

of specialists cut off from the rest of the population by their expertise, disturbed Mao. He wanted the PLA to remain a radical political force, not to develop into a political or conservative army of competent technocrats. The deterioration of relations with the Soviet Union in the late 1950s increased his suspicion of Russian practices in the PLA.

In 1959 at Lush'an the Central Committee, having considered the issue, decided that political reliability must take precedence over technical expertise; the soldier must be Red before he was expert. The Minister of Defence, P'eng Teh-Huai, protested. He was purged and Lin Piao was put in his place with orders to revive political life and revolutionary sentiment in the PLA. The political content of military training was increased, regular troops were sent off to work alongside peasants and in the factories to "re-integrate them with the people", and an attack was made upon the hierarchical structure of the Army. In 1965 this culminated in the abolition of all badges of rank and marks of status. Ranks were replaced by appointments.

Meanwhile, despite the internal turmoil, the PLA continued to defend the frontiers and police the interior of China. In 1962 PLA units seized and consolidated some small but strategic areas of territory along the border of Tibet with India. In the same year PLA troops had to deal with the first of a series of frontier incidents along the borders with the Soviet Union and the Mongolian SSR. In 1959 the PLA put down a major rebellion in Tibet, and in

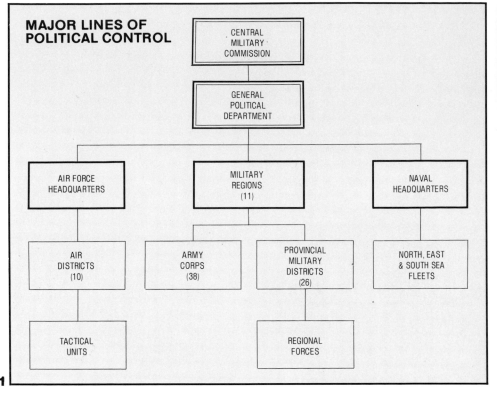

MAJOR LINES OF POLITICAL CONTROL

1962 it was forced to quell serious unrest in Sinkiang and Inner Mongolia.

From 1964 onwards the PLA was drawn inexorably deeper into internal politics by the development of the cultural revolution. At first, only the political commissars of the PLA were involved, sent as propaganda teams into cities and villages to revive revolutionary fervour. Later, the General Rear Services Department gave advice and logistic support to the Red Guards. When the Red Guards began to attack local party and administrative committees, the Militia and Local Forces

were drawn into the conflict usually on the side of the local bureaucrats. As civil order broke down completely the PLA Main Forces intervened to force an end to the activities of the extreme radical Red Guards, which they saw as a threat to national security. The structure of civil government had been destroyed by the violence of the radicals, so the PLA played a major part in erecting new machinery, based on Revolutionary Committees, and became predominant within it. By 1967 PLA Commanders were in control of China at all levels, and in 1969 Lin Piao was

units as guerrillas. Air and naval operations would be co-ordinated by Military Regional Commanders.
3. The rulers of China — Party and State leaders — at a grand rally. From left: Saifudin, Su Chen-hua, Chen Yung-kuei, Wei Kuo-ching, Wu Teh, Chi Teng-kuei, Li Hsien-nien, Hua

Kuo-feng, Yeh Chien-ying, Chen Hsi-lien, Wang Tung-hsing, Hsu Shih-yu, Li Teh-sheng, Wu Kuei-hsien and Ni Chih-fu. Hua Kuo-feng is Supreme Commander of the PLA. Before he was elected chairman of the Party he was Minister of Public Security. Ninth on left (on Hua's left)

stands Yeh Chien-ying, the Minister of Defence, an old fighter who, unlike Hua, went with Mao on the Long March. Teng Hsiao-p'ing, Chief of Staff, is not present. Teng remains the central character in the formulation and implementation of China's new policy line.

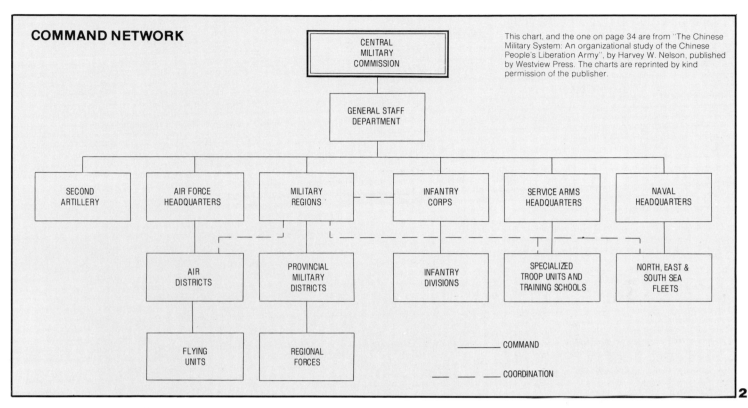

COMMAND NETWORK

This chart, and the one on page 34 are from "The Chinese Military System: An organizational study of the Chinese People's Liberation Army", by Harvey W. Nelson, published by Westview Press. The charts are reprinted by kind permission of the publisher.

CENTRAL MILITARY COMMISSION

GENERAL STAFF DEPARTMENT

SECOND ARTILLERY — AIR FORCE HEADQUARTERS — MILITARY REGIONS — INFANTRY CORPS — SERVICE ARMS HEADQUARTERS — NAVAL HEADQUARTERS

AIR DISTRICTS — PROVINCIAL MILITARY DISTRICTS — INFANTRY DIVISIONS — SPECIALIZED TROOP UNITS AND TRAINING SCHOOLS — NORTH, EAST & SOUTH SEA FLEETS

FLYING UNITS — REGIONAL FORCES

——————— COMMAND

— — — — — COORDINATION

2

named Mao's political successor.

However, Mao was determined to re-establish the principle established in 1929 that "politics comes first", and worked ceaselessly to reduce the political power of the Army leaders. By 1971 the position of Lin Piao had been seriously undermined, and he felt impelled to flee the country. An aircraft carrying him and his closest associates crashed in mysterious circumstances near the western border of Manchuria. The political position of the Army deteriorated swiftly. In 1973 most of the commanders of military regions

were redeployed, and were thereby cut off from the local power bases that in some cases had been cultivated since 1949. Meanwhile the representation of the PLA on vital committees at all levels of state and party organization steadily diminished. The 1975 Constitution made it clear that the PLA was to be 'led by the Communist Party of China', and therefore come under civil political control.

However, although the Army is no longer in direct control of day to day policy, it remains as it had always been, a powerful influence on political

life in China. After the death of Mao in September 1976 the PLA intervened in the subsequent power struggle to ensure that the "Gang of Four" led by Chiang Ching did not succeed in seizing power. Eventually the Army ensured the success and security of Hua Kuo Feng as Mao's political heir. Disorders instigated by radical supporters of the "Gang of Four" were firmly suppressed by the PLA, and the favourite target of radical spleen, Teng Hsiao-P'ing, returned to public life once more in 1977 as Vice-Premier and Chief of Staff of the Army.

3

Professor
Harold C. Hinton

Professor of Political Science and International Affairs, Institute for Sino-Soviet Studies, George Washington University, Washington D.C.

Teng Hsiao-ping signs the historic agreement to "normalise" relations between the People's Republic of China and the United States of America. Thus the process started by Chou En-lai and Richard Nixon reached fruition, although many Americans considered it wrong to ditch their former allies the Nationalists on Taiwan. Nevertheless, Teng's personality and honesty won him many friends during his 1979 tour of the USA, while the "hawks" were to a certain extent placated by his forthright comments on the dangers posed by the Soviet Union. It also seems fairly certain, in retrospect, that Teng must have warned his hosts of China's intended action against Vietnam and, while he did not gain their support, he did ensure that their criticism was muted. Teng is a great pragmatist.

China's influence on international affairs will undoubtedly increase in coming years. China's grand design, formulated by Chou En-lai in 1968, is to build an informal entente with the US, Japan and Western Europe to contain what China regards as an expansionist, aggressive and "hegemonistic" Soviet Union.

1. *A Soviet admiral visits the PLA-Navy at the high noon of Sino-Soviet fraternal relations in 1956. On 24 May in the previous year the Soviet Navy had vacated Port Arthur (now Lushun) the occupation of which had long been an affront to Chinese dignity. Also in* *1955 (on 1 May) the Soviet Union had signed the "Atomic Cooperation Agreement" with a number of Communist powers including China, which led to the supply of atomic material, the provision of information and the training of nuclear technicians. This laid the* *foundations of the Chinese nuclear programme, something which the Soviet Union has, no doubt, later regretted. On 7 April 1956, just before this photograph was taken, Anastas Mikoyan, one of the First Deputy Premiers of the USSR, had signed agreements in* *Peking on further Soviet economic aid to China. He also agreed to the completion of the Trans-Siberian railway, with the final link between Lanchow and Aktogai (near Alma Ata) being laid by the Soviet Union. On 28 October 1956 China publicly*

To an even greater extent than in the case of most other powers, the propaganda and declaratory policies of the Chinese leadership are not a very enlightening guide to its actual policies and behaviour. An understanding of the latter requires an analysis of Peking's record to date, in this case in the field of foreign policy.

China's external objectives, although never explicitly announced, appear not to differ much from what would be expected of a power in its position.

In the first place, China has always been profoundly committed to modernization and development, mainly as a source of increased national power and independence, and ultimately also as the basis for a better life for the Chinese people. This has also been the aim of all other Chinese nationalists since the late nineteenth century.

Secondly, China needs and seeks security from attack. Until the late 1960s, the main perceived threat came from the United States; since then, it has come from the Soviet Union. China has sought security from these threats by building up its conventional and nuclear military power and by taking a variety of political and diplomatic measures to be discussed shortly.

Thirdly, China seeks, at acceptable levels of cost and risk, influence for its own sake and in various environments: Asia, the rest of the Third World, the international left, and the circle of major powers.

Finally, Peking regards China as a divided country and seeks unification through the "liberation" of Taiwan. This is a much more important matter than the disputes over relatively small amounts of territory that China has with some of its neighbours, notably the Soviet Union and India. Taiwan was protected by the United States from mid-1950 to the end of 1979 and is the base of the Chinese Communists' hated enemy in the civil war, the Kuomintang, which cannot be said to have been fully defeated as long as Taiwan remains to be "liberated".

In foreign policy as in domestic politics, the Chinese leadership has been divided into two different, but not always conflicting, schools of thought; which are often labelled, with some but not serious oversimplification, as radical and moderate.

The former, led by Mao Tse-tung until his death (September 9, 1976), has stressed Marxist-Leninist ideology—the "thought" of Mao, "revolution", and the like—as the major value, and propaganda as the main, and also a relatively cheap and riskless, means of promoting it. This school began to decline in actual influence at the time of the fall and death (1969-71) of Mao's then designated heir, the radical Defence Minister Lin Piao. It virtually collapsed with Mao's death in September 1976 and the purge the following month of the remaining radical members of the leadership, the so-called "Gang of Four" including Mao's widow Chiang Ching.

The moderate school included a number of party figures, notably Vice Chairman Liu Shao-ch'i, who were purged by Mao before and during the Cultural Revolution (1966-68), but its main leader was Premier Chou En-lai until his death on January 8, 1976. This school, which has gained power and influence at the expense of the radicals, has stressed China's national interests—security and influence, in particular—as the major national value, and diplomacy and political manoeuvre as the main means of promoting it. Chou intended his successor as premier, and the next real leader of the country, to be Vice Premier Teng Hsiao-p'ing, who, however, was unacceptable to the radicals and therefore fell from office in April 1976—during the interval between Chou's death and Mao's—but who re-emerged as the most dynamic member of the leadership, although without the title of premier, in the summer of 1977.

China's reliance on the Soviet Union

The People's Republic of China was obviously too weak and backward, as of 1949, to develop without foreign aid or at least extensive foreign economic contacts. Accordingly, the PRC relied at first, largely for ideological and political reasons, on the Soviet Union as the main external source of credits, technology, capital equipment, and the like. But economic dependence on the Soviet Union was not only costly but carried the danger of political dependence, which was intolerable to Peking, and in any case Maoist theory stressed the virtues of "self-reliance" in economic as well as in other matters. In the second half of the 1950s, therefore, Peking disengaged itself from both the economic and the political aspects of its relationship with Moscow and indulged in a thoroughly Maoist exercise in attempted rapid development, through ideological and political mobilization of the populace, known as the Great Leap Forward (1958-60).

This programme was a disaster, however, and after its collapse China intensified its previously minor economic ties with Japan and Western Europe, which could and did provide much of what the Soviet Union had

previously provided in the way of economic support, without the dangerous political strings. This approach, combined with a restoration to the peasants of important economic incentives of which they had been deprived during the Great Leap Forward, produced a fairly rapid recovery from the economic effects of that misguided initiative.

But the Great Leap Forward had been Mao's brainchild, and he viewed the retreat from it, however necessary as an interim measure, as a threat to the revolutionary momentum that he desired for his party and his country. He failed to persuade certain other leaders, notably Liu Shao-ch'i, of the need to revert to something resembling the Great Leap Forward, and partly for this reason he launched the so-called Cultural Revolution in order to get rid of them and re-install revolutionary ideology as the guiding influence on domestic and foreign policy. He succeeded to a considerable extent, but only temporarily and at the cost of a setback to development comparable to the one inflicted earlier by the Great Leap Forward.

Accordingly, a retreat from the Cultural Revolution began under the direction of Chou En-Lai, but he proceeded cautiously on account of his clear recollection of the fact that Liu Shao-chi had fallen largely on account of his leadership of the retreat from the Great Leap Foward. Chou's hands were partially freed by the fall of Lin Piao, and at the end of 1972 he launched a substantial expansion of industrial imports, to be financed, it was hoped, largely by exports of coal and oil. This programme encountered a number of difficulties, including the disturbance of the international economy created by the Middle East war of 1973. Undeterred, Chou announced in January 1975 the "four modernizations" (of agriculture, industry, national defence, and science and technology), which were intended to make China a "powerful modern socialist country" by about the end of the twentieth century. Foreign economic relations were obviously expected to play an important part in this programme. Chou did not live long enough to see the "four modernizations" produce significant economic results, but he did see them generate strong opposition from

the radicals, who objected to their non-ideological overtones.

Since the death of Mao and the purge of the "Gang of Four", and above all since the re-emergence of Teng Hsiao-p'ing about a year later, the "four modernizations" have been fully reinstated, and "self-reliance" has been discarded in fact if not in theory. Chinese leaders, officials, and technicians are showing keen interest in various foreign developmental models, notably those of Yugoslavia and Japan, and perhaps also those of South Korea and even Taiwan. The overseas Chinese in Southeast Asia, and in the British crown colony of Hong Kong, are being treated more than ever as valuable sources of foreign exchange and skills of various kinds. Hong Kong has been virtually guaranteed a cooperative relationship with China for the indefinite future, and the Bank of China has begun to conduct lending and investment operations in the colony along fully capitalist lines. The United States and Western Europe have become significant sources of imports, including modern arms in the latter case. In a massive departure from Maoist "self-reliance", foreign credits and technical assistance, although not foreign investment in the usual sense, are being sought and received on a large scale, apparently in the belief that they can be repaid through drastically increased exports of onshore and offshore oil, of which China has substantial reserves.

For rather obvious geographic,

economic, and cultural reasons, Japan is by far the most important economic partner of post-Mao China. Expanding Sino-Japanese economic relations have been paralleled and facilitated by an expanding political relationship. The Japanese business community, whose home front and whose external relations in other directions including the United States are not doing very well, sees in China a source of potentially large export earnings. China, on its side, sees Japan as the most accessible and cheapest source of most categories of modern technology, and in fact the mainstay of the "four modernizations". In view of the current overvaluation of the yen, China prefers its credits from Japan to be expressed in terms of the dollar.

China's current development targets, as announced at the Fifth National People's Congress (February-March 1978), are very ambitious and may not be fully attainable. On the other hand, China's innate resources and dynamism and its present leadership and policies appear sufficient to produce substantial economic progress during the coming decades, except probably in the event of one or more of three possible catastrophies: serious political conflict approaching civil war, a Malthusian disaster involving an outrunning of the food supply by population growth to an extent not remediable through food imports, and a military defeat at the hands of the Soviet Union. Military modernization is the third of the "four modernizations" and in fact

CHINA'S FOREIGN POLICY AND NATIONAL INTEREST

1. For many centuries the reports of China's mineral resources have varied from glowing overestimates to cautious underestimates, and the true nature of the situation has always been difficult to establish. Like other maritime nations China is now searching for off-shore oil.

2. Some two-thirds of China's total energy production comes from coal, of which China has reserves claimed to be in the region of 100,000 million tons. Most coal deposits are in the north and north-west of the country, but there are also mines in Manchuria, which are exploited because of their nearness to the main areas of demand. One of the most unusual of these is the mine at Fushun, east of Shenyang (formerly Mukden), where coal has been produced for some 600 years. Here a bed of tertiary coal is exposed at the surface and dips down at some thirty degrees in a bed which varies in thickness between 32 and 394 feet, the thickest deposit of bituminous coal in the world. Mining is achieved by a mixture of shafts and large open-cast pits.

3. The earlier post-World War II oil

surveys were carried out with assistance from the Soviet Union, but since the mid-1960s China has carried on on her own. The first major oil strike was here at Taching in Heilungkiang, in northern Manchuria, an area worryingly close to the Soviet border. Other recent oil discoveries have been at Takang in Hopei province, Shengli (Shantung), and in Szechwan. Chinese oil production in 1976 was claimed to be 85 million tons.

4. The achievements and problems of China's steel industry have been well-documented in the Western press. The euphoria of the Great Leap Forward, with a miniature smelting plant in what seems like every back garden in the country, is long forgotten; attention is now concentrated on massive plants such as this at Wuhan. Even these plants are not without problems and many are undergoing massive modernization programmes with the help of Western experts. Steel production in 1976 was estimated to be 25 million tons compared with 1.3 million in 1952.

3

4

1. *The long-standing tension between China and India over the precise line of the frontier between the two in certain parts of the Himalayas led to open war on 20 October 1962. Massive Chinese advances in the Ladakh area of North-East Kashmir and* *across the "McMahon Line" in the North-East Frontier Agency (NEFA) resulted in deep penetrations into Indian-held territory. In Ladakh the PLA occupied the area up to the line which they claimed to be the true border and then stopped. In NEFA, however,* *they advanced for about one hundred miles until on 21 November they declared a unilateral cease-fire and moved back to a line some 12 miles behind the line of actual control on 7 November 1959. The PLA used its conventional* *tactic of a mass infantry advance supported by very heavy artillery fire, enabling the PLA to succeed against one of the most efficient armies in Asia.*
2. *An atmosphere of euphoria at Peking airport as Chinese Premier Chou En-lai greets a high-level*

1

has been a major goal of the Chinese leadership for most of the period since 1949. China lags so far behind the "superpowers" in strategic military power that its efforts to manage the threat believed to be posed by one or the other of them has necessarily had a very large political component, including the maintenance of a capability to mobilize the population as well as the armed forces in a "people's war" in the event of invasion.

Partly for ideological reasons and partly because of American support for the Nationalists during the Chinese civil war, the Chinese Communists regarded American "imperialism" not only as an adversary but as a threat from the time of their coming to power. Partly to cope with this perceived (or, more accurately, misperceived) threat, the PRC "leaned to one side", toward the Soviet Union. The most important single documentary landmark of this "tilt" was the Sino-Soviet treaty of alliance of February 14, 1950, which named Japan directly, and the United States indirectly, as the hypothetical aggressors. China's intervention in the Korean War later that year was conducted with Soviet approval and support and largely in order to prevent the United States from becoming a strategic threat to Manchuria and perhaps to China as a whole. During the ensuing three-year undeclared Sino-American war, the existence of

the Sino-Soviet alliance was one of the major factors inhibiting the United States from yielding to the temptation to carry the war to the mainland of China. It was also a major cause of the adoption by the United States of a strategy of trying to "contain and isolate" the PRC through political, military, and economic sanctions, a strategy which in turn made China perceive the American threat as all the greater. China's response, after the end of the Korean War, apart from relying with decreasing optimism on Soviet protection, was to cultivate good relations with non-aligned states, especially India.

People's diplomacy in the Third World

After Stalin's death in 1953, Mao showed less respect for his successors, and they in turn tended to take their alliance with China less seriously than Stalin had. This trend was especially noticeable at the time of the Vietnamese Dien Bien Phu crisis and the ensuing Geneva Conference in 1954. The Soviet leadership felt little interest in helping China to "liberate" Taiwan, and yet such Soviet support became all the more necessary to China after the United States concluded a security treaty with the Republic of China on

Taiwan at the end of 1954. The PRC coped with this seemingly disadvantageous and indeed dangerous situation largely through a marked expansion of its diplomatic contacts and "people's diplomacy", especially in the Third World. It also decided about 1956 to work toward its own nuclear weapons capability. By 1957, however, this approach had seemingly reached the point of diminishing returns, and Mao turned back to Moscow with a demand for a strategy of confrontation with the United States over Taiwan and West Berlin. When the then Soviet leader Krushchev prudently hesitated, Mao tried to galvanize him, or alternatively to compensate for his inadequacy, by launching a military crisis in the Taiwan Strait in August 1958. American and Soviet behaviour during the crisis convinced Mao that the United States was to be taken more seriously as an adversary than the Soviet Union was to be taken as an ally. After that, China soon came to regard the Sino-Soviet alliance as a virtual dead letter, and Moscow tended to agree inasmuch as it was coming under increasing polemical attack from China on ideological and other grounds.

About 1960 Peking, or at least the radical section of the Chinese leadership, adopted what is sometimes called a dual adversary strategy: ideological, political, and to some extent military struggle to be waged simultaneously against American "imperialism" and Soviet "revisionism" — a large order even for China. Fortunately for Peking, neither "superpower" took its behaviour seriously enough to attack it. There was a partial exception, to be sure, in the case of the United States, whose "escalation" in Vietnam in 1965 was initially motivated to a large extent by the essentially mistaken belief that Hanoi was acting as Peking's agent. In the spring of 1966, however, China and the United States reached a tacit understanding that the war in Vietnam would not be allowed to escalate into another Sino-American war, and after that Peking enjoyed a sense of freedom from serious external threat.

But not for long. Since the mid-1960s the Soviet Union had been observing with growing alarm certain aspects of China's behaviour, especially its acquisition of atomic weapons in 1964 (and nuclear in 1967), its rejection early in 1965 of a proposal by Krushchev's successors for "united action" in support of the North Vietnamese, its subsequent launching of the highly unorthodox and chaotic Cultural Revolution, and various Chinese statements beginning in 1963 that Tsarist and Soviet territorial expansion at China's expense might have to be rolled back. In the spring of 1966, the Soviet Union introduced major military units into the Mongolian People's Republic, and at about the same time

began to strengthen its forces in other sectors of the Sino-Soviet border region as well. The initiation of a series of particularly menacing anti-Chinese articles in the Soviet theoretical press in the spring of 1968 apparently completed the process of convincing Chou En-lai that the Soviet Union was becoming the major threat to China in succession to the United States. At the same time, President Johnson's decision to begin de-escalating the war in Vietnam and to intensify efforts to reach a settlement with Hanoi seems to have suggested to Chou the possiblity of some sort of future anti-Soviet arrangement with the United States as well as with Japan and Western Europe, the only other power centres at all comparable to the Soviet Union. The Soviet invasion of Czechoslovakia the following August made this aim still more desirable in Chou's eyes and somewhat more plausible in the eyes of some of his colleagues, apparently including Mao but not Defence Minister Lin Piao, at that time Mao's heir apparent.

Lin remained bitterly anti-American, as well as anti-Soviet. It was apparently he who organized an ambush of a Soviet patrol on the disputed island of Chen Pao in the Ussuri River that occured on March 2, 1969. This error produced a serious Sino-Soviet border crisis during the ensuing months, a massive Soviet military build-up near

the border that continues to pose a threat to the PRC, and the beginning of Lin's political decline.

Chou En-lai stepped forward to manage the threat by primarily diplomatic and political means, since Peking obviously lacked the resources to do so by military means alone. His problems were greatly complicated by the attitude of the extreme radicals, including Lin Piao, who believed that Russia should be defied with threats of a "people's war" and who opposed any improvement in Peking's relationship with the United States. Nevertheless, the Soviet threat, the tapering off of the Cultural Revolution, and a degree of support from Mao enabled Chou to send new ambassadors to China's foreign diplomatic posts (all ambassadors had been recalled by then, for reasons connected with the Cultural Revolution) beginning in the spring of 1969 to initiate talks with the Soviet Union on the border dispute (in October 1969), to seek new diplomatic relationships at the expense of Taiwan (notably with Canada in October 1970 and with Japan and West Germany in September 1972), to press for entry into the United Nations (achieved in October 1971), and above all to begin official contacts with the United States (notably the Kissinger and Nixon visits to Peking of July 1971 and February 1972 respectively, and the establishment of liaison offices in both capitals in the

2

1. *An historic handshake as Chairman Mao Tse-tung greets President Richard M Nixon. The enmity with the United States had lasted since 1949 and had nad an unsettling effect on international affairs for two generations. It took, therefore, two strong and determined realists to make the gestures necessary to heal the wounds of the Korean War, of backing opposing sides in numerous conflicts, and of years of mutual vituperation. By the time of President Nixon's visit the aura surrounding the ageing Chairman was such that to be invited to his bungalow was one of the supreme political honours of the time.*
2. *Such is the world of real politik, however, that at the time that the President was in Peking US troops were still in Vietnam fighting the North Vietnamese who were receiving substantial material aid from China. Rapprochement with China was one of the key elements in the strategy of Nixon and Henry Kissinger to achieve US disengagement and bring men such as this US Special Forces adviser back home. They*

succeeded, but lost Vietnam.
3. A relaxed interlude during President Nixon's historic visit to Peking. From left are: Chi Peng-fei, Minister of Foreign Affairs; William Rogers, Secretary of State; Premier Chou En-lai; President Nixon; Chiang Ching, wife of Chairman Mao; Mrs Nixon; Teng Ying-chao, Premier Chou's wife; and Dr Kissinger, special assistant to the President. Nixon's daring and imaginative initiative enabled China to make a long overdue emergence onto the world stage.

2

3

1. *The Peking government has always been sensitive about its relationship with the many "Overseas Chinese" communities scattered over the whole of Southeast Asia. Many of these communities are sizeable in number, and all have considerable* *financial influence; the host governments are, therefore, naturally apprehensive lest such important minorities should have split loyalties and start following lines being dictated from Peking. The government of Vietnam, however, started on a policy of deliberate* *harassment of the Hoa Chiao, the ethnic Chinese long resident in Vietnam, and the PRC was eventually forced to take an interest in what was going on. Incidents then developed on the Sino-Vietnamese border which appear to have been quite deliberately* *berately sponsored and organized by the Vietnam government. This picture was taken on August 25 1978 and shows uniformed Vietnamese hurling rocks across the border at the somewhat inappropriately-named "Friendship Pass". The man in the centre*

spring of 1973). There is little doubt that Chou's main purpose in conducting this remarkable diplomatic campaign was to enhance China's security against the Soviet Union, although there were significant gains for China's influence as well. In addition, Chou, with the help of his military colleague Yeh Chien-ying, inaugurated a programme of steady, although unspectacular and hence unprovocative, strengthening of China's strategic and conventional forces. These steps, which were facilitated by the fall of Lin Piao in September 1971, gave the PRC a very much stronger international position.

The deterrent effect of Chou's programme on the Soviet Union was evidently considerable, but not necessarily permanent. Russia's military modernization programme forged ahead faster than China's, and some would say faster than America's as well. The initially dramatic effect of the new Sino-American relationship on Soviet thinking began to wear off as that relationship reached a plateau until late 1978 short of a resolution of the Taiwan issue or the establishment of "normal" relations between the United States and the PRC.

The Soviet Union's anti-Chinese mood grew more intense than ever as the post-Mao leadership of Hua Kuo-feng and Teng Hsiao-p'ing chose to maintain Peking's confrontation with the Soviet Union rather than accommo-

date with it. China was (and is) very resentful of Soviet bullying, the massive Soviet military presence near the border and fears, probably correctly, that the real Soviet terms for an accommodation include a near-satellite status for China, which would of course be unacceptable.

Deterioration in Sino-Soviet relations

A series of events in 1978 served to heighten Russia's anti-Chinese feelings. These were the profound commitment of the new Chinese leadership, as evidenced at the Fifth National People's Congress (February-March 1978) to an industrial and military modernization programme largely unhampered by Maoist ideology; a new Chinese demand, made public at the same time, for a dramatic reduction of Soviet forces near the entire Sino-Soviet border; the dramatic improvement in Sino-Japanese relations, above all the treaty of peace and friendship of August 12, and the rapid expansion of economic and technological contacts between Peking and Tokyo; and Chinese involvement on the side of Cambodia (Kampuchea) in the latter's confrontation with Vietnam. China for its part was troubled by the Soviet Union's mood without being willing to yield to it, and especially by the Soviet-

Vietnamese treaty of friendship and cooperation of November 3, 1978, which was clearly intended to deter escalation of China's existing pressures (which included border incidents) on of interaction: the central military Vietnam. In December, however, Vietnam invaded Cambodia in force, and even the new Soviet-Vietnamese treaty did not prevent China from attacking Vietnam in February-March 1979 with the announced aim of teaching it a lesson.

China's current strategy for managing the Soviet threat was apparently devised conceptually by the late Chou En-Lai about 1968 and has been promoted since then first by him and more recently by Teng Hsiao-p'ing. Its essence is an effort to achieve a kind of informal anti-Soviet entente with the United States, Japan, and Western Europe. In this grand design, China has been encountering difficulties because the other prospective partners do not fully share its view of the Soviet Union. They do not see their own relationship with it as one of full-blown confrontation, they have a healthy respect for its power, and they have important economic relations with it. China's much greater sense of antagonism toward Moscow is fuelled by a sharp divergent interpretation of an ideology once held in common, a long common border and a resulting sense of acute threat, and a fear of possible satellitization.

appears to be carrying a bayonet, and the hatred is clearly portrayed; similar incidents occurred all along the common border.
2. A Chinese picture taken during the "punitive" invasion shows their soldiers distributing salt to Vietnamese villagers in the Cao Bang area. The propaganda war was fought every bit as fiercely as the military battle with cameramen accompanying troops on both sides.
3. The chart shows some of the more noteworthy treaties, alliances and "understandings" reached between the PRC and foreign countries. The great alliance with the USSR which was almost the first diplomatic act of the new Communist government in 1950 has long been moribund in all but name, but the legalistic Chinese have nevertheless thought it necessary to inform the USSR that they do not intend to extend it beyond its current expiry date in 1980. The restoration of relations with the USA has played a key role in China's emergence into world affairs, but the mutual antagonism between the PRC and the USSR bodes ill for the future.

CHINA'S TREATIES, ALLIANCES AND DIPLOMATIC RELATIONS

Afghanistan
Non-aggression pact, 1976

Burma
Non-aggression pact, 1976

Canada
Diplomatic relations established, 1970

EEC
China given "Most favoured nation" status, 1978

India
Diplomatic relations restored after 15 years, 1976

Japan
Diplomatic relations established, 1970

Kampuchea
Non-aggression pact, 1976 (China supplies free military aid)

Libya
Diplomatic relations established, 1978

Malaysia
Diplomatic relations established, 1974

N. Korea
Mutual defence treaty, 1961 (China supplies free military aid)

Nepal
Meeting between King of Nepal and Hua Kuo-feng, 1976

Oman
Diplomatic relations established, 1978

Portugal
Diplomatic relations established, 1979

Taiwan
Talks proposed, 1979

Thailand
Commercial maritime navigation agreement, 1979

United Nations
China became member, 1971

USA
Shanghai Communique, 1972 (President Nixon was encouraged by Peking to end US alliance with Taiwan). Liaison office opened, 1973
Normalization of relations agreement, 1979

USSR
Friendship and Mutual Assistance Alliance, 1950 (USSR has been informed by China that this Alliance is not to be extended beyond 1980. Russian advisers evicted, 1960

W. Germany
Diplomatic relations established, 1972

Note: A scheme, started in the early 1970s, to link China by road through Laos to Thailand and eastern Burma was held up because of Soviet pressure after the end of the Vietnam War

China fears that the United States is not doing enough, and is not interested in doing enough, to cope with the Soviet Union in any of their major fields of interaction: the central military balance, Strategic Arms Limitation Talks (SALT), Central Europe, the Middle East, Africa, and the Far East. The latter is, for obvious reasons, of particular interest to China, which wants the United States to maintain its existing political role and military presence in all areas but one—Taiwan—as a counterweight to the Soviet Union. The Korean case is only an apparent exception; China goes through the motions of publicly demanding an American military withdrawal from South Korea, but only for the sake of its delicate relations with North Korea, and its real aim is stability in the peninsula, an aim that it knows is best promoted through the retention of the American military presence in South Korea. China would like to work out a more direct form of cooperation with the United States, short of an alliance, for purposes of containing the Soviet Union and is gratified by the present United States administration's interest, in principle, in seeing a "secure and strong" China and in "playing the China card" against the Soviet Union. Both parties, however, are constrained by political and practical obstacles, by a desire not to overprovoke Russia, and to some extent by the Taiwan issue.

In dealing with Western Europe, China stresses the alleged "inevitability" of a war (possibly conventional) between NATO and the Warsaw Pact, the resulting need to strengthen NATO politically and militarily, and the urgent need for NATO not to reach some understanding with the Soviet Union (a "Munich") that would enable Moscow to divert more attention and forces toward China. Although the West Europeans (except perhaps for the West Germans) by no means fully share China's perception, they do appreciate its utility in tying down significant Soviet forces in the Far East and appear willing to sell China modern arms in spite of Soviet warnings not to do so.

China would probably like to establish some form of anti-Soviet military cooperation with Japan, but the political obstacles on both sides are formidable. When dealing with Japan in this connection, China stresses the Soviet drive for "hegemony" in Northeast Asia and the Northwest Pacific (mainly through a continuing naval buildup), Japan's right to its Northern Territories (the Kuriles, or at least the four southern islands) currently held by the Soviet Union, China's intent to abrogate the Sino-Soviet treaty of alliance of 1950 (which names Japan as the likely adversary), the need for Japan to maintain a close security relationship with the United States and continue building up its own Self Defence Forces, and the desirability of avoiding participation in the development of Siberian resources at any rate on Soviet terms.

Vietnam invades China's "client state"

For the first time in ten years, China's leaders saw a security threat in Southeast Asia, not so much directly to itself as to its client Cambodian (Kampuchean) regime of Pol Pot. Peking was apparently correct in asserting that the Vietnamese, whom it unfairly labels the "Cubans of Southeast Asia", were trying to establish a Hanoi-dominated "Indo-chinese federation" embracing Laos (already largely under Vietnamese control) and Cambodia, as well as Vietnam. Both under the former (before 1970) government of Prince Sihanouk and under the regime of Pol Pot (from 1975-78) Cambodia cultivated good relations with China as the best means of deterring Vietnam, which had been rightly perceived in Cambodia as the major external threat. In fact, Cambodia became a virtual client state of the PRC, which saw it as a valuable asset to his own effort to contain Vietnam even though it privately disliked the notorious brutality of the Pol Pot regime. China regards Vietnam as an enemy because it has invaded Cambodia, and even more because since about the time of Ho Chi Minh's death (September 3, 1969) his successors have departed from his policy of maintaining approximate political equidistance between Russia and China and have tilted strongly toward the former.

In late 1977, after Vietnamese-Cambodian antagonism had erupted

3

1. Modern China is a land of the most astonishing contrasts. On one hand the PLA, although faced with some very serious threats, is equipped with some obsolescent hardware, while in other fields China is virtually abreast of the world's leaders. Thus, she has her own nuclear weapons, her own missiles and—as shown here—a Chinese-designed and built digital satellite communication ground station. Priority was given to the electronics industry in 1970 as it is fundamental to progress, but the military communications systems do not yet seem to have profitted from these developments so far.

2. Peking, once almost closed to all except the most carefully selected foreigners, is now on many politicians' itineraries. Here Chairman Hua Kuo-feng stands with a group from the Central Executive of the Komeito, Japan's "Clean Government Party".

3 and 4. High technology factories such as this are still comparatively rare. It is reported that China has bought technology and know-how from Japan and the PLA wishes to order military computers from the

1

2

USA. Although Japan has reportedly won multi-billion-yen contracts for the supply to China of a variety of products — including ships, steel, TV tube glass, integrated circuits and ethylene — China appears to prefer to licence-produce indigenously.

3

4

1. *China is currently the fifth in the order of arms suppliers with 2 per cent of the trade, compared with the USA (38 per cent), USSR (34 per cent), Britain and France (9 per cent), and Italy (also 2 per cent). During the years 1970-76 the principal recipients were* Pakistan, Tanzania and North Vietnam, but the latter country is unlikely to receive any further arms for many years to come. The main exports have been aircraft, and especially the successful and reliable Shenyang F-6 (Chinese version of the Soviet MiG-19 fighter) and light coastal defence craft. Quantities of tanks have also been exported, but in minute numbers compared with the USSR. The recipients have virtually all been "uncommitted" countries, although the relationship with Romania is *interesting in view of the latter's continuing membership of the Warsaw Pact. Pakistan is particularly dependant on China.*
2. *China's record in peaceful overseas aid has been a good one in that the projects have been sensible and devoid of the political*

CHINA AS AN ARMS EXPORTER—RECENT EXAMPLES

Date of Agreement	Recipient	Weapons System	Number	Remarks
Early 1970s	Romania	P-4 class motor torpedo boats,	13	
		Hu Chwan hydrofoil patrol boats	12	
		Shanghai patrol boats	18	Now made under licence
Early 1970s	Albania	K-63 armoured personnel carriers	?	
		Hu Chwan hydrofoil patrol boats	32	
		Shanghai-II patrol boats	4	
		MiG-21 fighters	?	
1971	Pakistan	Shenyang F-6 fighters	100	
		Osa-class patrol boats	?	
		T-59 main battle tanks	100	
		Hu Chwan hydrofoil patrol boats	6	
1972	Sudan	Shenyang F-4 fighters	9	
		T-62 light tanks	20	
1972	Guinea	Shanghai patrol boats	6	
1972	Sri Lanka	Shanghai patrol boats	5	
1972	Tanzania	Shenyang F-4 fighters	24	Reported to have been an outright gift
1975	Cameroon	Shanghai-II patrol boats	2	
1976	Egypt	Aircraft components	—	Spares for refurbishing Soviet-supplied equipment
1976	Guinea	Shanghai-II patrol boats	2	
1976	Pakistan	Shenyang F-6 fighters	60	
1976	Bangladesh	Shenyang F-6 fighters	50	
1976	Tunisia	Yu Lin patrol boats	2	
1976	Zaire	T-62 light tanks	20	
1977	Pakistan	Hainan fast patrol boats	3	

1. This table is not intended to be exhaustive, but is meant to show the types of equipment supplied and some typical recipients.
2. Sources: ISS "The Military Balance"
   ISS "Strategic Survey"
   SIPRI Yearbook 1978

into border hostilities, Hanoi proposed negotiations but was rebuffed. Peking then sent Chou En-lai's widow, the highly respected Teng Ying-ch'ao, to Cambodia's capital, Phnom Penh, apparently in an effort to persuade the Cambodians to reconsider. In this she evidently failed, but China, apparently considering that Cambodia was China's country right or wrong, then shipped some heavy weapons to it, with which the Cambodians opened an offensive in the Parrot's Beak area in mid-March 1978. At that time, in an effort to help distract Vietnam, China began to apply a combination of none-too-well-considered pressures. It cut off all aid, including rice shipments, to Vietnam's already reeling economy, even though it must have remembered that a similar step by the Russians in 1960 had enraged China without bringing it to terms. China also incited a number of overseas Chinese living in North Vietnam to return to China, precisely because they were well integrated into the economy and society of their adopted country and Vietnam wanted them to stay. In reprisal, Hanoi began to squeeze out part of the Chinese population of South Vietnam, which was not integrated at all and which Hanoi was glad to get rid of. China protested at the resulting influx of

unwanted refugees but to no effect; no agreement has been possible on this issue.

Both sides sought outside support and understanding for their positions. Vietnamese Premier Pham Van Dong visited all five of the ASEAN (Association of Southeast Asian Nations) states (Thailand, Malaysia, Singapore, Indonesia, the Philippines) in September 1978, and at about the same time Cambodian Vice Premier Ieng Sary visited Indonesia and the Philippines, probably on Chinese advice and in an effort to improve his government's poor international image; Teng Hsiao-p'ing visited the remaining three ASEAN states, probably because they are the closest ones to Indo-china, in November 1978. On November 3, 1978, Vietnam signed a treaty of friendship and cooperation with the Soviet Union that appeared to amount to an alliance in everything but name.

This treaty evidently gave Vietnam the assurance it felt it needed to launch a full scale invasion of Cambodia, which it did on December 25. The Soviet Union incited and supported the operation, partly in retaliation for the normalization of relations between China and the United States (announced on December 15). Seeing the Vietnamese as Soviet proxies (the "Cubans of

Southeast Asia"), enraged at their invasion of Cambodia, and determined to strike at least an indirect blow at Russia in the hope of galvanizing the United States and others into taking a strong anti-Soviet stand, China launched an attack across the Vietnamese border on February 17, 1979. The result was some heavy fighting which, however, all parties concerned, including the Soviet Union, apparently wanted and tried to prevent from escalating into a crisis with genuinely global consequences, such as a Soviet attack on China.

There had probably never been a more threatening challenge to Peking's powers of threat management, except perhaps during the Sino-Soviet border crisis of 1969, or in early 1953 (when the United States threatened the PRC with nuclear attack if it did not agree to an armistice in Korea based on the principle of voluntary repatriation of prisoners of war, to which Peking objected because it would mean the non-return of most of the prisoners it had lost). In both these earlier instances Peking had backed down, in the former by agreeing to talks—inconclusive, as it turned out—on the border issue, and in the latter by accepting voluntary repatriation. This time, however, Peking defied the major adversary by striking at the lesser one; apparently it relied, successfully, on its new "normalized" relationship with the United States and on its growing nuclear deterrent, with which, it is by now targeting Soviet European as well as Asian cities, to prevent Soviet retaliation.

China's intrinsic and traditional importance, on the one hand, and the dynamism of its Communist leadership, on the other, render it neither illogical nor surprising that the nation should aspire to a degree of international influence limited only, it appears, by a fairly realistic estimate of the possible risks and costs.

For obvious geographic and cultural reasons, Asia is the primary theatre of China's quest for influence. The Chinese radicals, notably the late Defence Minister Lin Piao in his tract *Long Live the Victory of People's War* (September 3, 1965), have generally emphasized an unconventional strategy for China in Asia centring on "support" for more or less "self-reliant" (Lin's term) "people's wars" that would

2

"strings" attached to aid from countries such as the USSR. The epitomy of such an approach has been the Tanzam railway linking Tanzania and Zambia. This was started in October 1970 and finished on 14 July 1976. Here Presidents Nyerere and Kaunda

inspect a worksite shortly after the project had started. When it was finished Nyerere said that he had had reservations about Chinese involvement, but they had never interfered in either country's affairs.
3. Two Chinese-built locomotives pull a train across a viaduct on the

Tanzam line. The route is 1,156 miles (1,860km) long, with 147 stations, 23 tunnels and over 300 bridges. The project was financed by an interest-free loan from China of US $415million (£220million) repayable over thirty years, starting in 1983.

supposedly bring into being Asian Communist regimes that were autonomous and yet to a significant degree pro-Chinese; obviously such a strategy, even if successful, could not create a satellite empire such as the Soviet Union controls in at least the northern half of Eastern Europe as the result of World War II. From 1949 to 1952, approximately, China supported (with propaganda, arms, etc.) Communist revolutionary movements in Southeast Asia, but the only one that succeeded was the one in Vietnam, which incidentally was the one that received the greatest amount of Chinese support; the others (in Burma, Malaya, Indonesia, and the Philippines) were failures. China therefore abandoned them; in any case, it needed the good will of the governments of Asian countries, and of India above all, because of its dangerous confrontation with the United States centring on the Korean War. In 1965, after a period of ambiguity in its attitude towards "people's war", China was somewhat sobered as to its utility as a grand strategy. In South Asia, the Indian Army retaliated effectively against China's friend Pakistan for the latter's attempt, probably on Chinese advice, to start a "people's war" in Indian-held Kashmir. In Southeast Asia, Vietnam at the beginning of 1965 escalated the "people's war" it had been fostering in South Vietnam by sending in regular units of its army and thereby bringing on the retaliatory commitment of massive American forces to the struggle. Since then, China has been far more cautious and selective about support for "people's war". Its target of choice, since 1968, appears to be Burma, which is accessible, completely nonaligned, and rather vulnerable. The Burma Communist Party has had a kind of sacred quality in radical Chinese eyes because in 1967 it became the only foreign Communist Party to follow Peking's advice to have a Cultural Revolution of its own; as a consequence, all its major leaders were dead by 1968, and China stepped in to rebuild the party and its military arm in the Sino-Burmese border region with cadres, arms, and the like. China has a special dislike for Burmese President Ne Win, because in 1967 he condoned large scale violence against Chinese in Burma who had been conducting demonstrations along

3

the lines of the Cultural Revolution. The case of Chinese revolutionary involvement in Burma, which continues down to the present, is enough to show that China has not completely dropped "people's war" in practice. Nor has it done so in principle; during his November 1978 trip to Southeast Asia, Teng Hsiao-p'ing refused explicitly, and at some political cost, to pledge that China would discontinue support for foreign Communist Parties (and, presumably, for their future efforts at armed revolution). China treats this as a matter of Leninist and Maoist principle; in addition, it likes to use support for local Communist Parties as a lever in dealing with governments, and it probably fears that abandonment of "fraternal" parties would drive them into the arms of Vietnam or, worse still, the Soviet Union.

"Overseas Chinese" in Southeast Asia

Another unconventional approach to possible influence much favoured by Chinese radicals has been close emotional, cultural, political, financial, and sometimes subversive ties with at least some elements of the large overseas Chinese populations of Southeast Asia. China likes their monetary remittances and finds them a valuable

pool of skills. It is therefore unwilling to abandon them and is willing on occasion to try to manipulate them. The problem is that the overseas Chinese communities, although economically strong, are politically weak. In most cases they are not interested in being manipulated by China, being nevertheless disliked and distrusted by the political elites of the Southeast Asian countries (except for Singapore, where Chinese make up a large majority of the population, and Thailand), and are highly vulnerable to physical and other forms of attack by mobs, armies, police forces, political parties, Muslim extremists, and so on. The problem is particularly acute in predominantly Malay areas, Indonesia above all, and less so in other areas. In the mid-1950s, accordingly, when China was cultivating Asian goodwill during the so-called Bandung (after the Asian-African Conference at Bandung, Java, in April 1955) phase of its foreign policy, the declaratory policy of the PRC on the overseas Chinese came to be the following: they were free, although not specifically urged by China, to take out local citizenship, and if they did so they were expected to accept its obligations and own no further allegiance to China. If they preferred to retain Chinese citizenship, they were nevertheless told to respect the laws and customs of their countries of residence. The governments of the latter were

1. *China's trade with the rest of the world jumped from £1957.5million in 1967 to £7527.5million in 1977. By far the leading trading partner is Japan, although trade levels have not regained their 1975 level. Hong Kong occupies a special position,* *importing the bulk of her foodstuffs from the mainland as well as acting as a re-exporter. The high positions of Australia and Canada are due to a recent increase in Chinese grain imports. It is noteworthy that despite the acrimonious diplomatic exchanges the USSR is* *still number 8 in the list, her main imports from the PRC being foodstuffs and clothing, and the exports being generating machinery, trucks and aircraft (presumably civil types). The trade figures show that the Communists have lost none of the Chinese* *skills, the overall balance being in China's favour.*
2. *A Chinese team inspects the Lockheed aircraft factory during a tour of the USA. China desperately needs a larger and more efficient civil air fleet, but once again the problem is one of*

CHINA'S PRINCIPAL TRADING PARTNERS

Country	Total Trade (Million US $)		Ranking	
	1976	1977	1976	1977
Japan	3,052	3,509	1	1
Hong Kong	1,620	1,779	2	2
W. Germany	952	826	3	3
Australia	380	631	7	
Romania	451	600	5	5
Canada	309	459	9	6
US	351	391	8	7
USSR	417	338	6	8
Singapore	295	324	10	9
UK	277	284	12	10

1

CHINA'S TRADE BALANCES

Year	(Billion US $)		
	Exports	Imports	Balance
1977	2.1	2.2	−0.2
1971	2.5	2.3	0.2
1972	3.2	2.8	0.3
1973	5.1	5.2	−0.2
1974	6.7	7.4	−0.8
1975	7.2	7.4	−0.2
1976	7.3	6.0	1.3
1977	8.0	7.1	0.9

Note: Data are rounded.
Source: China: International Trade
CIA National Foreign Assessment Center. Dec. 78.

3

2

finance. Principal suppliers are the USA, Britain and France.

3. Vice-Premier Teng Hsiao-P'ing inspecting the Space Shuttle during his highly successful tour of the United States. While a visit to the Space Center is a standard part of all VIP tours Teng's visit had real purpose because China is very much in the space business. A total of eight launches have taken place so far (see table on page 174) and there are strong indications that they wish to reserve payload on the Shuttle for some of their own experiments.

China's programme is modest but well-planned.

4. Teng inspects a space capsule. Again, there are reliable reports that China is actively considering a manned programme, which would, in fact, be a logical extension of her present activities.

China is not going to undertake space "spectaculars" on the American or Soviet lines as the leaders are most unlikely to be prepared to allocate the vast sums of money necessary. In the space programme top priority is given to reconnaissance satellites.

4

1. *A significant step in restoring friendly relations between China and Japan was made when the instruments of ratification of the Treaty of Peace and Friendship were exchanged in Tokyo on 23 October 1978 in the presence of Teng Hsiao-ping (one of the* *Chinese Vice Premiers) and Mr Fukuda, the Japanese Prime Minister. This cleared the way for the extension of the existing trade agreement from 1985 to 1990, and China agreed to increase oil supplies to Japan in the years 1983-85 from 30 million tonnes to* *50 million, while importing more technology—especially in the construction of factories—from Japan. Under this extension the trade between the two countries is forecast to increase from US$20million in 1985 to US$80million in 1990. This table* *shows the more recent contracts signed with Japanese firms. The emphasis on the construction of factories is very clear, but the orders for ships suggest that China's trade is growing at a rate greater than her shipbuilding industry can build new ships. The*

encouraged to grant citizenship to resident Chinese seeking it, but not to force it on them regardless of their wishes as President Ngo Dinh Diem did in South Vietnam in 1955, and not to persecute them if they retained Chinese citizenship. No overseas Chinese could hold dual citizenship. China disclaimed any desire to interfere on behalf of overseas Chinese, regardless of their citizenship, but admitted to retaining an interest in their welfare. This is not only China's declaratory policy but, to a considerable extent at any rate, its actual policy on this question, at least in relatively normal times.

In 1964, however, China allowed itself to be carried away by excitement over such developments as the fall of its hated adversary, Krushchev, its own debut as a nuclear power, and the rapid leftward movement of the political climate in Indonesia into forming a close although informal alliance with President Sukarno and the Indonesian Communist Party (PKI), to which China encouraged overseas Chinese to contribute funds. Buoyed up by China's support, among other things, and yet alarmed by an apparent collapse of Sukarno's health, the PKI, with China's knowledge but seemingly without its active encouragement,

attempted a coup against the army leadership on September 30, 1965, that backfired disastrously. In the ensuing slaughter many Chinese were killed, and Peking could provide them no effective protection. Since then Peking has reverted essentially to the normal, relatively cautious policy just described. During the Cultural Revolution, militant Red Guards accused the Foreign Ministry of not doing enough to promote the interests of the overseas Chinese. Recent developments in Sino-Vietnamese relations show that deviations toward a more forceful overseas Chinese policy are still possible. During his November 1978 visit to Southeast Asia, Teng Hsiao-p'ing found a restrained welcome in Singapore and Malaysia, where the Chinese communities are officially regarded as a serious political problem (and Vietnam is not much feared), and his warmest welcome in Thailand, where the Chinese community is fairly happily assimilated (and Vietnam is viewed with great suspicion).

The Chinese moderates, who have essentially dominated China's foreign policy since about 1970, place relatively little stock in unconventional approaches such as support for "people's war" and manipulation of overseas Chinese communities. They

place much more emphasis on diplomacy, and above all on cultivating good relations with most states—South Africa is an obvious exception—in order to cope with the perceived main adversary—the United States until the late 1960s, the Soviet Union since then.

China is engaged not only in a cross-border confrontation with the Soviet Union, but also in a contest with it for comparative influence nearly everywhere, and above all in Asia. Since 1969 the Soviet Union has been proposing a "collective security" system for Asia resembling the Helsinki Agreement of 1975 for Europe. Russia denies that its purpose is anti-Chinese, but nobody believes it, least of all China.

Articulate Chinese opposition to "collective security" is a major reason why the idea has made no progress toward fulfilment. As its counter the PRC has proposed to other governments since the early 1970s that they express opposition to efforts at "hegemony" on the part of any power or group of powers; "antihegemony" clauses were included in the (Sino-American) Shanghai Communiqué of February 1972, the Chou-Tanaka Communiqué of September 1972, and the Sino-Japanese treaty of peace and friendship of August 1978. The PRC says unilaterally,

RECENT CHINESE/JAPANESE COMMERCIAL TRANSACTIONS

Company	Approx. value	Product	Comments
Mitsui Corp.	£44 million	Four ships	One 1,500-ton supply ship—8,000 bhp diesel engine; Three 1,200-ton supply ship—6,000 bhp diesel engine
Mitsui Corp.	£7 million	Two geophysical survey ships	
	£27-36 million	Five suction dredgers Four pile-driving vessels	Probably for use in building an integrated steelworks near Shanghai. A cargo-handling area is also to be built by the Japanese.
Nippon Yusen Kaisha	—	Used bulk carriers	
Marabeui Corp.	—	Secondhand dry cargo ships	
Nippon Steel	£890 million	Steel	Plant to be constructed at Shanghai. Eventual annual capacity: 6 million tons.
Nikki Marubeui	£55 million	Ethylene	Plant to be constructed at Taching.
Hitachi Toshiba	£33-44 million £31 million	Integrated circuits	Plant to be constructed at Chengyang; Plant to be constructed at Wushi.
Asahi Glass	£29 million	Tube glass for colour TV	Plant to be constructed at Chengyang.
Kurasay	£16 million	Synthetic leather	
Mitsubishi Corp.	£5 million	Ethylene	Plant to be constructed at Kirin.
		Jack-up type offshore drilling rigs	Enquiries have been made.
		Joint project for the manufacture of aircraft jet engines	An engine is now being developed by the Ministry of International Trade and Industry (MITI) and the Agency of Industrial Science and Technology to use in a short take-off and landing (STOL) plane. The aircraft should be ready to fly in 1982.

RECENT CHINESE/US COMMERCIAL TRANSACTIONS

Company	Approx. value	Product
US Steel	£500 million	Iron ore mines and processing facilities
Bethlehem Steel	£50 mil +	Iron ore mines and processing facilities
Kaiser Engineers	£2.5 mil	Iron ore mines and processing facilities
Intercontinental Hotels/Hyatt	£500 mil +	15 1,000-room hotels
Fluor	£400 mil	Copper mine development
Boeing	£75 mil	Three 747
—	—	Cyber 72*

* Ostensibly for processing geophysical data in oil surveys and in earthquake detection, but apparently could be adapted for use in air defence and anti submarine systems.

aircraft engine project is very significant.

2. The Chinese government has obviously qualified its desire to import new technology with the proviso that no one foreign country will be able to achieve a strangle-hold as did the USSR in the 1950s. These orders placed with firms in the USA are evidence of such diversification.

3. Another milestone in China's foreign policy was achieved when Vice-Premier Teng Hsiao-ping visited the United States between 28 January and 5 February 1979. Despite the message on this banner he did not visit New York as both that city and San Francisco have large Chinese communities and it was feared that there could be hostile demonstrations. Instead, he followed his stay in Washington with visits to Atlanta, Houston and Seattle. He scored a considerable personal triumph, although his outspoken comments on the Soviet Union's "plans for world hegemony" caused some dismay in Washington and considerable annoyance in Moscow.

and loudly, that the Soviet Union is seeking such "hegemony". Russia denies it and objects strenuously to "antihegemony" clauses; for this reason the Japanese government insisted on including an article in its treaty with China to the effect that nothing in the treaty affected the relations of either signatory with any third party, but without succeeding in mollifying Soviet objections.

China has been somewhat more adroit in projecting an image of approval for ASEAN and for its announced goal of "neutrality" for Southeast Asia than has either the Soviet Union or Vietnam. China by now has diplomatic relations with three of the ASEAN states—Malaysia, the Philippines, and Thailand—the other two, Singapore and Indonesia, are holding out mainly because of their nervousness over the possible impact of a PRC embassy on their large Chinese communities. On the whole, for geographic and cultural reasons, and because of its usually deft diplomacy, China is considerably ahead of Russia in the contest for influence in Asia; the main exceptions are Vietnam and Afghanistan, both of which worry China considerably. Soviet influence in India, although still a problem for China, is much less under the Desai government than it was under the preceding government of Mrs. Gandhi.

Japan practices a nominal policy of "equidistance" between the two giant Communist adversaries, but this is mainly because of the proximity of dangerous Soviet military power and attractive Siberian natural resources. In all other respects Japan prefers China as a genuinely Asian neighbour with whom it has had a long, although not always friendly, relationship and by whom it does not feel threatened. For its part, China currently regards Japan as its main Asian friend and partner. The PRC tries to minimise the potential for Soviet influence on Japan by such tactics as encouraging the Japanese to build up the defensive capabilities of the Self Defence Forces and maintain a close security relationship with the United States, supporting the Japanese demand for the return of the Northern Territories, and urging abstention from involvement in the development of Siberian resources.

For some years China has been

3

trying to increase its own oil exports to Japan, both as a means of paying for its expanding imports from Japan and as a means of reducing Japanese interest in Siberian oil. Especially since the treaty of August 1978 and Teng Hsiao-p'ing's triumphant visit to Japan shortly afterwards, Sino-Japanese trade and the negotiation of Japanese credits to cover new imports of Japanese technology and capital equipment have proceeded at an astonishing pace. The only real current problem is China's ability to pay, which remains uncertain. China would evidently like to work out some form of defence relationship with Japan, but this aim is hampered by serious political obstacles on both sides, as well as by concern over the Soviet response.

China favours stability in Korea

As already indicated, China's policy toward that perennial trouble spot in Northeast Asia, Korea, is one of favouring stability as the best guarantee for its own security. This means, among other things, encouraging North Korea to take a political rather than a military approach to reunification and to avoid provoking the United States. On the other hand, it is essential for China, as the weaker party to the Sino-Soviet dispute, to maintain at least a

moderately friendly relationship with Kim Il Sung, if only to prevent him from inclining toward the Soviet Union, for example by giving Soviet troops unopposed access to the Korean-Manchurian frontier in the event of a Sino-Soviet war. China's task in cultivating the irascible North Korean dictator is made easier by the fact that Russia takes little trouble to conceal its dislike for him or its preference for a "German" solution (one nation, two states) for the Korean question. The Soviet Union has even gone so far as to initiate some non-diplomatic contacts with South Korea, and it seems possible that China may follow suit, but more cautiously because of its problem with North Korea.

Until recently, the PRC took a keen interest in the affairs of the South Asian subcontinent. It had a generally poor relationship with the Indian governments of Nehru and his daughter Indira Gandhi after the late 1950s because of their pro-Soviet leanings and the existence of a Sino-Indian border dispute. To help balance India, China maintained a confrontation of sorts with it and cultivated a very close relationshp with India's enemy, Pakistan, under the presidencies of Ayub and Bhutto. All this is now changed.

The Sino-Indian border dispute has not been acute since China's resounding victory in the brief war of October-November 1962, and there are signs that India may be prepared to accept

1. The PLA's predominant concern in peacetime is the maintenance of an unceasing watch on the northern borders. The existence of the People's Militia ensures that local knowledge and expertise is always available to help the regulars of the Main Force.

Further, the PLA is always prepared to use the most suitable means of transport, such as here in the Gobi Desert where the Bactrian camel is ideal. The long, dark winter coat and short sturdy legs of Camelus bactrianus enable it to cope well with work in the

mountains and cold desert conditions of the Gobi. Herds of wild Bactrian camels still roam the Gobi desert existing on what little amount of vegetation they can find. The PLA would not fight to defend territory such as this, but would encourage the Soviets to

overextend their communications.
2. *Further East, China's strategic worries are increased by the situation in the Korean peninsula where the activities of the Pyongyang government frequently cause concern. The perpetual animosity between north and south*

1

—typified by these watchful North Koreans—could, if it explodes, drag in the USSR, China and the USA, since the latter still maintains a substantial force in the south. The North Koreans sided with China over the Vietnam-Kampuchea dispute, and they depend heavily upon China for oil supplies, but North Korea also owes the USSR more than £800 million and depends upon Russia for sophisticated military equipment. The USSR has recently wrested a warm water port out of the North Koreans at Najin, north of Wonsan, in return for the rescheduling of this massive debt, an object lesson for those taking credit from the USSR. **3.** The official caption for this picture states that it shows Korean People's Army fighters practising shooting with "deep hatred for the US aggressors". This sort of rhetoric underlines the dangers of the situation which most Western countries do their best to forget, although many, including the United Kingdom, still have a legal obligation to return to the aid of South Korea should it be attacked by the North.

1. *A crowd watches the delicate operation of lowering a Chinese-made hydroturbine generator into its housing at the Liuchiahsia hydro-electric station in 1974. Situated on the Yellow River in Kansu province this hydroelectric station has an output of* *5,700million kilowatt-hours per year, and supplies power to the three provinces of Kansu, Shensi and Chinghai. The dam and reservoir on the Yellow River enable the Chinese to achieve their ancient dream of regulating the flow of water, thus preventing floods in* *the wet season and ensuring a constant supply in the dry season for the irrigation schemes nearer the sea. The lot of the long-suffering peasant in China has been to struggle for a living, with his efforts regularly brought to nought either by natural disasters or by the* *depradations of war. The Communists have done more to improve the standards and prospects of life for the peasants than any previous government in China, and schemes such as this, allied to the measures to relieve famine and disease, will ensure*

1

the *de facto* compromise based on the status quo that China has proposed at intervals since 1960: retention of the eastern disputed area (the Northeast Frontier Agency, between Assam and Tibet) by India, and retention of the western disputed area (Aksai Chin, between Kashmir and Sinkiang and Tibet) by China. The Indo-Pakistani quarrel, China's other main source of leverage on the international politics of the subcontinent, has tapered off since Pakistan's defeat by India in 1971, the sundering of Bangla Desh (East Bengal) from Pakistan, and the reluctant acceptance by Pakistan of a clearly secondary position as compared with India. Since the fall of Bhutto in 1977, Pakistan has entered the latest of its phases of acute internal difficulty, one in which China can be of little influence; in any case, the PRC feels much less friendship for the right wing government of President Zia than it did for that of Bhutto.

Since the fall of Mrs. Ghandi in 1977, the Indian government has maintained a much less close relationship with the Soviet Union and a considerably closer one with the United States, and it has shown signs of wanting a closer one with the PRC. In essence, the states of South Asia have quite properly turned their almost undivided attention to their pressing internal problems and de-emphasized foreign policy; this they are fortunately in a position to do because the subcontinent is shielded to a high degree from the outside world by mountains and ocean.

On the whole, China in its current nonradical mood is respected, although not always liked, in Asia. The quest for Chinese influence in Asia is doing well, except in South Asia, and there is no reason why the PRC should try to accelerate it by more aggressive approaches, even when and if Chinese power becomes considerably greater than it is now. In any case, the PRC for practical purposes is militarily contained by the Soviet Union, as it once was by the United States. It is also balanced, politically and diplomatically, not only by the "superpowers" but by Japan and by the other regional states.

Next to the "superpowers" and Asia, China reserves a special place in its foreign policy for the "second world"— the developed countries other than the "superpowers". Japan having already been discussed under the rubric of Asia, there remains principally Western Europe, which is important to China chiefly for strategic reasons already described but also for others as well. China fears "Finlandization"—in other words, the possible falling of Western Europe, with or without a war, under a degree of Soviet influence approximating that which the Soviet Union exercises over Eastern Europe, or more precisely Finland. Much as China's European policy (which is more active than is generally realized even though the results to date have not been very obvious except in the field of diplomatic relations and in trade) was once aimed mainly at countering American influence in Europe, so it is now aimed mainly at countering Soviet influence in Europe. China favours West European regional organizations such as the Common Market, with which it has recently established an official relationship. China dislikes Eurocommunism, nominally because of its "revisionist" tendencies but actually because of its potential as an entering wedge for Soviet influence.

China's influence on other communist parties

Although much less intensely than in the 1960s, when Maoism was a major influence on Chinese foreign policy, the PRC tries to counter Soviet influence and enhance its own on what is left—collectively speaking—of the international communist movement and on the extreme leftist "fringe" or "splinter" groups, whose emergence in the early 1960s owed much to Chinese influence. In the former case, China's attention is lavished mainly on parties, such as the Yugoslav and Romanian, that have maintained a significant degree of independence from Soviet influence. Yugoslavia is currently of great importance to China as another Communist state threatened with Soviet pressures after the death of

that there is broad-based support for the Party, at least among the older generation.
2. Another hydroelectric project, this time at Tanchiangkou in Hupeh province, which includes a 900,000 kilowatt power station. China is rich in energy resources, having plentiful supplies of coal, oil, and water for hydroelectric schemes such as this. In none of these three fields have they tapped the full potential, however, and this receives due priority in each successive economic plan, but China has many priority problems.

its leader, and of great interest as a source of ideas on how to move toward "market socialism" from a previously Leninist society; dozens of Chinese missions, including one led by Hua Kuo-feng, have visited Yugoslavia since Tito's visit to China in the summer of 1977. China's relations with Albania, once a close friend of China's because of its hostility (after 1960) to the Soviet Union, have cooled sharply in the 1970s, not because Albania has turned back to Russia (it has not) but because the primitive-minded Albanian leadership objects to China's cultivation of the United States and NATO, which appears opportunistic from Tirana's perspective. For similar reasons and to Chinese annoyance, Tirana has tended to supplant Peking as the mecca for the fringe groups of the far left.

China's main concern in the Third World beyond Asia—the Middle East, Africa, and Latin America—has been essentially the same as elsewhere—opposition to American influence until the late 1960s, opposition to Soviet influence since then. Given the collectivist, "one-man democracy" bent of the political elites of so much of the Third World, China's task was probably easier in the earlier stage than it is in the current one. For China, as for Russia, opposition to the United States can require little more than making trouble under the banner of anti-"imperialist" revolution; opposition to the Soviet Union, on the other hand, requires the offering of something more constructive by way of an alternative.

The beginning of China's shift from a largely troublemaking to a more constructive role in the Third World dates from about 1965, a year of setbacks when China faced not only escalation in Vietnam, an anti-Communist massacre in Indonesia, and military defeat for its friend Pakistan, but also a series of anti-Communist and anti-Chinese military coups in Africa and, worse still, the failure of the Afro-Asian Conference to meet at Algiers, on which Peking had pinned high hopes for the advancement of its influence in the Third World. From that period dates the initiation of China's most important single contribution to the Third World, the Tanzam (Tanzania-Zambia) Railway, as well as the decline of China's troublemaking ("revolutionary") activities. The PRC rejoiced at the anti-Soviet turn taken by Egypt under Sadat after 1970.

At present China is greatly concerned over the difficulties of the Shah of Iran, whom it esteems for his anti-Soviet stand, and over the obvious possibility that turmoil in Iran may somehow benefit Moscow's interests. In Africa, China is understandably worried by the successes of the Soviet-Cuban axis in Angola and Ethiopia, without being able to do much to counter them beyond offering some support to Somalia since it turned against Russia. In remote Latin America, the PRC has never exercised much political influence, and less in leftist circles than does Castro, whom China has long considered excessively pro-Soviet.

In its quest for worldwide influence, China, while disclaiming any desire to be a "superpower", has not done badly considering its material weakness. It benefits from the errors made and resentments generated by the "superpowers", as well as from the peculiar attraction exercised on the minds of so many foreigners by the image of China—its ancient and complex culture, its size, its potential power, its dynamism, etc. As soon as the United States ceased its opposition, China entered the United Nations in lieu of the Republic of China in 1971, and in the process acquired a permanent seat on the Security Council, with a veto of course, a prestige symbol possessed by no other developing country. The PRC is also the only state in the latter category to be a major nuclear power. It

CHINA'S FOREIGN POLICY AND NATIONAL INTEREST

1. China's efforts to make friends have been strenuous, although some of the choices seem to have been unwise. This 1977 visit to Peking by Pol Pot, the former dictatorial ruler of Kampuchea suggested that the Chinese supported his brutal, inhuman methods, which was not so.

2. When Vietnam invaded Kampuchea in December 1977 China was at first unable to intervene, although she later carried out a "punitive attack" against the Vietnamese. China's diplomatic efforts have covered both small "Third World" countries and major Western powers: Chairman Hua Kuo-feng is seen here with (**3**) President Ziaur Rahman of Bangladesh, (**4**) Mrs Margaret Thatcher, now British Prime Minister, (**5**) President (now Emperor) Bokassa of the Central African Empire, and (**6**) Prime Minister Somare of Papua New Guinea.

7. Far more crucial is the relationship with the USA. Teng Hsiao-ping's visit was a great success although his accusations against the USSR were quite explicit.

1

2

China's trading relationship with the United States has improved tremendously over recent years: in 1978 US trade with the PRC rose more than three times the level of 1977, and US exports to China in 1979 expected to reach $1.25 billion, with Chinese exports to the US around $400 million. With China's relaxation of ideological restraints on exporting raw materials in large quantities to the industrial West, the first exports of Chinese oil to the US were expected in 1979. China is committed to a Ten Year Plan (1976-85) designed to provide the basis for a modernization of agriculture, industry, national defence, and science and technology, a Plan that would propel China into the front ranks of the industrialized nations by the year 2000. The investment needed for this plan is estimated to be in the region of 600 million dollars, and procurement of the capital equipment for the Plan has already started. China is having to borrow on the international market to cover the gap between earnings and expenditures.

1. *When the Chinese leaders decided that there was no alternative but to import both modern technology and goods their political and military leaders began a series of tours all over the Western world, making contacts, inspecting products and assessing what would be most cost-effective for their country's needs. These much-publicised tours gave rise to a considerable degree of euphoria in Western business circles as the prospect of a civil market of 900million opened up, while the arms sales-men saw the chance of orders to re-equip the numerically largest armed force in the world. However, the Chinese have proved to be much more hard-headed and pragmatic than many Westerners had expected; each equipment area has been inspected meticulously and orders have only been placed after the most thorough consideration, which has included, among many other factors, the desire not to become too dependent upon any one supplier in any area. Here Vice-Premier Wang Zhen is*

has diplomatic relations with most other countries, aid programmes of its own, and in short nearly all the trappings of great power status.

It is a curious thing that China has enhanced its influence most effectively in those areas and respects where classical Maoism would have predicted the least success, and vice versa. This is only one among many current testimonials to the essential irrelevance of the Great Helmsman's "thought".

China inherited from previous history a series of border disputes with most of its neighbours. The seriousness of these has varied inversely with the level of the political relationship between China and the country in question and has therefore been greatest in the cases of India and the Soviet Union. In the early 1960s, China **1** signed boundary treaties on a more or less compromise basis with Burma, Nepal, Pakistan, and Afghanistan, mainly in order to isolate and pressure India on the border question, and also with the Mongolian People's Republic, in the vain hope of countering the over-whelming Soviet influence over that isolated country. In 1970, Peking reached an informal boundary agreement with North Korea on their mutual territorial differences. A similar dispute currently exists with Vietnam with respect both to two island groups in the South China Sea (the Paracels and the Spratlys) and to the common land frontier; the tense general relationship between the two parties, and the early 1979 war above all, render the resolution of this dispute in the near future improbable.

The most serious territorial dispute is of course with the Soviet Union. Since 1969 China has denied seeking more than minor rectifications of the border created through Tsarist and Soviet expansion, and the Soviet Union has recently shown a tendency to concede that this is in fact China's position. The Soviet Union is still very sensitive to China's assertion that there remain small "disputed areas", of which the most sensitive is in the immediate vicinity of the Soviet Far Eastern city of Khabarovsk. Except in this area, Moscow has conceded in principle China's position that the international boundary along the Amur and Ussuri Rivers runs along the middle of the main channel, rather than **2**

RECENT CHINESE/EUROPEAN COMMERCIAL TRANSACTIONS

Country	Company	Product	Comments
UK	Rolls-Royce	RB 168-255 augmented turbofan aircraft engines	Value £80 million; agreement includes supply to China of some engines, plus manufacturing licence and assistance in establishing production at Sian. (Possibility that China intends to produce the engines for a new indigenous fighter, "F-12"—see fold-out, pages 114-117). Date 1975.
UK	—	Westland WG 34 helicopters	1978-79
UK	Hawker-Siddeley	Harrier VTOL aircraft	Interest has also been shown in purchasing the Sea Harrier
UK	National Coal Board	Design, construction and equipment for 2 2 coal mines	
UK	GEC and Babcock	Equipment for power station	China is to build the station in Hongkong
UK	British Shipbuilders	Equipment for developing offshore oil reserves	The Chinese are welcoming finance from abroad to help develop their oil reserves.
UK		Laser sight system and missiles now under development	
UK or West Germany		100,000 metric tonnes- a year methanol plant	
West Germany		4 Bolkow Bo-105 helicopters. 100 more to follow, specially equipped for military missions	Ostensibly to be used as aids in oil prospecting, they could be adapted for anti-tank purposes.
France/Germany	Euromissile	HOT and MILAN anti-tank missiles	MILAN is a NATO missile, sales of which have already been made to Syria.
Italy	Aeritalia, Electronica San, Giorgio, Selenia, SIT-Siemens	Electronic guidance systems	
Italy		Agusta helicopters	Manufactured under licence in Italy for US-Bell, so export of these helicopters could be vetoed by the USA.
Italy	Oto-Melara	76/62 AA and AM guns	
W. Europe		370/142 computer	For processing geophysical data in oil surveys and in earthquake detection, but could be adapted for use in air defence and anti-submarine warfare systems.
W. Europe		Strategic metals, including aluminium and manganese	Possibly for use in the production of new fighter aircraft

An agreement in principle has been made to guarantee, through the UK Export Credits Guarantee Department, a line of credit of £2.5bn, to be raised by UK banks to support a £7bn economic cooperation agreement, 1980-1985.
An EEC-China consortium for trade agreements is now under consideration.

shown visiting a British Aerospace factory, where he is examining a Hawk trainer. The PLA-Air Force urgently needs a new advanced trainer to replace its aging fleet of two-seat adaptations of the F-2 (Chinese version of the Soviet MiG-15) and F-4 (MiG-17). The

BAe Hawk is not just a trainer, however, and it possesses a very effective ground-attack capability, which could prove invaluable to the PLA. No orders have yet resulted from this visit.
2. This table shows some of the most recent Chinese commercial

transactions with Western Europe, together with some of the more serious enquiries. Comparison with orders and enquiries made in Japan and the United States (see page 54) shows just how carefully China is spreading her interests.
3. In early 1979 the former British

Secretary of State for Trade, Mr Eric Varley, led a delegation to the People's Republic of China, and he is shown here signing the resulting Economic Trade Agreement, with his Chinese counterpart, Mr Li Ch'iang, Minister of Foreign Trade.

along the Manchurian bank as previously asserted by the Soviet side. The actual territorial differences between the two sides are not very great, and a compromise agreement could undoubtedly be reached if it were not for the extremely bad state of the general relationship between them.

China's most serious territorial problem is not with a foreign but with a domestic rival. China is a divided country, although of course a most unequally divided one. Taiwan remains under the control of the Republic of China dominated by the Kuomintang, which challenges the PRC's right to rule not merely Taiwan but the mainland itself. For reasons relating mainly to the inequality of the division — in other words, ultimate confidence on China's part, rigidity engendered by a sense of weakness on Taiwan's part — no solution of the issue along "German" lines (one nation, two states coexisting more or less *de jure*) is in sight, at least in the near future. Since China displaced Taiwan in the United Nations in 1971, it has done the same in dozens of foreign capitals. By 1978 only three major states — the United States, the Republic of Korea, and Saudi Arabia — still recognized Taiwan, and all three of these wanted to change to China. The United States did so at the beginning of 1979, while continuing its alliance with Taiwan until the end of the year and planning to sell defensive arms sales to it after that. Unlike the

radicals, China's moderates are in no great hurry to achieve the "liberation" of Taiwan, a process that would present considerable difficulties if only because of the vast economic and social differences between the two Chinas. The moderates are trying to bring Taiwan to terms through a process of gradual isolation, with the largely hypothetical threat of military action as an ultimate sanction. In addition to the diplomatic strangulation already mentioned, the PRC has been trying to reduce the economic and cultural ties of the overseas Chinese with Taiwan, and above all to bring the United States to break off the official aspects of its relationship with Taiwan.

For, although American abandonment of Taiwan is probably not a sufficient condition for the "liberation" of the island, or for the unification of China in some less dramatic way, it is almost certainly a necessary condition. The main problem has been that, whereas the United States would have liked to "normalize" its relations with the PRC (i.e., establish full diplomatic relations in lieu of liaison offices) without abandoning in full its commitment to the security of Taiwan, the PRC insisted that the latter was a precondition for the former.

Beginning in 1973, China has put forward three conditions for "normalization": the cutting by the United States of all diplomatic ties with Taiwan, the withdrawal of the few remaining Ameri-

can military personnel from Taiwan, and the abrogation by the United States of its security treaty with the Republic of China. The first two of these demands did not present much of a problem for current American policy, but the third did, for a variety of ethical and political reasons, notably the possible impact on American "credibility" in the eyes of such other allies as Japan. At any rate, the United States was unwilling to abrogate the security treaty without some convincing assurance that China would not use force against Taiwan, and the PRC has refused to give such an assurance both as a matter of principle and out of concern that to do so would weaken its bargaining power with respect to Taiwan. The search for a compromise formula continued until December 1978, when the United States finally abandoned its demand for an assurance from Peking on Taiwan's security and Peking agreed to tolerate continued sales of American defensive arms to Taiwan.

China will remain an international influence

Unless it encounters some disaster of the kind mentioned earlier, China, whether it succeeds in achieving unification with Taiwan or not, is likely to remain a major influence in international affairs, and in Asia above all. Apart from a disaster, a serious policy error on China's part (such as reversion to active promotion of "revolution" in Asia and the rest of the Third World) could endanger China's prospects for influence, but such an error seems unlikely at least in the near future. China's foreign policy is now being conducted, and will probably continue to be conducted, in the spirit of Hua Kuo-feng's recent statement that what the PRC needs most is a period of stability in its international environment as the best guarantee for the success of the "four modernizations". On the security front, the outlook is somewhat less promising; the Soviet Union remains dangerous, and China occasionally seems to underestimate the possible results of the dislike with which it is viewed by the entire Soviet elite, and by the military perhaps most of all.

THE ORGANIZATION OF CHINA'S GROUND FORCES

Professor Harvey W. Nelsen

Associate Professor, International Program, University of South Florida.

The People's Liberation Army (PLA) is 3,600,000 strong and its mainstay is the infantry—tough, well-trained and resolute. These young soldiers on parade know that they are members of an élite institution whose value to the State has been proved in both war and peace. The PLA needs lots of infantrymen to cover its vast areas of responsibility and these would undoubtedly be able to deal with most of the tasks. But the problem is on the northern borders where the Soviet Union has strong, modern forces, well-equipped with tactical missiles, self-propelled artillery and large numbers of tanks. The challenge facing the PLA is how to counter this threat: could the traditional methods of "people's war" suffice, or must a massive and costly re-equipment programme be undertaken?

The ground forces of the People's Liberation Army are 3,600,000 strong and are divided into three elements: the Main Force, Regional Forces and the People's Militia. The Main Force comprises 40 Army Corps, and independent units including 10 to 12 armoured divisions, three airborne divisions, as well as artillery, engineer and railway troops. Training and morale of the soldiers are good, but much of the equipment, though rugged and reliable, is old and needs replacement.

1. The political battle for the hearts and minds of the officers and fighters of the PLA is unceasing and the value of the programme was tested — sometimes almost to breaking-point — during the Great Proletarian Cultural Revolution. During that time there were periods when the integrity of the nation rested on the shoulders of the PLA; the Main Force stood the test, but the Regional Force, very occasionally, faltered. Here a Main Force unit holds a political rally, the commissar atop the T-59 leading the slogan-shouting.

2. Parades of military might serve a number of purposes: they show the soldiers and equipment to the Party and the people, and they also demonstrate to the soldiers that it is the Party that is in charge. These detachments are 152mm guns of Soviet design.

3. China is divided into 11 Military Regions, which in time of war would become autonomous "Fronts" and take command of all military forces within their boundaries. In peace, however, the Main Force units are controlled from Peking with Military

The ground forces of the People's Liberation Army of the People's Republic of China constitute between 80 and 85 per cent of military personnel — about 3.6 million of the 4.3 million total. If paramilitary forces are also considered, the ground forces make up about 97 per cent of the grand total. The regular PLA ground forces also have the best military capabilities of the three services. While inferior in equipment, mobility and firepower to advanced military systems, the ground forces come much nearer to equalling the Soviet and US militaries than do the technologically backward naval and air forces. The massive size of the infantry combined with fine individual and small unit training and high morale do much to offset the firepower and mobility disadvantages.

Ever since General Douglas Macarthur warned Americans against engaging in a land war in Asia, it has been axiomatic that the US should avoid a conventional war on the Chinese mainland. The USSR seems to have reached the same conclusion, since the 1969 border clashes have not led to an escalating conflict. This understandable reluctance to fight a land war in China is partly due to its large size, difficult terrain and vast population. But much of the credit should go to the effective deterrent provided by the PLA ground forces.

The deterrent and defensive nature of the ground forces is reflected in their organization. They are divided into three major components — main forces, regional (sometimes called "local") forces, and the militia and other paramilitary units. The main forces are intended to do battle with the enemy divisions. Regional forces are responsible for local self-defence, organiza-

tion and leadership of guerrilla units, and light infantry support to main force units in major engagements. The militia serves as the manpower reserve since there is no other reserve system. In wartime, they would make up the bulk of guerrilla troops and provide logistical and intelligence support to the other forces.

Strategically, the concept has been

Regions responsible mainly for administrative matters. This map shows the boundaries of the Military Regions and an estimate of the disposition of the Army Corps of the Main Force. The majority faces the Soviet Union, but note those around the Lop

Nor nuclear centre and facing Vietnam. The Regional Forces are relatively static, but Main Force formations are redeployed according to the threat. In 1978/79, for example, three Army Corps moved to face the border with Vietnam; two of these had

been facing Taiwan and the third Hong Kong.
4. The organization of a Main Force Army Corps of the PLA. This Corps is very strong in infantry (37,818 all ranks in three divisions) and the men are well-trained and highly motivated, but

they are only foot-mobile, with no armoured personnel carriers or passenger-carrying trucks. All artillery weapons are towed. There are also fewer logistics resources than would be found in a Western formation of this size; however, the logistic requirement is smaller.

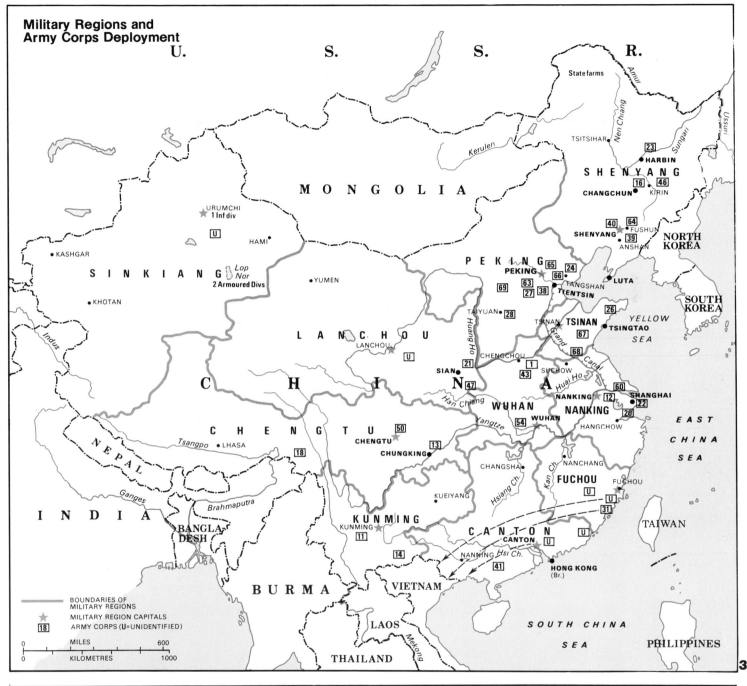

Military Regions and Army Corps Deployment

3

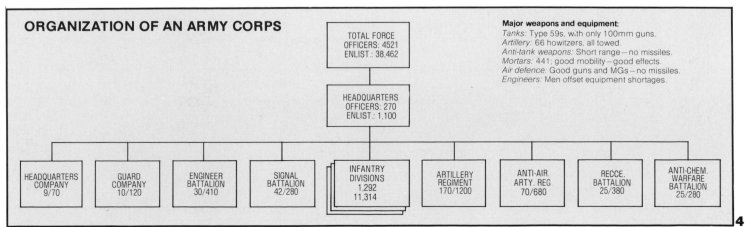

ORGANIZATION OF AN ARMY CORPS

TOTAL FORCE
OFFICERS: 4521
ENLIST.: 38,462

HEADQUARTERS
OFFICERS: 270
ENLIST.: 1,100

| HEADQUARTERS COMPANY 9/70 | GUARD COMPANY 10/120 | ENGINEER BATTALION 30/410 | SIGNAL BATTALION 42/280 | INFANTRY DIVISIONS 1,292 11,314 | ARTILLERY REGIMENT 170/1200 | ANTI-AIR. ARTY. REG. 70/680 | RECCE. BATTALION 25/380 | ANTI-CHEM. WARFARE BATTALION 25/280 |

Major weapons and equipment:
Tanks: Type 59s, with only 100mm guns.
Artillery: 66 howitzers, all towed.
Anti-tank weapons: Short range—no missiles.
Mortars: 441; good mobility—good effects.
Air defence: Good guns and MGs—no missiles.
Engineers: Men offset equipment shortages.

4

1. The PLA, like armies the world over, encourages professional pride and a sense of achievement through a system of tests, with success being marked by certificates and public acknowledgement. Throughout recent years the only way to judge the difference between officers and soldiers has been through the number of pockets on the uniform jacket. The officer on the left has four pockets but there is no visible distinction to indicate his rank or grade, while the soldiers' jackets have only two breast pockets.

2. Mao's dictum that "Political power grows out of the barrel of a gun" is well known, but the equally important second part is often forgotten: "The Party commands the gun and the gun must never be allowed to command the Party". Party control is assured through a system of political control and education, achieved through two parallel structures: the Party committees and the political department. Here the most essential element – a unit Party cell – is conducting its daily meeting.

3. All insignia indicating rank and

branch of service were abolished in June 1965, but merit badges were retained and other badges may be on their way back. This truck driver has badges on his red collar tabs—possibly indicating rank—together with three merit badges. The left badge indicates

that he is a "Good-in-Five" soldier with exemplary standards in political attitude, military training, discipline, physical fitness and the "3-8 work-style". His carefully tended truck is made in China, but low production rates result in desperate shortages.

4. PLA soldiers are resourceful and brave and this rope exercise is by no means as easy as it looks. This spectacular picture was taken among the karst hills of Kweichow, where spires of limestone rise almost vertically to heights of 600 feet, or so. Level land is seldom

more than half-a-mile in extent, leading to a shortage of airstrips and very difficult surface movement. This is just the sort of terrain in which the PLA infantry comes into its own, and Type C army corps with only light equipment operate well.

4

1. *The single greatest asset of the PLA is its magnificent corps of infantry. They are well-trained, highly motivated and very skilful in the traditional infantry arts. The PLA has made careful study of the lessons of the Korean War and is unlikely to use the same methods* *again unless it is felt that there is no option if an enemy (such as the USSR) is to be halted. Note the use of "cold steel".*
2. *A fine shot of "that most necessary article". This alert infantry soldier is preparing to lay a satchel charge.*
3. *The organization table of an infantry division of the PLA. The basic pattern is a conventional 3+1, ie, three infantry regiments, each of three battalions, each of three companies, etc, and with an equivalent fire support unit at each level. Compared with Western* *infantry divisions it is very weak in tanks; only one regiment of 32 MBTs, where the Soviet equivalent has 266 and the US mechanized infantry division 270. Further, the Western infantry divisions are all fully mobile on tracks and wheels, with the infantry almost entirely*

to draw the enemy deep into Chinese territory, trading space for time, until his lines of communication are extended, his troops partially tied down in garrisons and units dispersed. The invading army is to be drawn into pre-selected battle fields. Meanwhile, regional and militia forces would harass the enemy behind his lines, while the main forces prepared to launch a massive counter-offensive which would eventually annihilate the enemy or drive him from Chinese territory. This long-established strategy has been revised over the past decade. Even a powerful enemy attack will now only be allowed limited territorial penetration in order to protect China's industry and capital city. The heavy concentration of main force units in the Shenyang and Peking Military Regions indicates that the Chinese will hold those areas with a forward defence strategy, although the PLA still would not attempt to stop a major attack at the border. In the less developed, more remote regions of China, the "people's" war strategy would still apply.

Organizationally the ground forces are unlike the Air Force and Navy in that they do not have their own service arm headquarters. Instead, the entire high command of the PLA serves in that capacity. The top of the pyramid is the Military Affairs Committee of the Chinese Communist Party Central Committee, usually referred to by the Chinese as the "Central Military Committee" (CMC). Orders are transmitted from the CMC through the Ministry of National Defence and three General Departments—Political, Staff and Rear Services (i.e. logistics). Although the primary role of the CMC is policy making, it frequently involves itself in operational decisions and carries out an inspectorate role. The Defence Ministry is responsible for mobilization plans, training manuals, conscription—demobilization, civil defence, administration of the military budget, many personnel functions, and liaison with the ministries of machine building to oversee military production. Thus, unlike many military systems, the Defence Ministry has little policy making or operational authority.

Each of the three General Departments have their own chain of command and control leading down through the ground forces. Each also has its own advanced military school for specialized officer training. In wartime, the General Staff Department (GSD) is the most important of the three since it serves as the ground forces headquarters. It supervises the eleven military regions, which can be flexibly combined into fronts or theatres. The GSD also maintains skip-echelon command capability so that orders can be issued directly to main force units down to regimental level without the necessity of passing through the chain of command from military regions to army corps to divisions. The GSD also supervises most of the ground force service arms, i.e. artillery, armour, signal and anti-chemical warfare forces.

The General Rear Services Department (GRSD) handles military logistics including planning, procurement and distribution. It supplies fuels, munitions, a broad range of general commodities, and provides and repairs equipment. PLA equipment testing and improvement are also done by GRSD technicians. It is responsible for all medical services and facilities for the PLA and serves as the military paymaster. The GRSD has operational control over the Railway Engineering Corps, the Engineer Corps and the Capital Construction Engineer Corps, and staff supervision over combat engineer elements attached to infantry and armoured units. (Staff supervision entails handling training, career management and defining and implementing doctrine.)

One logistics function perhaps unique to the PLA is the supervision and coordination of industrial side-line production carried out by regular PLA units. Many medium and large units have established small and medium sized industrial facilities such as metal works and processing plants for locally available raw materials. The income from such operations is used by and for the benefit of the units—usually to provide amenities not otherwise avail-

mounted in armoured personnel carriers. The PLA infantry division does not have even one such carrier, as far as is known. However, the logistical demands of such mechanized forces would place an almost unbearable load on the Rear Services and upon the lines-of-communication. There can be no doubt, however, that the PLA infantry division is hard hitting and able to move in the more remote parts of the country, as was demonstrated in the recovery of Tibet, the Sino-Indian War and the operations against Vietnam in early 1979; the real challenge, however, is the USSR. (In the chart the first figures refer to officers, the second to enlisted men.)

4. A platoon commander leads his men across an improvised floating bridge. Once again the pistol is a sure sign of an officer.

2

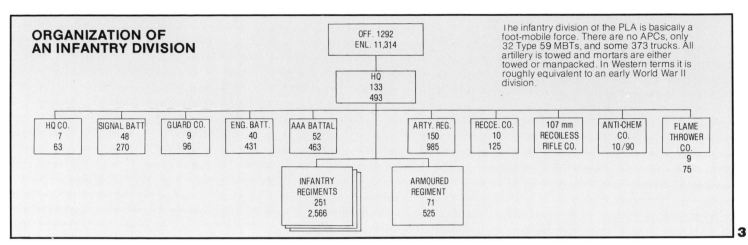

ORGANIZATION OF AN INFANTRY DIVISION

The infantry division of the PLA is basically a foot-mobile force. There are no APCs, only 32 Type 59 MBTs, and some 373 trucks. All artillery is towed and mortars are either towed or manpacked. In Western terms it is roughly equivalent to an early World War II division.

OFF. 1292 ENL. 11,314

HQ 133 493

| HQ CO. 7 63 | SIGNAL BATT 48 270 | GUARD CO. 9 96 | ENG. BATT. 40 431 | AAA BATTAL 52 463 | ARTY. REG. 150 985 | RECCE. CO. 10 125 | 107 mm RECOILESS RIFLE CO. | ANTI-CHEM CO. 10/90 | FLAME THROWER CO. 9 75 |

| INFANTRY REGIMENTS 251 2,566 | ARMOURED REGIMENT 71 525 |

3

able, improve base housing and the like. Abuses of the system have occurred, primarily misuse of profits in partying and lavish banquets, expropriation of civilian property for profit making purposes, and creating extra-legal business ventures of a capitalist nature, often in conjunction with local civilians. Most units also engage in agricultural production for their own food consumption. The benefits of encouraging maximum self-sufficiency far outweigh the occasional abuses. The programme causes the ground forces to be one of the least expensive in the world on a per/man basis.

The partial self-sufficiency of PLA units is only one reason for the army being such a bargain. The second reason is low pay. Monthly pay for new recruits is just over £1.50 ($3), and for a squad leader, it goes up to only about £3 ($6). Of course, all necessities are provided and senior enlisted men who are allowed to marry, receive family and housing allowances. Junior officers receive £9-£17.50 ($18-$35) per month, field grades £20-£50 ($40-$100), general officers, up to about £90 ($180). Longevity pay adds 1 per cent to base salary for every year of service over five years. With the family allowances, provision of necessities and most entertainment, travel, and eventual retirement pay for career soldiers, the low individual pay has not been deleterious to morale.

The Chinese army is often incorrectly described as rankless. It is true that there have been no visible badges of rank since 1965—only some distinctions in the tailoring of uniforms between officers and enlisted men. However, there are 24 pay grades in the officer corps and about six for enlisted men which are equivalent to rank.

Returning to visible badges of rank was debated by the leadership in 1978, and rejected.

The General Political Department (GPD), as the name suggests, oversees the Chinese Communist Party's control of the armed forces. It also oversees military justice, discipline and morale. The chain of command is a pyramid of Party committees within every military unit reaching through battalion level. Companies have Party branches. The committees consist of the political commissar, the unit commander and a few elected Party members, usually from other leading officers. In peacetime, unit Party committees wield collective leadership. In wartime, the commanders have authority to make quick and independent decisions,

4

1. An anti-tank squad armed with the Chinese Type 56 40mm launcher. This is a copy of the Soviet RPG-2, but fires a Chinese Type 50 grenade.

2. The PLA exhibits an extraordinary preoccupation with water. Swimming soldiers are, however, particularly vulnerable, and the military value of being able to fire in this way is doubtful, to say the least. The weapon is a straight copy of the Soviet PPS-43 7.62mm sub-machine-gun (SMG), which was rushed into production during the Korean War. A blowback-operated weapon, it has a 35-round magazine and an effective range of 100 metres.

3. Once again swimmers, but this time a mortar team moving under cover of night. It appears to be the intention that the mortar should be capable of being fired from its raft but as this weapon has a fixed firing-pin, and the round must be dropped down the barrel the chances of success appear remote. The mortar is the Type 63 60mm, which is a development of the Type 31. It has a range of 1530

3

metres and can fire up to 20 rounds per minute, depending upon the standard of training of the crew. It fires high-explosive bombs.
4. Although the PLA may have discarded badges of rank there is no surer indication of officer status than carrying a pistol! These men

with their simple buoyancy tubes are armed with Chinese-designed Type 68 rifles, easily recognized by their gas regulators.
5. The People's Militia are often used to assist the regular units of the PLA, and here a supply team arrives with more ammunition for

these machine-gunners. The weapon in the foreground is the Type 56 LMG, a copy of the Soviet 7.62mm RPD.
6. More swimming soldiers of the PLA, but armed this time with the Type 56 7.62mm Assault Rifle, a copy of the Soviet AK-47.

4

5

6

1. *This picture of a flight simulator for training fighter pilots in air defence tactics probably sums up the present state of China's armed forces better than any other. Most air forces use multi-million dollar simulators depending upon very sophisticated electronics to achieve* *realism and training value. This machine moves in only two dimensions and, while obviously better than nothing, cannot give the "pilot" any true feelings of realism. China's air force has had no combat experience since the Korean War.*

2. *China is a great believer in the efficacy of ground defences, even against modern jet aircraft, and this was reinforced by the great success of the North Vietnamese air defences against the attacks of the United States Air Force. These men at practice camp are firing the* *Type 54 heavy machine-gun, the Chinese version of the Soviet 12.7mm Degtyarev DShK M1938/46. The special double-ring anti-aircraft sight can be clearly seen. Many thousands of these weapons are operated by the Regional Troops and the Militia.*

figure. Before a battle, he exhorts the men, promising recognition of merit, appealing to patriotism, and he obtains oaths and pledges that the men will fulfill their duties. After battles and during lulls, mutual criticism and self-criticism meetings are held at squad, platoon and company levels to correct mistakes and strengthen the group through the catharsis of confession and forgiveness. The battle post-mortems help identify and resolve command, tactics and communications problems. They also provide a major motive for conformity and obedience, reducing the need for overt coercion. Public shaming of men and officers largely substitutes for corporal punishment except in cases of severe infractions such as desertion. This Chinese version of the Soviet political commissar system was severely tested in the Korean War. While successful in the early stages, it was unable to prevent serious deterioration of morale and organizational control in the later stages after the army had taken heavy losses and was continuously retreating. However, it is doubtful that any other means of morale maintenance would have fared much better.

though they must later account for their actions to the committees. The political commissar has veto power over decisions of the commander. However, political commissars are not given the intensive military training received by commanders. Thus it would be very unusual for a commissar to attempt to over-rule a commander in a combat situation. Any disagreements between the two unit leaders are to be resolved at a meeting of the Party committee. Should that fail, the dispute is referred to higher echelon. In units down to battalion level, the Party committee has a political department which is its administrative arm. It handles political warfare, prisoners of war, personnel matters, morale, education, recruitment and demobilization and most other unit matters except those directly related to operations. Political departments at regiment level and above are divided into subdepartments responsible for education and propaganda, organization, personnel, political warfare, youth and culture, and "mass work" — i.e. civil military relations.

In wartime, political commissars play a vital role. The PLA, far more than

either the US or Soviet armies, operates on the assumption that carefully articulated and inculcated political motives provide the basis of good morale. Primary group solidarity, pride, loyalty and camaraderie which serves as the basis for morale in the US Army is seen by the Chinese as insufficient. Without political indoctrination, small group loyalties could be counter-productive under severe circumstances. It is up to the unit political officer to provide that indoctrination and to make it relevant to the tasks in hand. The PLA does value small group relations as a factor in morale maintenance — since the 1930s they have subdivided infantry squads into groups of three men each to serve both as fire teams and as morale supporting primary groups. Unlike Western armies, political commissars choose the leaders of these teams on the basis of political indoctrination as well as leadership ability.

The political officer's methods include camaraderie as well as authority. At company level, he de-emphasizes difference in rank and attempts to become at one with the enlisted men, or at least to serve as a friendly father-confessor

Reorganization in Defence Ministry

The system of political control has gone through many vicissitudes in the past few decades. P'eng Teh-huai, the Defence Minister in the 1950's, favoured centralization of authority in the hands of unit commanders. As a result, Party branches at company level withered or disappeared and Party committees played ancillary roles in higher level units. Lin Piao, the Defence Minister from 1959-71, initially rebuilt the political control apparatus but much of his work was undone by the Great Proletarian Cultural Revolution in the mid and late 1960's. The General Political Department was suspended in 1967 due to its alleged failure to properly implement political guidelines for the armed forces in the midst of civil turmoil. Over 40 per cent of the GPD officers were imprisoned and some suffered permanent disabilities and even died as a result of maltreatment. The GPD was reconstituted in the early

3. *The Type 55 37mm light anti-aircraft gun is a copy of the Soviet M-1939 weapon, made in China. It has a cyclic rate of fire of 360 rounds per minute and a maximum effective AA ceiling of 1500metres. It weighs 2 tonnes and is mounted on a four-wheel trailer. It is used only with optical sights, ie, it has no computer, but even so a battery like that shown here with six guns properly sited would prove very worrisome, even to the most modern high-speed aircraft. These weapons were also used extensively by the North Vietnamese and had many successes against low-flying US aircraft. China's great weakness, however, it that it has only the old SA-2 missile and thus it would be difficult to force enemy aircraft down to heights where guns such as these could be effective.*

1970's with civilians appointed to head it from 1975 to the present.

From 1967-77, the political control system was the scene of ideological and power struggles pitting revolution against professionalization within the army units and administrative echelons. Subordinates were encouraged to question orders of superiors and openly to defy those they believed to be politically incorrect. This caused serious factionalism and deterioration of discipline in many units. The promotion system, based on seniority and merit, was undercut by "helicopters"—the Chinese term for young, bold political activists who were suddenly vaulted to high level positions; in one case from a squad leader to the director of a regimental political department.

Re-establishing discipline and morale

In the years following Mao Tse-tung's death in 1976, Defence Minister Yeh Chien-ying and the current incumbent, Hsu Hsiang-ch'ien, moved to re-establish discipline and personnel routine, and to restore the political control system to its traditional role. Officers and men who had actively challenged their orders and leaders were subjected to intensive criticism. Many were demoted or dismissed. In 1978, Hua Kuo-feng, the Chairman of the Central Military Committee, publicly admitted that three or more years would be required to restore the army political apparatus to its former prestige and power. It has, however, clearly returned to its traditional role of maintaining morale and heightening the fighting capabilities of the troops. Moreover, the morale and prestige of the enlisted men and most of the officer corps seems to have survived these political difficulties remarkably well. Indeed, the Chinese soldier can hold his own with any in terms of motivation, dedication and morale.

Militarily, the best men and morale are in the "main force" units. In the ground forces, the term refers to the approximately 38 army corps, and troops of the combat and support arms. The army corps are the largest, best trained and equipped units of the ground forces. Most have proud unit

histories dating back to World War II or the 1930's. There is a very strong *esprit de corps* within each corps due to the army's unusual promotion system. Officers are chosen from the enlisted ranks. They are promoted up a single command chain; e.g. a regimental Party committee will select the commanders and political commissars of its subordinate companies while the Party committee at corps level selects its own regimental commanders. Thus, in any given army corps, the overwhelming majority of officers will have served their entire careers in that unit. This greatly improves the longevity of training effectiveness, though at some cost to combined arms expertise. Enlisted men are also not normally transferred to other units. The officers at each echelon, with their shared career patterns, become tightly knit groups.

Organizationally, there are two different types of corps. Type "A" is the more modernized with relatively more vehicles, medium artillery and armour.

Most of the 38 corps are type A, and the accompanying table of organization and equipment is for those units. Type "B" has more draught animals, light and pack artillery, less armour and fewer vehicles, but about the same manpower. Such units are stationed in mountainous terrain. Ground forces are mostly triangular in organization, i.e. each unit contains three units of the next lower echelon. Thus the vast majority of army corps contain three divisions each. In addition, there are about nine "independent" main force infantry divisions not subordinate to corps level headquarters.

The other main force combat arms components are 11-12 armoured and three airborne divisions. Combat support elements include twenty artillery, fifteen railway engineer and construction divisions and eleven signal and a few anti-chemical warfare regiments. There are also several independent transportation regiments under the control of the General Rear Services Department and twenty anti-aircraft

1. A soldier of the PLA with a Type 56 anti-tank grenade launcher. The grenade is the Type 50; this has a high explosive anti-tank (HEAT) warhead which will penetrate 265mm of armour at 0°, which is considerably better than that achieved by the Russian RPG-2 round. The projectile weighs 4lb and has a maximum effective range of 162 yards.

2. A battery of 37mm anti-aircraft guns M-1939 in action. They are being manned by militia; note the girls among the crews.

3. An instructor showing two attentive soldiers the vulnerable parts of a Soviet T-62 main battle tank. There can be no doubt that the PLA takes the Soviet threat very seriously, and especially the tank threat. The heaviest Chinese tank gun is the 100mm on the T-59 which cannot deal with the Soviet T-64 and T-72 at long range, particularly if the reports that these MBTs have "special armour" are true. The PLA must then depend upon their anti-tank guns, such as the 57mm, 75mm, 82mm and 90mm recoilless rifles, but these are only short-range weapons. The

1

man who will bear the brunt when all these deficiencies bear fruit will be the soldier in the infantry regiments, and it is at the insistence of the front-line commanders that an order has recently been placed in France for wire-guided anti-tank missiles.

2

3

1. Tactics such as this are reminders of the "mass-attacks" practised at such cost by the PLA in the Korean War. The tank is a T-59.
2. Much hilarity as a visiting officer challenges one of the tank men at Tai Kung Tau, a form of one-armed wrestling. Pictures such as this afford evidence of an easy and relaxed relationship between fighters (soldiers) and officers, but one based firmly on respect. These tanks are Type 60/63, a Chinese designed and built reconnaissance vehicle, based closely on the Soviet PT-76, but with a welded turret mounting an 85mm gun. The fume extractor on the barrel can be seen very clearly.
3. Armoured Corps Commander (equivalent to lieutenant-general in Western armies) Chu Pao-Chuan spending some time serving as a soldier to learn about their problems and opinions at first hand. The Corps Commander (centre foreground holding the shell) seems to be doing more talking than listening, and the soldiers in the background are awaiting their turn!

1

2

artillery divisions under Air Force control. Most signal and anti-chemical warfare troops are integrated into the army corps, as are the combat engineers. The independently controlled combat and combat support units serve as strategic reserves to reinforce the regular infantry as needed.

In peacetime, the Railway Engineers build most of China's new rail lines, signal units help string new lines of communication—civil as well as military—and engineering regiments help in capital construction and disaster relief. For example, they provided immediate emergency services after the massive T'angshan earthquake of 1976 and later helped in the rebuilding process. It is however, a moot point whether or not Chinese ground forces are more heavily involved in economic construction and disaster relief than are most other armies.

Special security Unit 8341

There is yet another unit which might be categorized as belonging to the main forces—at least because of its elite status. This is known only as Unit 8341 which has some parallel to the militarized security forces of the USSR. Its organization seems atypical, although it must be of division echelon or higher. Headquartered in Peking, it is charged with providing security for high level officials and foreign diplomats, much like the US Secret Service. It also carries out investigations for the Central Military Committee and the General Office of the Party—which has had operational control of Unit 8341. There are some recent indications that the CMC may now control this unit. It also has broad security powers within the PLA, and may have some connection with the Party General Offices at province level. In other words, it may be a nation-wide militarized security force above and beyond the normal police forces and functions.

Over the past decade, China has gradually narrowed the conventional capabilities gap between its ground forces and those of the West and USSR. Artillery production has gone up markedly in the 1970s and China now has as many guns as the USSR and

3

4. *The organization table for an Armoured Division of the PLA. The PLA is reported to be equipped with some 10,000 main battle tanks, with the T-59 (Chinese version of the Soviet T-54) the most modern in service. There are also T-62 light tanks and T-60/63* *amphibious reconnaissance tanks. The T-59s are distributed in tank regiments of infantry divisions (32 tanks per division) and the balance in 10 to 12 tank divisions, which are usually held in strategic reserve. There is no doubt that the PLA is weak in tanks, and that this* *weakness could be critical in any battle with the Soviet Union in the northern border areas. The T-59 would be hard pressed in any fight with Soviet T-64 and T-72, being both out-armoured and out-gunned, and the PLA is in urgent need of a suitable replacement.*

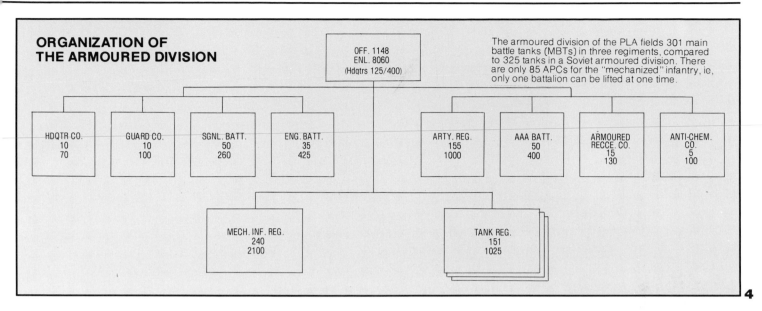

4

three times as many as the US. Of course, because of the immense size of the ground forces, there are still fewer artillery pieces per unit than in the Soviet or American armies, and in some specialized artillery categories such as conventional and "FROG" rockets, China still trails badly. All light and medium guns are indigenously produced versions of post-World War II Russian designs. They are not obsolete. Their ranges are longer than equivalent US weapons. While fire control systems have been unsophisticated, in 1978, China announced the development of a laser/computer range finder fire control system. PLA artillery pieces are mostly towed rather than self-propelled, but that is probably a plus factor rather than a weakness; towed guns are more easily maintained, and if necessary can be moved by muscle. Guns which rely on their own engines and tracks are useless in the case of mechanical failure.

Two long standing weaknesses— anti-tank and anti-aircraft weaponry— are now being ameliorated. The PLA still relies mainly on World War II style anti-armour defence systems, i.e. conventional artillery, mines, and for small infantry units, shoulder-fired anti-tank rockets—the RPG-7. However, China has been shopping in Western Europe for more sophisticated laser- or wire-guided missiles to improve their infantry anti-tank capabilities. In late 1978, China contracted to buy the "HOT" optically guided anti-tank missile, It is a vehicle mounted unit which represents the state of the art in

Western systems; it is more advanced than anything in the Soviet inventory at present. About the earliest that the "HOT" would be in the inventory would be 1981, meanwhile, the Chinese version Type 69 RPG-7 is still capable of disabling a modern tank, and it is very effective against armoured personnel carriers. In early 1979 the PLA was considering its replacement with the "MILAN" light anti-tank weapon, but no contract had been signed. Finally, the British built "Harrier" jet attack aircraft contracted for in 1978 will also serve as a potent anti-armour weapon.

Need for light air defence missiles

Air defence for the main forces has posed a similar problem. Most radar guided conventional AAA pieces are controlled by the Air Force AAA divisions. These are deployed to defend strategic targets. The ground forces have ample heavy machine guns and light AAA cannon to provide a reasonable curtain of fire against low level attacking aircraft, but they could do little against medium altitude tactical bombing. The PLA has long needed infantry- or truck-portable surface to air missiles effective against medium (and low) attack aircraft. In 1978, they bought "Roland" which is effective at low altitude and in early 1979, were negotiating over the "CROTALE"—a medium altitude SAM.

As for armour, China is producing three types of tanks and an armoured personnel carrier. All Chinese armour is obsolete. In total numbers, the PLA has over 10,000 tanks, about the same as the US, but only between 26 and 30 per cent of the Soviet total. Since most Russian armour is deployed in Europe, the imbalance is not as severe as the bare numbers indicate. Unfortunately for the PLA, in 1977-78, Russia began deploying many of its new T-72 main battle tanks along the Sino-Soviet border. China is capable of producing about 1000 tanks annually, although it has averaged about 600-800 in the 1970s. Production may have been slowed awaiting the development of a new main battle tank, but so far it has not been forthcoming. At present, there are only about 4000 armoured personnel carriers in the inventory.

Until 1977-78, China accorded low priority to improving PLA mobility either through heliborne capabilities or mechanizing the infantry forces. Production levels of armoured personnel carriers has been sufficient to upgrade several army corps to type "A" units, but the infantry remains tactically foot-mobile and strategically rail-mobile. In the Maoist "people's" war strategy, the sheer size of the world's largest ground forces is relied upon to offset the lack of mobility.

Inadequate measures have been adopted to offset the lack of tactical mobility, e.g. reliance upon night fighting and "hugging" tactics wherein infantry are deployed as close as possible to enemy positions to offset

1. Great emphasis is placed upon the ability of Regional Troops and the People's Militia to deal with enemy tanks. Although the effectiveness of such unsophisticated anti-tank defences may appear doubtful to Western eyes, the fact that every city, town, village and commune produces many such teams presents a daunting prospect to any potential aggressor. These tanks are Soviet-designed T-34/85s, World War II machines now being rapidly replaced in the PLA by the Type 59, and probably now relegated to training duties such as shown here.

2. One of the most important branches of the PLA is the artillery. The standard of training is very high, and the PLA Artillery is equipped with towed guns of 122mm, 130mm and 152mm calibre, although it is reported that a self-propelled howitzer has been developed, using the K-63 armoured personnel carrier and a 122mm howitzer, Type 54. Self-propelled guns would be necessary in Manchuria.

3. The crews of a tank company being briefed by their company

1

commander. Organization is based on threes; ie, three tanks in a platoon, three platoons in a company, three companies in a battalion, etc. Each Type A army corps of the PLA includes only 96 tanks: 32 in the tank regiment of each of the three infantry divisions. In addition, there are some 10 to 12 armoured divisions held in central reserve under the control of the Ministry of National Defence. This gives a grand total of somewhere in the region of 10,000 tanks, all old designs, which is a very small number when the task of the PLA is considered. The design of a more modern tank is well within the capability of the PLA and it could well be that a new tank is under development now. Especially critical is the need for a more powerful tank gun than the 100mm DT10.

4. The Tank Corps of the PLA is also highly trained, but it cannot be denied that its equipment is somewhat dated. Men such as this tank commander realize this and their requests for more modern equipment are now causing the leaders to take notice.

1. *The PLA must be able to operate in every type of terrain and these mountain troops are reminders that China owns many mountainous regions including the Himalayas. These men carry the Type 56 assault rifle, the Chinese version of the Soviet 7.62mm AK-47.*

2. *This weapon training class is dressed in the standard cold weather working uniform, with padded jacket and trousers and fur-lined hat. The instructor is holding a bagged explosive charge mounted on a short board, while the soldier centre rear grasps a wooden stick*

grenade. All the men have Type 68 rifles, a Chinese design which incorporates some features of both the Soviet AK-47 and SKS rifles. The Type 68, however, has a gas regulator (the small cylindrical object above the barrel) and a folding bayonet of cruciform cross-

section. Chinese infantry weapons are all simple, well-designed, easy to use and maintain, and very reliable. In comparison Western infantry weapons are very complex, vastly more expensive, but with virtually identical ranges and combat effectiveness.

their superior firepower and tactical nuclear weapons. In the 1980s, this weakness will be gradually ameliorated. The Chinese leadership has resurrected a 1975 Central Military Committee directive which had been shelved for three years due to civilian political opposition. It calls for the priority development of motorized, modern transporation for the PLA and major emphasis on science and technology in future force building programmes.

The leadership frankly admits that this can only be accomplished in conjunction with China's overall industrialization and modernization plans, and that the equipment and weaponry of the 1980's will still be inferior to that of the "enemy"—i.e. the USSR. Therefore, the "people's" war strategy, hotly debated in 1977, is still being retained. A political-economic trade-off seems to have been made. In return for the PLA allowing its modernization to be geared to the indigenous industrial and technological base, the civilian leadership gave the go-ahead for the PLA to spend billions of pounds buying "most needed" weaponry from Western Europe and Great Britain. The ground forces of the mid-1980s will undoubtedly have greater mobility and they will almost certainly be equipped with tactical nuclear weapons. An April 1978 nuclear test was less than twenty kilotons, indicating that the Chinese are making steady progress toward tactical nuclear capability. When the test warheads become operational, a forward linear defence of all border regions might be feasible if China were willing to be the first to use nuclear weapons in a limited war mode. At present, the oft-repeated 1964 pledge "never to be the first to use nuclear weapons" has not been modified.

The regional forces comprise about half of the total regular ground forces. They are equipped as light infantry. Organizationally, the top tactical echelons are independent divisions and regiments.

These regional units are much more closely tied to the civilian government than are the main forces. Their most important peacetime role is militia training. Other peacetime missions include internal security, capital construction projects, aid to agriculture and political work with the civilian

1

population. Until the mid-1960s, a paramilitary organization known as the People's Armed Police were the basic internal security organization. That force of about 600,000 men was absorbed into the regional forces and no separate militarized public security force now exists, apart from the highly specialized Unit 8341 described above. Locally controlled police deal with routine functions such as traffic control and crime.

Most regional force divisions and regiments are under the operational control of the military regions, although some seem to be controlled by provin-

cial and large urban garrison districts. The political commissar of each provincial military district is normally the first Party secretary of the province, and the commander of the district is usually concurrently appointed as a vice-governor or a Party deputy secretary. Below the province level, special districts which equate geographically and administratively with military sub-districts, generally have an independent regiment. Thus the civilian political and military leadership are inextricably linked. In wartime, these close civil-military ties are expected to pay off in local defence

3. *The PLA's airborne forces comprise three parachute divisions held in strategic reserve in Wuhan Military Region. Unlike many Western forces the parachute divisions are under control of the air force and not of the ground forces. Roles for the airborne include the* *seizure of important areas in advance of major ground thrusts, sabotage attacks on enemy nuclear delivery means, the disruption of enemy rear areas and assistance to guerrillas. They suffer from limitations due to their light equipment and logistical shortages, and any* *major force will need to be joined quickly by a ground advance. Here a battalion commander regains control as his men move off the Drop Zone (DZ). Note the Soviet-style protective headgear and the Type 63 manpack radio set with its unique pentaform antenna.*

benefits. The regional forces would mobilize the militia to carry out guerrilla war and self-defence operations. Guerrilla governments would be easily established where needed, and the provinces would not have to rely upon centrally deployed main force units for protection.

Regional officers: problems of morale

The regional forces engage in the same individual and small unit training as the main forces, but the training cycle is briefer and few of the independent units have experienced combined arms training. Morale among the enlisted men is excellent, but there are some problems with the officers. In some ways, the regional forces are the step-children of the PLA. They get little priority for modernization and their officers have much less opportunity for promotion to high rank than do main force cadres. The latter receive first priority for training in advanced officer schools. On the other hand, regional force officers are better able to put down local roots and maintain a normal family life, since their units are almost never relocated, and they are not apt to be isolated on large military reservations. The regional forces peacetime mission consists of unglamorous donkey work, e.g. public security, recruitment/demobilization, militia organization and training, and civic action. There is no reason to believe that these roles detract from their capability to carry out provincial and local self-defence in wartime. The only serious danger posed by the active peacetime roles of the regional military is that it would take them some time to achieve a wartime footing and a surprise attack could overrun regional units in the border provinces before they could mobilize for effective resistance. The existence of border defence divisions theoretically should prevent that from happening, but those lightly armed units would not seriously hinder a major combined arms attack.

The third element of the protracted war defence triad is the paramilitary component. Militia make up the bulk of these forces. Militia control and financing are decentralized. There are

two national level organizations having some militia responsibilities. The Mobilization Department of the General Staff keeps records, distributes arms, coordinates PLA training of militia, and, as its name suggests, develops mobilization plans in case of war. The Mass Work Department of the General Political Department is concerned with civil/military relations generally, and thus provides guidance to the PLA regarding local militia organization, control and political training. At the next lower level, military regions have mobilization departments and "people's armed departments" (PAD). The PAD are the records keeping and arms control offices while mobilization departments handle war planning, civil defence and the militia role as a reserve system. However, it is the provincial military districts which have primary responsibility for militia organization and control. They have been directed to devote top priority to improving militia organization and effectiveness.

In theory each county has a militia

"division", each commune a militia "regiment", each of the commune production brigades a militia "battalion" or company, and each of the village level work teams has a militia platoon. All such "units" above the company level are administrative echelons only. Factories and enterprises have equivalent echelons depending upon the size of their work force. This echelon system exists primarily on paper and as a wartime mobilization plan. Except in frontier and border areas, most communes seem to have only one or two companies of armed militia who receive a few weeks of annual military training at PLA bases. The national total of armed militia is estimated at 7 to 12 million. A large number, perhaps 20 to 30 million, belong to the basic militia which engages in periodic drills, is taught civil defence procedures and attends occasional lectures on military tactics and weapons. A 1961 directive ordered that each militia battalion was to have one basic militia company, but it is not clear if that goal has ever been achieved. The majority

1. One of the main tactical considerations for the PLA is to endeavour to overcome weaknesses in equipment by achieving close contact with the enemy. They also believe that this will prevent the use of battlefield nuclear weapons, at least among the forward troops. At such close quarters the infantry soldiers of the PLA are second to none and one of the skills they are taught is Kwang Tau, one of the several Chinese arts of self-defence. This particular form concentrates on the use of any handy implement, such as a stick, and turning it into a deadly weapon.

2. Arguments rage in Western armies about the value of the bayonet and whether it is redundant in the nuclear age. The PLA has no doubts.

3 and 4. Just as the PLA regards Kwang Tau as a realistic form of combat in modern times, their training in uncomfortable conditions bears the mark of realism: on the bamboo bridge the fate of the loser is obvious!

5. A platoon of Type 59 MBTs, showing the 12.7mm Type 54 anti-aircraft machine-gun to advantage.

This is the Chinese-made version of the Soviet Degtyarev DSh K-38, which is belt-fed and has an effective range of 2000m.
6 and 7. These nurses are regular soldiers of the PLA, and are working under field conditions. Chinese medicine makes great use of herbs and still relies to a great extent on traditional methods. The standard of nursing is as good as anywhere in the world.
8. A patient is hurried from an ambulance to a hospital tent in tropical southern China, possibly near the Vietnamese border.

5

6

7

8

1. *One of the many unusual characteristics of the PLA is that many units are required to achieve a high degree of self-sufficiency. Complete farms are run by military units and soldiers are seen here cultivating pak choy, a Chinese cabbage.*

2. *A sight which most people would think had been relegated to the history books—a cavalry charge with drawn swords! While horsed units are of undoubted value for reconnaissance in some areas, this sort of charge against a Soviet unit would be a military disaster.*

The PLA still maintains a substantial body of cavalry. They are especially useful in mountains, heavily wooded areas and deserts. Furthermore, grass and grain are more freely available and cheaper than petrol. Mules were used in 1979 invasion of Vietnam.

of militia members belong to the common militia which numbers 100 to 200 million or more. These men and women receive no individual or small unit training. In wartime, the armed militia under the leadership of regional force PLA units, would provide the bulk of the guerrilla fighters and serve as a manpower pool for the PLA. Armed militiamen, except for leadership cadre, are restricted to the 18 to 25 age group and women constitute only a token portion of the force. Most armed militiamen are recently discharged PLA veterans—a "ready reserve". Basic militia would be used for logistic support and labour, and the common militia would provide a militarized framework for the population-at-large.

The best trained and equipped armed militia companies are those in the border provinces, especially in the north and opposite Taiwan. All armed militia have weapons arsenals in local people's armed departments down to the commune and factory level. Until the 1970s, militia weapons were almost exclusively rifles, hand grenades and side arms. Over the past several years, they have begun acquiring infantry and

3. *There is no current evidence that China has an offensive capability with chemical weapons, although the country undoubtedly has the technical capability. However, the Soviet Union has a considerable chemical capability and China, like NATO, must make preparations* *accordingly. There are anti-chemical warfare units in the PLA and much training in protective drills is conducted for both military units and the civil population. This crew of a 37mm Type 55 Anti-Aircraft Gun are wearing the standard equipment, comprising a* *suit of special material, rubber gloves and a respirator. It would appear, however, that at least one soldier has neglected to wear his gloves, a fatal oversight with some chemical agents. There does not seem to be any neck protection for these men which, again, would be* *fatal. The long hose from the respirator leads to a filter unit in the carrying satchel. This is a clumsy arrangement dropped some time ago in the West in favour of a filter mounted on the respirator itself. Decontamination equipment is widely issued.*

anti-aircraft machine guns, land mines, mortars, and anti-tank weapons, such as the RPG-7, and recoilless rifles. Side arms and rifles have been a hodge-podge of captured US, Japanese and Chinese Nationalist weapons—a logistician's nightmare. The armed militia is now largely equipped with standard PLA AK-47 and SKS assault rifles. The hand-me-down weapons are mostly used by basic militia for drill practice. Armed militia, unlike basic and common, receive remuneration while on duty such as on border patrols or internal security operations. They are paid by the government organization utilizing their services. The military capabilities and readiness of the armed militia has markedly improved in the 1970s. In addition to its expanded arsenal, its training has been better systematized and PLA veterans serve as full time militia cadres at grass roots levels.

Some harm was done to the militia in the power struggles surrounding the political succession to Mao Tse-tung. The leaders of the Cultural Revolution who emerged in key political and military posts in the early 1970s attempted to redefine the militia mission. They attempted to use the militia as the cutting edge in advancing China's domestic socio-political revolution. In urban areas, this too often devolved into vigilante activity whereby persons were arbitrarily arrested or beaten. Organizationally, they obtained

national directives removing the PLA from control of the militia, set up urban "militia commands" under leadership of their own choosing, and attempted to form a national militia headquarters. This would have provided an invaluable power base to consolidate the leadership of the ideologues in the post-Mao period. Naturally, this was strongly resisted by the PLA and many, if not most, provincial military districts continued to play a major role in militia organization and training, at least in the rural areas where three-fourths of the population live. This effort to create a counter-armed force to the PLA came to an abrupt end in late 1976 with the arrest of the "Gang of Four". Militia commands were abolished in 1977 and the people's armed departments have re-established control. However, the status and prestige of the militia was badly damaged.

Other paramilitary forces include the PLA Capital Construction Engineering Corps, various civilian led provincial agricultural production "divisions", and "production construction corps". The size and military capabilities of the Capital Construction Engineering Corps has remained a well kept secret since 1967. The largest—about one million personnel—and oldest of the production construction corps (PCC) is in Sinkiang. Newer and smaller PCC are in Heilungkiang, and Inner Mongolia. These PCC in the northeastern,

northern and northwestern regions are organized in units up to regimental level, with a few "divisional" titles which are actually administrative echelons. Each regiment has one fully armed company and all personnel receive military training. Unlike the militia, both PCC and agricultural production divisions are full-time occupations. The agricultural production divisions are mostly in interior provinces and their military capabilities are probably not much above that of the basic militia. The total manpower of all production-construction elements is around four million.

The deployment pattern for main force army corps is shown on the accompanying map, with one or two possible additional corps omitted, e.g. there are unconfirmed reports of an army corps in the Shanghai area, and two additional corps may have been moved to the Vietnam border region as a result of bilateral tensions and the Vietnam-Cambodia war.

Chinese invasion of Vietnam, 1979

During the Chinese invasion of Vietnam of February-March 1979, about 150,000 troops were massed and 50-100,000 participated in the invasion. In addition to the two corps already present, at least one was redeployed from the Fukien Front along with another, possibly from the Wuhan Military Region. The latter houses "strategic reserve" army corps, artillery and armoured divisions—centrally located and with good rail connections in any direction. There were reports that every military region except Sinkiang contributed some forces—mostly specialized units such as engineering regiments and anti-aircraft artillery divisions. It would seem likely that the PLA will have to keep at least three army corps with supporting elements along the Vietnam border for the indefinite future, and the accompanying map reflects those 1979 redeployments.

With the exception of the North Korea-Soviet-Chinese border triangle in Eastern Manchuria, there are no corps located on the Sino-Soviet border. Most of the Manchurian units are in the Southern and central

1. In a setting of great natural beauty women soldiers of the People's Militia carry out firing practice. It is interesting how many pictures released by the PLA show coastal defence, indicating something of a fixation with anti-invasion measures.

2. The men of the Ninth Motor Company of the PLA were the heroes of a "Save Petrol" campaign, having reportedly economised to the tune of 10,000 litres in the course of a year, without prejudicing their operational tasks. Measures taken included the fitting of home-made valves to reduce the petrol flow while coasting downhill. Such nationwide campaigns tend to come and go, being pursued with religious fervour for a time, with regular meetings and many slogans, but are then forgotten when the next policy is announced **2**

3. *One of the great achievements of the Communist Party has been to ensure that the PLA is an army which belongs to the people. The Chinese have suffered over many centuries from the depradations of marauding soldiers, especially in the years from about 1910 to 1949.*

Strong and stern measures have always been taken since the founding of the PLA to ensure that its officers and soldiers do not, either deliberately or through neglect, cut themselves off from their roots, while the people as a whole are constantly exhorted to

achieve unity with the armed forces. This young officer of the PLA is helping a group of young militia men and women in the interpretation of a field training manual. These youngsters carry the Type 53 7.62mm carbine, a Chinese version of the Soviet

Mosin-Nagant M-1891/30.
4. *Men of an anti-aircraft unit of the People's Militia engaged in "earnestly studying Marxism-Leninism-Mao Tse-tung thought and trenchantly criticising Lin Piao's counter-revolutionary revisionist line".*

3

4

1. A group of the Village Militia is briefed by their leader for an exercise. Such groups operating from underground bases are the very essence of Mao Tse-tung's "People's War" and would cause incessant problems for any occupying force.

2. A scene high in the Pamirs, where little has changed for centuries. The cavalry patrol returning past the yurts (low tents made from hide) could be reporting to Ghengis Kahn were it not for the slung rifles. The PLA tries to keep on good terms with minorities.

3. These women members of the People's Militia are firing hand-held 81mm mortars, a process which could well be as dangerous for the firers as those at the target! The addition of a simple tripod rest would not only make them much safer but also much more accurate.

4. A patrol of frontier guards and People's Militia of Mongolian nationality working together on China's northern border. Mongolia is more of a geographic expression than a political or ethnic entity. Many of the boundaries have never been properly surveyed and changes

portions of the Shenyang Military Region. This is done to prevent a Soviet blitzkrieg attack from the Maritime province in the east and the Mongolian border in the west from cutting off the Chinese main forces in Manchuria. That was the plan of attack used successfully against Japanese forces in the USSR's 1945 conquest of Manchuria. That attack used 75 divisions, and the total now along the entire border is only about 46. However, there are about as many tanks and artillery pieces in the Maritime province as there are in East Germany and the Soviets have been steadily improving the capabilities of the ground and air forces all along the border; thus the Chinese are understandably reluctant to risk forward deployment of their primary defence units.

There are no army corps in the Northwest. This is a lightly populated, arid region with poor lines of communication. Only one main line plus branch lines in Tsinghai and Sinkiang, serve the entire area and there are few natural barriers. The highly mobile Soviet mechanized forces could easily outflank

have taken place as recently as 1945 when the Soviet Union absorbed Tannu Tuva which had long been accepted to be part of Mongolia. There are many areas of dispute both in Sinkiang, and in the East between the Mongolian People's Republic and Inner Mongolia which is an integral part of the PRC. For military purposes the PLA divides Inner Mongolia between the Shenyang Military Region and Peking Military Region. Russian penetration of the Mongolian People's Republic (there are at least three divisions in the country) causes great concern in Peking since one of the shortest invasion routes lies through Chahar region straight towards the Chinese capital. Rather like the Poles, the Mongols find themselves inescapably stuck between two major powers, a notoriously sad fate.

well fortified with artillery and armour, and a cluster of army corps. In the defence of this line, the PLA might be forced to use its main battle tank—the T-59—like self-propelled artillery, usually firing from dug-in stationary positions. The fire control system could not hope to match that of sophisticated Soviet tanks in open field battle where first-hit capability is vitally important. Defensive doctrine calls for the scarce armoured personnel carriers to be held in tactical reserve units in order to be able rapidly to shore up weak points in the line or to protect against outflanking manoeuvres.

The deployment of regional forces would be difficult to depict on a single map, even if their locations were all known. About a dozen divisions are equipped and deployed as border defence units, although in that mode they are no longer technically regional forces, since they are in direct communication with the high command in Peking. These divisions are small—only about 6500 total personnel, with no armour and very little artillery, but they can claim the unique distinction of having 150 guard dogs each. Other regional forces are garrison divisions and regiments and similar units in emplaced coastal defence fortifications and watch posts. This leaves the majority of the regional units scattered throughout China in an internal defence mode.

As part of the "four modernizations" (agriculture, industry, science and military), the PLA is to be continuously upgraded over the last two decades of this century. The high costs of advanced military technology, competing domestic economic priorities and China's scarcity of capital will probably combine to prevent the ground forces from closing the gap between their capabilities and those of the USSR. Despite the new European defensive weapons purchases, the nation in general and the ground forces in particular will remain vulnerable to air and naval attack in conventional or nuclear modes. However, the PLA's objective capability and lethality will continuously increase so that the ground forces will remain a strong deterrent against military attack of any sort. At least that is what the Chinese leadership seems to be counting on in the absence of any viable alternative.

and isolate regular Chinese units in this region. There are some border defence divisions there, but the best they could do would be to delay briefly and harrass a Soviet attack. In case of war, the Chinese leadership is prepared to sacrifice most of that territory, while developing guerrilla resistance behind enemy lines. There are few strategic prizes in the area. The nuclear test range at Lop Nor is little more than a blast area wasteland with few permanent installations, no production facilities, and no permanent warhead storage. The city of Lanchow has considerable military importance as a research and development centre, and the nuclear gaseous diffusion plant is nearby, but it is doubtful that a single sustained Soviet offensive could penetrate that far. There is an army corps and several independent divisions in the Lanchow Military Region. In Inner Mongolia, a quick Soviet thrust could over-run the missile test facility at Shuang Cheng-tz'u (northwest of Paot'ou), but that would have no immediate effect on China's strategic forces.

The strongest defence line is that which protects Peking to the north and northwest, and the mountain passes separating Manchuria from North China. These natural barriers are very

THE DEFENCE OF CHINA'S HOMELAND

Colonel William V. Kennedy
Armor, United States Army Reserve*

"CHARGE!" While dramatic and impressive in a photo, the tactical sense of APCs charging in line across open ground is a little doubtful. The K-63 APC is a very neat, workmanlike vehicle, carrying a commander, driver and an infantry section of 9-10 men. It has a combat weight of 10 tonnes and is amphibious. Because they are in short supply these APCs are not part of infantry battalions, but are held centrally in transport battalions of armoured divisions. Also shown very clearly are the Type 54 12.7mm heavy machine-gun mounted on the commander's cupola and the Type 68 assault rifles, with the characteristic folding bayonet and knurled gas-regulator. Although the men are wearing respirators, chemical protection is, in fact, poor as they have large areas of exposed skin.

Although it is the largest land force in the world, the PLA has many problems. Strategy, tactics and equipment all need to be reviewed and brought up-to-date to meet the perceived threat from the Soviet Union and other potential enemies. China has embarked on a programme of military modernization by the year 2000. Will her enemies wait that long?

*The opinions and findings contained in this chapter are those of the author and should not be construed as an official US Department of the Army, Department of Defense or US Government position, policy or decision, unless so designated by other official documentation.

1. China takes the protection of its people very seriously, indeed, and firmly intends that the great majority of the population will survive, whatever the form of attack. This diagram, copied from a Chinese domestic magazine, shows the type of underground complex which a commune is expected to construct. Such a system is valuable both for resistance to conventional ground attack and for nuclear survival. The tunnels on the left enable the resistance fighters to move around underground, while the non-combatant elements shelter on the right.
2. Local defence is a task for the local Party Committee and the People's Militia. A female member of the militia guides a child through the tunnels; she is armed with a carbine, but it is doubtful whether there are enough to arm every militiaman in China.
3. It is surprisingly easy to construct effective shelters to give protection against nuclear weapon effects; all that is required is determination, some limited tunnelling skills and a lot of

1

The Chinese Army—that is, the part of the People's Liberation Army responsible for land warfare—is listed by the International Institute for Strategic Studies (IISS) as the largest in the world, with a strength of some 3,625,000 regulars.[1] That probably is the most misleading military statistic in the world today. The manoeuvre elements of the Army as distinguished from a large force of local defence units, consist of some 121 infantry divisions, 11 armoured divisions, three airborne divisions and 40 artillery and air defence divisions.[2] These are organized on the Soviet model, but, according to the US Defense Intelligence Agency (USDIA), at a much lower level of equipment.[3]

The Red Army of the Chinese Civil War and the Korean War was armed with whatever it could lay its hands on. This resulted in a mixture of European, Chinese, Russian, Japanese and American equipment. Modernization and standardization got underway with the receipt of large quantities of Russian equipment during the Korean War and the years of relatively good relations with the Soviets that followed. The deterioration of Sino-Soviet relations in the late 1950's brought this process to a halt. With the end of Soviet assistance the Chinese were thrown back on their own inadequate resources.

The Chinese armament industry has developed sporadically since the initial Manchu reform efforts of the late 19th century, through the era of the war lords, the Nationalists and the subsequent Russian influence. Despite a mixture of antiquated industrial equipment and methods, it has managed to produce serviceable small arms, crew-served weapons and tanks and artillery of 1950's Russian-pattern technology. Current tank production capacity and associated logistical support is inadequate to build and maintain an armoured force on the scale of China's requirements.

The USDIA says, "The Chinese require that their equipment be relatively simple to operate, maintain and repair. This requirement results partly from a scarcity of skilled technical personnel and, in some instances, of spare parts."[4]

The shortage of skilled manpower has been compounded by a decade of turmoil in which Mao Tse-tung's "Cultural Revolution" disrupted education and scattered many graduates to the agricultural communes.

In China's militarized society, the logistics base of the Army is the same as that which supports all the rest of Chinese society and industry. This civilian base was affected even more grievously than the Army by the Cultural Revolution.

Three principal characteristics must be kept in mind, therefore, in evaluating the potential effectiveness of the Chinese Army:

1. It is primarily a foot-mobile army.
2. Its weapons were designed to fit China's severe technical and financial limitations, not to match the capabilities of a first-class enemy.
3. Particularly in terms of mechanized warfare against a first-class foe, what logistics capabilities there are will decline quickly as the distance between deployed forces and the largely immobile civilian logistics base increases.

Supporting the large regular ground

2

establishment are two forces whose significance is of endless speculation and debate in the West. At one extreme is a presumably growing force of nuclear-tipped strategic missiles. At the other is a citizen militia counted in the millions or the tens of millions under varying criteria.

It appears that the Chinese possess a few missiles of intercontinental range and several hundred smaller weapons mated to delivery systems ranging from intermediate range missiles to aging Soviet-designed bombers.

Whether this combination of nuclear weapons and citizen militia is capable of deterring an invasion of China by one of the current superpowers, i.e. the United States or the Soviet Union, or of defeating such an invasion by "people's war" or "human sea" tactics if one occurs is debatable.

Whether China free from interference by the superpowers could use its existing and likely potential military strength to dominate East and South Asia is perhaps easier to ascertain.

What the Chinese Army or any other military force can do or fail to do is a

physical effort. These young men and women are building a shelter for their commune which will, at its simplest, give protection against blast, heat and radiation, except in the unlikely event of a direct hit. Some of the shelters under large cities such as Peking

include shops, hospitals and even transport systems.
4. PLA tactics in the attack, as depicted by the US Defense Intelligence Agency. Successful though it has been against Vietnam in 1979 and India in 1962, a Chinese infantry division would

find it difficult to conduct the sort of attack shown here in most of the terrain along the Sino-Soviet border. Soviet air power coupled with long-range reconnaissance would make it possible to spoil such an attack while it is still in the battalion approach march phase.

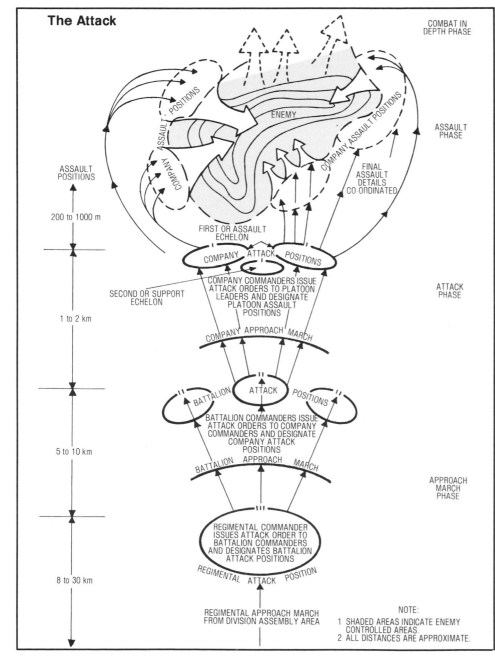

The Attack

COMBAT IN DEPTH PHASE

ENEMY

ASSAULT PHASE

ASSAULT POSITIONS

200 to 1000 m

FIRST OR ASSAULT ECHELON

COMPANY ATTACK POSITIONS

FINAL ASSAULT DETAILS CO-ORDINATED

COMPANY COMMANDERS ISSUE ATTACK ORDERS TO PLATOON LEADERS AND DESIGNATE PLATOON ASSAULT POSITIONS

ATTACK PHASE

SECOND OR SUPPORT ECHELON

1 to 2 km

COMPANY APPROACH MARCH

BATTALION ATTACK POSITIONS

BATTALION COMMANDERS ISSUE ATTACK ORDERS TO COMPANY COMMANDERS AND DESIGNATE COMPANY ATTACK POSITIONS

5 to 10 km

BATTALION APPROACH MARCH

APPROACH MARCH PHASE

REGIMENTAL COMMANDER ISSUES ATTACK ORDER TO BATTALION COMMANDERS AND DESIGNATES BATTALION ATTACK POSITIONS

8 to 30 km

REGIMENTAL ATTACK POSITION

REGIMENTAL APPROACH MARCH FROM DIVISION ASSEMBLY AREA

NOTE:
1 SHADED AREAS INDICATE ENEMY CONTROLLED AREAS.
2 ALL DISTANCES ARE APPROXIMATE.

4

product of several principal factors: doctrine (how it says it will fight); geography; logistics; military populations; history; the enemy.

All of these forces are operative in any conflict or potential conflict and any one of them can be the controlling factor at a given time. In the international environment of the 1980's, the dominant influence in Chinese military policy is likely to be the threat posed by a massive array of Soviet military power on the northern borders and, by proxy, along the southern border with Vietnam and Laos.

The Soviets and their Vietnamese allies are by no means the only potential enemy, at least in Chinese eyes. The United States has been relegated to "Enemy No. 2", for the time being. The old frictions with Japan have not been eliminated by the Sino-Japanese Treaty of Peace and Friendship concluded in 1978. They are latent in such issues as offshore oil exploration and Taiwan. The Nationalist Republic of China government on Taiwan continues to offer a political alternative to Chinese Communism and, perhaps even more dangerous, a striking economic contrast to the general poverty and economic stagnation of the mainland. India, in particular the Indian Army, harbours a latent resentment over border incursions and humiliation by China in 1962. Pakistan and Afghanistan are areas of existing and potential trouble as China, India and the Soviet Union vie for influence among local factions.

Within the context of the pervasive Soviet relationship, the locally dominant factor with regard to the United States, Japan and Taiwan is geographical: that

1. An open-air class in aircraft recognition. There must be an interesting practical problem of fire control in the event of war since so many of the PLA Air Force's aircraft are identical to Soviet machines. Secondly, it is doubtful that adequate communications exist to enable "hold-fire" messages to be passed so that the PLA Air Force can ensure that its own aircraft are not shot at by the People's Militia.

2. A militia unit from a steel works on anti-aircraft training. Such activities look amateurish and more hopeful than harmful to aircraft, but there is no doubt that in north Vietnam such a defensive system caused many US losses.

3. An anti-aircraft gun crew study their field-training manuals. One problem seldom discussed is the logistics for the People's Militia. The vast numbers of automatic AA guns and MGs must need much ammunition in peacetime practice, while their demands in war would be insatiable. Therefore, there must be an elaborate network of ammunition depots around China to back up the first-line stocks held with the units themselves. Further,

1

2

3

since ammunition deteriorates in storage, there must be some form of inspectorate to check on stocks.
4. A chemical reconnaissance team on a training exercise. The Chinese are clearly concerned about the possibility of chemical weapons being used against them, and rightly so, because the Soviet Union has very large stocks of chemical weapons and a great variety of delivery means. Further, Soviet military literature makes it clear that they regard chemical weapons as an integral part of their armoury; although they might still hesitate to be the first to use them, such hesitation might be less against the Chinese than against NATO. The Soviets have chemical shells for most of their larger guns; there are chemical warheads for the surface-to-surface missiles; and there are also air-delivered chemical bombs. The Chinese have chemical weapons also, but on nothing like the scale of the Soviet Union, while their delivery means are much more limited. Targets for chemical attack could include China's airfields, nuclear sites, communications centres and ports.

4

1. *The PLA firmly believes in the value of rapid and bold offensive action, particularly in what is termed the "meeting engagement", ie, the collision between two forces on the move. Here, an advance guard carries out a rapid infantry/armour attack.*

2. *The motor-cycle enjoyed a vogue in many armies from about 1910 to 1950. It is starting to make something of a come-back in Western armies, but the PLA has always been convinced of its value. Reconnaissance patrols such as this will operate some 10 to 15 miles ahead of the main body and here the radioman is passing a sighting report back to his headquarters, using a Type 63 high frequency set.*

3. *Positional defence is organized in depth and is designed to deny vital areas to the enemy, or to halt his attack and inflict heavy losses in both men and material. According to US DIA 4, the area is divided into three positions: the Security Position, the Main Defensive Position (MDP), and the Postion in Depth (DP). The Security Position. This is lightly manned by*

1

is, the ocean. In regard to India, Pakistan and Afghanistan the dominant factor is extreme geography of another sort—the mountains. The Soviet problem aside, history and population dominate China's military relationship with Indo China.

Under Mao Tse-tung, China evolved a military doctrine that supposedly could cope with the threat of superpower invasion with or without nuclear weapons. This was the concept of a "people's war" by which an enemy would be drawn into the interior of China, worn down by guerrilla warfare and then driven out by conventional counterattack. In this, the regular army serves as a sort of glue. It provides, successively, the framework for initial resistance, it breaks up into many parts to form the nuclei around which local forces and the militia gather for guerrilla resistance, and then it reconvenes, as it were, to drive out the weakened enemy.

Maoist doctrine was a product of history; that is, of Chinese Communist history. Human will and grit saw the PLA through the Long March and the Civil War. A tide of infantry rolled back United Nations forces from the Yalu River during the Korean War. That was the experience of the old men who stayed on and on in command positions throughout the PLA. Like old soldiers everywhere they have tended to become prisoners of their experience.

Powerful political, psychological and logistical factors reinforced the "human sea" doctrine. It is the logistical factor,

however, that dominates the others. Simply put, China lacks the means to support any other doctrine. It is much the same situation as existed in the early American colonies. Reliance on a universal militia (the-rifle-over-the-mantlepiece) was the only military system early America could afford, so it became enshrouded with enough myths to perpetuate public acceptance.

For the Chinese of Mao's day to have accepted the idea that they must have some other recourse than a "human sea" doctrine would have been to accept the inevitability of defeat and of a long period of military and political subjugation, something that no people and certainly not the Chinese Communist leadership can accommodate.

If you do not have the means to pursue a strategy of victory, therefore, and if you are not psychologically capable of accepting almost certain defeat, myths are a reasonable avenue of escape, particularly when they are politically attractive. Such was the case with the "human sea" idea. It fitted Mao's concept of the role of the masses and of a self-imposed isolation.

Since the Maoist doctrine was defensive in nature, it served nicely to support Peking's claim of non-interference in the affairs of other nations. Chinese offensives in Korea in 1950-51, against India in 1962 and against Vietnam in 1979 do not conform very well either to the Maoist military doctrine or to the announced foreign policy. They do, however, "track" very well with the development of the

Chinese Communist war machine over the past 30 years. History, therefore, is a better guide to the character and methods of the PLA than examination of theoretical doctrine.

Because it was so long and fervently declared to be so by Mao and others, many outside China assumed that the Chinese Civil War was won entirely by the "people's war" approach. That is not the case. The victories that enabled the Communists to gain a decisive advantage over the Nationalists were won in Manchuria, almost entirely by large-unit conventional operations. The concept of "people's war" enabled the Communists to survive the long period of inferiority in the 1930s and early 1940s and thereby create the base from which the large units used in Manchuria and later in the rest of China were formed. It was and remains, however, a defensive, indeed a survival doctrine.

The distinguishing mark of the early Chinese Communist armies in the offensive mode, whether as guerrillas or conventional armies, was determination born of political indoctrination.

The PLA acquired from the Russians a system of political commissars extending down to the lowest ranks. These infused the PLA with a sense of mission. The Nationalists long since have acknowledged that this was their fatal weakness and they have worked hard to correct it since reorganizing on Taiwan.

The grievances of the peasantry, of women and other large groups coupled with the patriotic impulses of the anti-Japanese war and resentment against foreigners in general gave the commissars of the PLA plenty with which to work. The results of their work were to be seen in the fanatical dedication of the Long March in the 1930s and in the suicidal "human sea" tactics employed during both the Civil War and against United Nations forces in Korea.

Although the commissar system was adapted from the Russian model it produced a distinctly different relationship between the Army and the Party than was the case in the Soviet Union. This was due to the fact that only a few years elapsed between the Russian Revolution in 1917 and the emergence of a fully organized Soviet bureaucracy. The Soviet commissars remained a distinctly different bureaucratic group from the military commanders. In

mobile troops with the divisional reconnaissance company well forward, and a company from each of the forward regiments some 3-6km in front of the FEBA. Each of the forward battalions also puts a reinforced platoon some 2km forward. The MDP. The bulk of the division is sited in depth in the MDP with two regiments forward. Mutually supporting positions are expected to hold out even if bypassed or surrounded. The PD. The aim of the PD is to stop deep penetration and to provide a firm base for counter-attacks by the mechanised battalion of the regiment in the PD. **4.** This dramatic picture is unlikely to be typical of a warlike operation as massed tanks in open terrain are very vulnerable to anti-tank fire from other tanks, anti-tank guns and, in particular, missiles.

China, the line between the two is much less distinct, at least among the older generation of leadership. By necessity, many of the Chinese political officers of the Yenan period developed into competent commanders and the commanders often were fully as proficient in the political realm as the commissars. Thus the military and the party in China have been more closely intertwined than has been the case in Russia. This means, also, that the Army has been pulled more deeply into political intrigue than has been the case in the Soviet Union.

From the time of the Great Leap Forward in 1958-59, major Chinese military figures have been deeply involved in the factional political struggles at the top of the Communist Party and the government. Regional commanders and local military units as

well were involved in the factional warfare during the upheavals of the Cultural Revolution, 1966-69. What effect has this had on the morale of the soldier?

It has been almost impossible for ordinary Chinese or even high-ranking local and regional party members to sort out the euphemisms and convolutions of the contending political lines. It seems reasonable to conclude that to some unknown and as yet unknowable degree, the early fanaticism of the PLA has been dulled by decades of inter-necine Communist feuds. Signs of cynicism detected among the civilian population by foreign travellers in recent years seem certain to have affected the military to some degree.

A more practical guide than the Maoist "thoughts" to the tactical doctrine of the PLA during the past 30 years is to be found in such purely professional tracts as Lin Piao's "Principles of Combat", first published in 1946.

Briefly, these constitute a relatively cautious doctrine emphasizing the following:

Mobility achieved through the toughness and endurance of the individual soldier.

Extensive reconnaissance to locate enemy flanks and gaps between enemy units.

Flanking and encirclement through multiple attacks in preference to frontal attacks.

Positional Defence: The Division

FEBA

REGIMENTAL MAIN DEFENCE POSITIONS

POSITIONS IN DEPTH

6 to 15 km

DIVISION SECURITY POSITION

3 to 6 km

2 km

750 m

DIVISION MAIN DEFENCE POSITION (DIVISION FIRST ECHELON)

3 to 6 km

GP (SUPPORTING)

GP (SUPPORTING)

GP (SUPPORTING)

GP (SUPPORTING)

(MOBILE ELEMENTS OF DIVISION SECOND ECHELON)

3 to 7 km

(MTZD)

GP (LONG RANGE)

6 to 12 km

DIVISION POSITION IN DEPTH (DIVISION SECOND ECHELON)

3 to 5 km

GP (LONG RANGE)

8 to 12 km

1. The diminutive Chinese T-62 shown here is virtually a scale model of the T-59 and pictures need to be examined carefully to confirm which of the two is depicted. This tank weighs 21 tonnes and is armed with an 85mm main gun, a coaxial 7.62mm machine-gun and a 12.7mm machine-gun for anti-aircraft protection. By scaling down the T-59 the PLA has obtained a light tank with a minimum of design and development problems. One of the tenets of armoured doctrine is to move tanks where the enemy thinks it impossible, and this small, ingenious tank can do just that.

2. These men are probably two of a special anti-tank team. Such teams are normally composed of three to five men and are formed to seek and ambush enemy tanks in the main defensive position.

3. A scene which will be familiar to soldiers all over the world: gun crews compete in an ammunition handling contest, with the battery commander (right foreground) leading the cheering. All ranks and insignia were abolished in mid-1965 in an attempt to counter

Soviet-style "professionalism". Officers were referred to by their task, ie, "Company Commander", while soldiers were referred to as "Fighters". This fine theory has been tried many times before, but has eventually broken down because someone has to make plans and give orders, and someone else has to do what he is told and get on with the job. Pay differentials have, of course, remained and a Squad Leader (corporal equivalent) receives 10 Yuan per month, while his Platoon Commander receives 50 Yuan. All officers start in the ranks, except for doctors and some technical experts.

4. People's militia practising their anti-tank tactics, this time against T-62s. The tank crews would have to be very inept to allow anti-tank teams to get so near in open country such as this, but in close country and built-up areas it would be quite another story, as was shown in the streets of Prague during the Soviet invasion of Czechoslovakia. The nearest soldier is armed with a Type 56 Rocket Launcher (the Soviet RPG-2).

3

4

1 and 2. *China's concern over the threat from the Soviet Union is typified by these cavalry patrols, in which the military expertise of the soliders of the PLA is reinforced by the local knowledge of the People's Militia. The men in the second picture are Kazakhs.*

3. *The PLA has to fight not only in every sort of terrain from desert to mountain, but also in every sort of climate. Their mountain troops are skilled in all aspects of "winter warfare", including skiing. These troops were particularly successful in the Sino-Indian conflict of 1962.* **3**

4. *Mobile defence comprises a series of defensive battles fought on designated lines of resistance forward of a "final interception line". The aim is to inflict casualties on the enemy and not to hold ground. As with positional defence the area is divided into a Security Position, the*

A willingness and ability to withdraw and disperse in the face of superior force.

In applying these principles during the Chinese Civil War, the PLA was aided by the chaotic situation that followed the defeat of Japan. Large areas were uncontested. What strength the Nationalists had was used to occupy cities and lines of communication. Even in the large-unit warfare in Manchuria, the PLA was relatively free to assemble, launch multiple attacks and exploit or fade away into the unoccupied countryside if resistance was too great. Emphasis on camouflage, foot mobility and small unit discipline founded on political indoctrination enabled large Communist units virtually to disappear in the face of a superior force, to reassemble and fight again at some distant and more favourable point.

These same tactics served the PLA well in the early stages of the Chinese intervention in Korea. Large forces were effectively concealed in the mountainous terrain. Attacks were delivered from many directions against United Nations columns separated by distance and difficult terrain. The dissolution and destruction of the enemy that was supposed to be the product of such tactics did not follow, however. UN firepower decimated the attacking Chinese units. Even as they retreated, the UN units collected substantial numbers of Chinese prisoners who had been demoralized by failure of the early attacks. Once a continuous UN front was re-established, the PLA found itself denied room for large unit manoeuvre. Local successes based on infiltration and multiple attacks could not be expanded. Worse, **2**

a terrible price was exacted by superior UN firepower from land, sea and air units.

When they had run out of tactical ideas in the Civil War, the PLA commanders had exploited the dedication of their soldiers by "human sea" mass infantry assaults in which columns advanced over what became literally carpets of their own dead. The same thing occurred in Korea with even more horrible results in the face of UN firepower. The late Chou En-lai told American visitors in later years that China had been staggered by these losses and that the entire Korean intervention "probably was a mistake".

The PLA tactic of careful preparation and superiority at the point of attack was evidenced again in the 1962 attack on India. Here again the static, widely separated Indian border posts and the inadequacies of Indian defence policy of the time enabled the Chinese to follow the Civil War "book" almost to the letter.

The incursion against Vietnam in February-March 1979 again followed the same general pattern in that there was a careful build-up, an attack against relatively weak border forces and withdrawal before the main strength of the Vietnamese army could be brought to bear. This, however, was a more complex combined arms operation than had been conducted by the PLA at any time in the past. How well Chinese armour, infantry and artillery worked together is unknown since foreign news coverage on both sides was severely limited. The limited

nature of the conflict and the very favourable overall strategic relationship the Chinese enjoyed relative to Indo China make it unwise to draw any conclusions about the prospects for future Chinese success against a first class opponent.

Concerning the aspects of PLA tactical doctrine that led to success in the past, the following observations can be made:

The most extensive of the past PLA successes were against Chinese rather than foreign opponents, and under conditions of mutual inadequacy in modern military technology and training.

The mobile tactical doctrine of Lin Piao and his colleagues was based on foot mobility. China probably still has a major advantage in this area, but if war comes with a major modern power it is the mechanized enemy who will have superior mobility.

"Human sea" tactics against modern firepower will produce losses that not even China can afford.

Modern means of battlefield surveillance, in particular the scout helicopter, will negate much of the Chinese emphasis on camouflage and dispersion as a means of large-unit concealment.

The stagnation of the Chinese economy over the past 30 years means that the military logistics system, wholly dependent upon the civilian economy, is not much better than it was at the time of the Korean War. It was unable then to sustain continuous

Main Defensive Position and the Position in Depth. The Security Position: The security force determines the enemy's strength and direction of approach, and also fights delaying actions to force him to deploy. Its task done, the force withdraws. Main Defensive Position:

Two regiments are deployed forward, but within these, battalions, companies and platoons deploy one-third of their strength forward and two-thirds to the rear in reserve, which is in complete contrast to positional defence. Small-scale defensive battles are fought by

combined-arms teams with the aim of delaying, fragmenting and exhausting the enemy to the point where they can be defeated completely by a large-scale counter-attack. Once the forward regiments have been fought back to their Final Interception Line, mobile defensive

operations within the division cease, and mobile defence at Army Corps level is started. Position in Depth: The third regiment is responsible for position type defence on the Final Interception Line, and minor counter-attacks. (Such tactics would need air superiority, or parity.)

foot-mobile offensive action over a relatively short distance from the most highly developed part of China. It is doubtful that the system can support sustained operations by the relatively few modern divisions China now possesses, much less the large number required to match a first class opponent.

Pressures for modernization within the PLA and acceptance of defence modernization as one of the four principal goals of the post-Mao leadership indicate that China recognizes its military deficiencies. Teng Hsiao-ping and others among the post-Mao leadership have implied in public statements that political activity and excessive time spent on civic action projects have compounded the problems of diverting time and energy from military training. Recognition of these problems by the

leadership and the dispatch of military delegations to the West and Japan, the search for some form of satellite reconnaissance capability, and the effort to rebuild an educational system shattered by the Cultural Revolution indicate that the entire Chinese military system is in a state of transition.

The existing structure and tactical doctrine of the Chinese Army is described in a US Defense Intelligence Agency handbook published in 1976. The picture drawn is that of a 1950's era Soviet-model army prepared to operate as "fronts" consisting of various numbers of armies, each of which consists of three divisions organized on the World War II Soviet scale. There has been virtually no direct observation by foreigners of Chinese military training and operations during the past 20 years. There is no

way to be sure, therefore, that the structure portrayed in current Western publications is accurate. It can be said with more certainty that whatever does exist now will change very rapidly as new ideas and new equipment are imported. Rather than attempt to describe the inadequacies of present Western information, it would seem to be more profitable to examine the challenge to which the Chinese forces must respond if they are to emerge during the next decade as a fully creditable modern force. The two principal components of that challenge are geography and relative military technology.

In terms of geography, China has both great vulnerabilities and great strength. The vulnerabilities lie principally in the northern region, along the 4,500-mile border with the Soviet Union. China's geographic strength lies principally where it is not needed, along the border with lesser, or less likely foes — Vietnam and India.

The principal strategic feature of the Sino-Soviet border is Mongolia. The old domain of Genghis Khan and the Golden Horde is now divided into the People's Republic of Mongolia, under Soviet control, and Inner Mongolia, a Chinese province where the Han Chinese population is now dominant. Russian-dominated Mongolia was described by Mao Tse-tung as "the fist in China's back". It has been the central element of the Sino-Soviet border dispute that broke into the open in the 1960s. Invariably, China suggests that a resumption of amicable relations depends upon Russian willingness to withdraw its forces from Mongolia.

Mongolia divides the Sino-Soviet borderland into three distinct regions: Sinkiang and the Kansu Corridor; the Gobi Desert and Inner Mongolia; Manchuria.

Sinkiang is largely a desert rimmed by mountains. It was inhabited originally by non-Chinese tribes, principal among them Turkic peoples with kinship to the Turkic peoples of Soviet Central Asia. Although conquered by China and Russia during the 19th century, these people have a political, cultural and religious (Muslim) heritage that is neither Chinese nor Russian. Chinese immigrants are often the products of forced campaigns, such as **4** the imposed exile of large numbers of

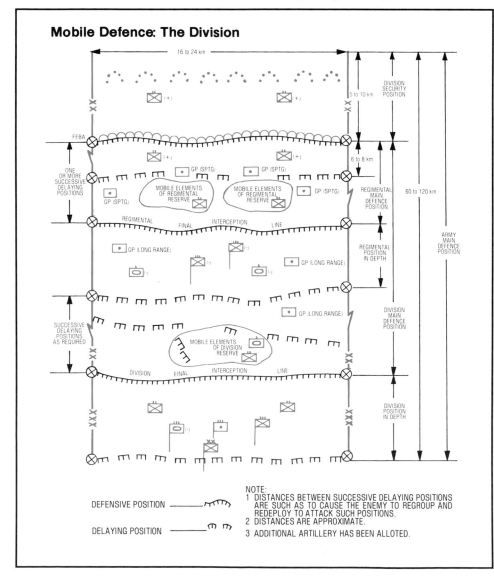

Mobile Defence: The Division

NOTE:
1 DISTANCES BETWEEN SUCCESSIVE DELAYING POSITIONS ARE SUCH AS TO CAUSE THE ENEMY TO REGROUP AND REDEPLOY TO ATTACK SUCH POSITIONS.
2 DISTANCES ARE APPROXIMATE.
3 ADDITIONAL ARTILLERY HAS BEEN ALLOTED.

DEFENSIVE POSITION ——————
DELAYING POSITION ——————

1. A medical team rushes forward to collect casualties. There are first-aid men at company headquarters and an aid station with each battalion. Like so much in the PLA the medical system is simple and straightforward but very effective. The medical services were given a thorough test in the punitive attack on Vietnam in early 1979, when very heavy casualties were incurred and most TV coverage shown in the West included shots of field dressing stations in requisitioned Vietnamese villages. The inherent stoicism of the Chinese eases the doctors' task considerably.

2. A dramatic picture of the forward defences on a river-line; the men are probably regional troops as the weapons are quite old. In the foreground is a Type 53 7.62mm heavy machine-gun, a Chinese-produced version of the Soviet SG-43. The riflemen are armed with 7.62mm Type 53 carbines, while a Type 50 7.62mm submachine-gun and a Type 53 7.62mm light machine-gun can also be seen. In the foreground an ammunition party rushes along the trench with machine-gun ammunition. Note the

1

2

absence of steel helmets which are standard in most other armies.
3 to 6. One of the main tactical considerations of the PLA is to achieve close contact with the enemy both to prevent the use of battlefield nuclear weapons and to negate, to a certain extent, equipment deficiencies. It will also enable the bravery and skill of the PLA infantry to be used most effectively. A real close-quarter weapon is this flame-thrower with a range of some 30 to 40 meters and an attack on an enemy trench would not be anything like as simple as appears from this sequence of pictures. Even though the two men are working together, they would need considerable protection from accompanying riflemen to achieve any sort of success. The flamethrower is now seldom used.

3

5

4

6

1. One of the main threats facing the PLA is large numbers of Soviet tanks, and there is no doubt that anti-tank defences are weak. This D-44 85mm anti-tank gun uses the same tube as the obsolete T-34/85 tank and would not be effective against modern Soviet tanks except at critically short ranges, and even then the "special armour" of the T-64 and T-72 tanks could defeat the old-fashioned armour-piercing shells used in this weapon. **2.** T-59 tanks and infantrymen of the PLA advance along a dirt road into Lang Son province of the Democratic Republic of Vietnam in early 1979. This operation must have taught the PLA General Staff many invaluable lessons. The PLA was quite unable to strike at the time of the Vietnamese invasion of Kampuchea, which robbed the punitive operation of some of its strategic and diplomatic impact. When the attack did start it was slow and ponderous and quite unlike the lightning operations mounted by the Israelis. Most reports also suggest that the PLA suffered very heavy casualties 20,000 according to sources in

youths from the cities under Mao. In any case, they are competitors of the indigenous population for political and cultural control and they are ultimately a threat to the survival of the Turkic identity.

Mongolian independence from China has the effect of channelling communications between Sinkiang and Central China through the Kansu Corridor, a rugged neck of terrain between the southern border of Mongolia and the mountains. A single Chinese railway stretches through this corridor, the lifeline of Chinese administration and the Chinese presence in Sinkiang. The principal geographic feature of the border between Soviet-controlled "Outer" Mongolia and Chinese Inner Mongolia is the Gobi Desert, homeland of the bubonic plague and generally inhospitable to life in any form.

These arid regions stretching from Dzungaria in Central Asia to the eastern border of Mongolia have much of the military characteristics of the Middle East. Since antiquity they have been controlled by whomsoever commanded greater mobility and firepower and the military organization to use them effectively. Greater numbers in this context could be a liability. In modern terms the military means to dominate the region lie in a complex combination of air power, helicopters, tanks and armoured infantry, with extensive mobile cannon and missile support. Nuclear weapons in the range of 100 kilotons or so and fired at high air burst would provide the means to control vast expanses of territory by observation and long-range delivery systems without incurring the disadvantages attributed to such weapons by Western nuclear theorists. Of at least equal importance is the need for an extensive logistical base that can regenerate equipment quickly through a combination of battlefield repair and resupply from depot rebuild and new production.

China does not have the means to control, or so much as seriously contest control of, the air over the northern border regions and will not attain such a capability in the 1980s unless either Soviet air and missile forces are diverted to other areas or China receives the help of large allied forces. These could come only from the US.

If China cannot control the air in the northern border regions, then she cannot manoeuvre her limited armoured and mechanized formations, nor can she supply them over open terrain subject to continuous aerial observation and attack. China would have to attempt, therefore, to conduct a static defence of principal invasion routes and of important economic and military centres, husbanding what tanks and other armoured fighting vehicles she possesses for local counterattacks. As soon as these forces began to fight, however, they would use up quantities of ammunition and fuel. Resupply would depend largely on a railroad system that fans out from central China and which grows thinner and more vulnerable every kilometer of the way west and north.

Static defence means essentially extensive fortifications. Both the fortifications and the supplies stockpiled therein or brought in from elsewhere would be vulnerable to chemical and biological attack, of which the Soviets have a formidable capability.

Assuming no immediate involvement by allied, that is, American, forces on a scale large enough to change the force relationships, Chinese defence of Sinkiang and most of Inner Mongolia would be foredoomed. If the Soviets chose to fight on World War II terms, that is, without chemical, biological and nuclear weapons, the Chinese might be able to conduct a prolonged defence of fortified areas. But if the Soviets attacked with all of the means at their disposal, excluding strategic nuclear weapons, the battle would be over very quickly.

"Human sea" tactics in this region would be out of the question. Mao's vaunted guerrilla warfare concepts depend on "secure rear areas". There is no such thing in the desert reaches of Sinkiang and the grasslands of Mongolia. Life in those regions depends upon scant supplies of food and water. Once the Soviets controlled those they would have the population at their mercy.

Along the eastern reaches of the Sino-Soviet border, geography is more promising for a successful Chinese defence, but only marginally so.

The mountains and swamps that rim the Manchurian plain tend to channel and delay an attack in either direction. They were not sufficient to save the Japanese Kwantung Army from destruction in 1945 and the Soviet means to overcome the terrain obstacles are much greater today. Again, the key would be control of the air. Although the rimland of Manchuria is more favourable than the Western deserts to resupply along concealed and relatively protected routes, the potential volume

2

Washington. Even so, the main aim was to serve notice on both Vietnam and the Soviet Union that China would not sit idly by while Vietnam brought Southeast Asia under its domination and in this it succeeded. China also showed up the shortcomings of the United Nations, because all the rhetoric against the Vietnamese interference in Kampuchea had achieved nothing and only China showed herself prepared to take resolute action.

3. Most countries have disbanded their coastal defence artillery many years ago, but China has an acute problem, with an enormous coastline and relatively weak naval and air forces to defend it. The threats are from the Soviet Pacific Fleet and the Nationalists on Taiwan. Guns such as these are of only limited value.

3

of demand is greater due to the increased density of forces. Here again, Soviet chemical weapons superiority could play a decisive role. Chinese fortress garrisons would not be likely to be able to withstand such an attack, and it would be difficult or impossible for the Chinese to conduct large-scale resupply in the face of air-delivered chemical attack.

At best, the Chinese, in their present circumstances and those likely to prevail at least through the 1980s, could hope to conduct a delaying action and attempt to stabilize a front somewhere south of the old Chinese Eastern Railway—the original eastern span of the Trans-Siberian. Such a withdrawal would place the Soviets in control of a large Chinese population and, in theory, create the sort of situation on which the Maoist doctrines are based.

It is generally acknowledged by Chinese and other authorities that the Japanese succeeded in pacifying Manchuria. Conducting a large-scale guerrilla war in the bitter winter climate and open terrain of the Manchurian Plain would be difficult. Further, it has yet to be shown that guerrilla war can succeed anywhere in the face of nuclear, chemical and biological weapons.

China's border with North Korea abuts Soviet territory and forms part of the overall Manchurian defence problem. Here China must be prepared against the possibility of being drawn into another Korean war, or of North Korean alliance with the Soviet Union in the event of a Soviet attack on China. China's doubts about the wisdom of the first excursion into Korea and the necessity of maintaining good relations with Japan and the United States as a counterweight to the Soviet Union make it increasingly unlikely that China could or would support North Korea if it were to attempt again to conquer South Korea. North Korean alliance with the Soviets against China would compound the Chinese defence problems, but because of the overall weakness of the Chinese strategic position along the entire border such an alliance would not change the existing power relationship other than to hasten a Chinese defeat. North Korean neutrality would favour China's defence of Manchuria, but not enough to change the present balance of forces.

China's seaward flank is secured by what the Peking government plainly regards as quasi alliances with Japan and the United States. Extension of Soviet naval power south of the Korean Peninsula would be certain to engage Japanese and American interests. The defence of the China coast, therefore, lies primarily in the field of politics.

The threat posed by Taiwan is political and ideological rather than military. Here, also, the international ramifications of Chinese military action to neutralize the threat by conquest makes questions of technical military capacity of secondary importance. China has demonstrated a limited amphibious warfare capability, but it has not indicated any intention to build the forces necessary for invasion and conquest on so large a scale.

Along its southern land frontier, China has demonstrated that geography, population base and relative combat power overall enable it to punish what it believes to be Vietnamese transgressions whenever it chooses, so long as the Soviet Union does not interfere directly. A Soviet decision to intervene in Vietnam itself or along the northern borders would dispel very quickly any lingering Chinese notion that regional Chinese commands could be expected to maintain a "small war" entirely from their own resources—another of the old Maoist themes. If the Soviets were to become directly involved, every bullet and every can of petrol expended anywhere on the Chinese periphery would lessen China's capability to cope with the main threat.

India has shown no disposition to regain by force the territory taken by China in 1962. If Chinese control over Tibet were to be weakened, as by Soviet advances into Sinkiang, India would be tempted to regain not only the mountain outposts lost in 1962, but the much more favourable position India enjoyed when Tibet was independent of Peking. Here again, China's ability to defend its positions on the Indian frontier is likely to be determined more by events elsewhere than by geographical or force relationships in the immediate area of dispute.

Barring a major international alignment, therefore, the PLA's doctrine, tactics, organization for combat and ability to maintain its strategic position during the 1980s are likely to be dominated by the dispute with the Soviet Union. The fundamental question in all of these areas is: How far would the Soviets be likely to penetrate in an attack on China?

The assumption, widespread in the West and Japan, that the Soviets would be "swallowed up" in China is rooted in the belief that the Soviets would be out to "conquer" China. The traditional Russian objectives, pursued with consistency throughout the 19th and 20th centuries, are much less ambitious. As defined by Gen. Alexei Kuropatkin in a memorandum to the Czar in 1916, the

1. One aspect of service shared by the Soviet Army and the PLA is that both are tasked with defending huge land masses, which include not only vast distances, but also virtually every conceivable variety of terrain and climate. Here a detachment of the PLA is encamped in the highlands of Sinkiang. At China's Western extremity, they are very close to the Soviet border, but a long way away from the Chinese heartland in the east. Their supply and reinforcement would thus be most difficult in time of war.

2. A convoy of military trucks winds its way through the narrow valleys of Yunnan province in south-west China, taking supplies to the forces engaged in the brief war against Vietnam in early 1979 Twenty-four years previously the Chinese trucks were using this same road to take supplies to the Vietnamese, but then they were aiding their fellow-Communists in their fight against the French colonial power. Roads such as this are very difficult to attack from the air and, if hit, are very easy to repair, especially using mass labour.

3. In the lowlands an infantry unit practises the attack. In the campaigns fought by the PLA — against Chiang Kai-shek, the Japanese, the UN in Korea, the Indians in 1962 and the Vietnamese in 1979 — the soldiers have shown themselves to be very brave, well disciplined, hardy and stoical. The recurring tactic, however, is that of very heavy artillery bombardments followed by mass infantry assaults. This works well against enemies such as the Indians and the Vietnamese, but it did not work effectively for too long against the much more sophisticated United Nations Forces in Korea. Nor could it be expected to work for long against the highly mobile, heavily armoured forces of the Soviet Union. Its main proponents are the elderly senior officers, some of whom are now in their seventies and still in active command, and when these depart the new generation can be expected to undertake a thorough review. Their influence is already being seen in the persistent demands for more modern and effective equipment.

3

1. The PLA places great emphasis on the ability to continue operating at night. This mortar crew is taking part in a competition. The weapon is the Type 53 82mm mortar and the 3-man crew split the loads into barrel (right), base-plate (centre) and bipod (left).

2. A 3-man machine-gun crew at night-firing practice. The tracers give an unusual opportunity to observe how the shots spread, the extent depending upon weapon design and upon the skill of the firer. The man on the left is carrying a satchel charge.

3. An anti-aircraft battery on a night deployment exercise, with the city lights blazing out behind them. Their weapon is the Type 55 37mm light anti-aircraft gun, a straight copy of the Soviet M-1939. Unlike the weapon shown on page 75 this mounting has only one gun.

4. The PLA manual on reconnaissance is quite explicit: "Every commander must organize reconnaissance within his unit's zone of activities. He must not wait for instructions . . . Each new mission requires immediate organization of reconnaissance.

aim to Russian policy should be to establish a buffer against the growth of Chinese power. To achieve this, Kuropatkin maintained, it would be necessary to secure a border that runs from the Khan Tengri Mountain in the Tien Shan range to Vladivostok. The Soviets achieved approximately half of the Kuropatkin objective when they gained control of Mongolia. Throughout the 1930s they continually pressed forward in Sinkiang, and in 1945 they forced the war-weakened Chinese Nationalist government to grant concessions in Manchuria that all but returned Russia to the favoured position it occupied prior to defeat by Japan in 1905. Ironically, these advantages had to be surrendered when the Communists came to power in China.

Reassertion of Russian control in Manchuria down to at least the line of the old Chinese Eastern Railway (Tsitsihar - Harbin - Vladivostok), to include re-entry of the Russian Pacific Fleet into Port Arthur and possibly Tsingtao would effectively cripple the development of China as a power capable of challenging Russian control of the Maritime Province. If this—and not the "conquest" of China—is assumed to be the Russian objective, then it can be concluded that the Russian penetration would stop short of the point at which the Chinese "people's war" doctrine could be effectively brought into play.

It is axiomatic among students of Chinese military history that "he who controls Manchuria controls all of China north of the Yangtze River". This stems from the lack of defensible

terrain between Manchuria and the river.

It can be further concluded, therefore, that a Russian victory in Sinkiang and Manchuria would effectively cripple Chinese military power in all of North China and give the Soviets unlimited access to the North China ports.

If the "people's war" approach is ruled out, the Chinese Army would be faced with a major dilemma: If it could not draw the Soviets into an endless campaign in Central China, then it would have to defeat the Soviets in open combat before they achieved their objectives in Sinkiang and Manchuria.

As shown earlier, the Soviet strategic position in Mongolia makes it almost impossible to defend Sinkiang under the best of circumstances. The Soviets would merely have to cut the Kansu Corridor using airborne and airmobile forces. This they could accomplish with conventional means alone, given their margin of technical superiority. Use of chemical and battlefield nuclear weapons would make the job that much easier.

Even if the Chinese were to double their present armoured force (estimated at 11 divisions) and re-equip the whole with up-to-date vehicles, communications and weapons it is doubtful that they would have the logistic resources to sustain a mobile defence of Inner Mongolia.

From what journalists and other Western and Japanese visitors have been able to observe of the frontier dispositions, the Chinese have acknowledged this situation by holding back their main forces in reserve positions in Central China.

China has ample forces with which to build and garrison the outer Manchurian defences, but it would be hard-pressed to resupply them once they began to consume large stocks of ammunition. Employment of a central reserve of armoured forces—even assuming that such a reserve could be created on an adequate scale—would depend on control or at least parity in the air, an unlikely prospect. No matter how successful the defence of Manchuria, however, the Chinese forces there would be almost certainly cut off by Soviet thrusts southeastward from

Mongolia toward Peking and south-westward from the vicinity of Vladivostok. Here again, the Soviet presence in Mongolia would force the defenders to fight, in a strategic sense, back to back with constant worry about the security of their lines of communication and retreat to the south. That is the reason that Chinese diplomacy emphasises getting Soviet forces out of Mongolia.

If the Chinese Regular Army could not hold the Soviets at bay, and if the Soviets were to stop before China's citizen militia could become engaged, what of the chances of the nuclear deterrent?

Soviet satellite photography almost certainly has recorded the location of every Chinese missile unit capable of launching an attack on the Soviet Union. With this Soviet superiority of reconnaissance and a parallel communications intelligence and electronic countermeasures (ECM) capability, it is difficult to believe that the Chinese could launch their missiles in time or with a sufficient degree of coordination

to preclude a disarming Soviet strike. Use of the long range missiles under any circumstances would invite destruction of Central China when it is likely the war otherwise would not have touched that centre of population.

Use of China's entire array of smaller nuclear weapons would incur a similar liability to Soviet pre-emption and a massive Soviet response that would cause far more damage to the Chinese than anything the inadequate Chinese delivery systems and communications capabilities could bring to bear on the Soviets.

The only extensive field test of tactical nuclear warfare to date was Joint US Strike Command Exercise *Desert Strike,* in May 1964. This exercise demonstrated that a defending force faced with defeat in a conventional conflict must deliver a rapid, highly coordinated nuclear response before major friendly and enemy units become intermingled. This requires secure mobile communications and delegation of authority to use nuclear weapons to the military commander on each major

front. The Chinese do not have a communications capability of that order and it is doubtful that they are willing to delegate such responsibility to a regional military commander. Even to contemplate use of nuclear weapons in such circumstances presupposes an ability to gain a military advantage or at least to cover the retreat. *Desert Strike* indicated that, when both sides have a tactical nuclear capability and when there is a great disparity in overall strength in favour of the attacker, initial use by the defender is only likely to increase the scale of devastation with no change in the ultimate result.

There remains some chance that the Chinese could destroy one or more major Soviet cities. The argument for and against use of the Chinese nuclear force turns, then, on an assessment of whether the Soviets would be willing to put at risk the lives of a large number of their citizens in return for gaining a decisive strategic objective not only over China, but over Japan and the United States as well.

Japanese military officers and journalists have been told by Chinese military sources that China expects the Soviets to attack. The Chinese have said that they hope to complete modernization of their economy and their armed forces before the attack begins. They have embarked on just such an effort by seeking military technology and military hardware wherever they can find it. The scale of the building required and the amount of money needed to achieve it make it doubtful that any such objective can be reached if China must rely on its own resources.

Much has been made of the defensive power of precision guided munitions (PGM) and some Western observers have suggested that these might provide a quick solution to the Chinese strategic problem. The fact remains that Sinkiang is indefensible by any combination of weapons so long as the Soviets enjoy their present margin of military superiority and their access to Mongolia. As is the case with nuclear weapons, Soviet air and ECM superiority would give them both unlimited reconnaissance and the ability to "blind" Chinese command and control systems before the defending Chinese forces could acquire targets.

The utility of PGM to defending

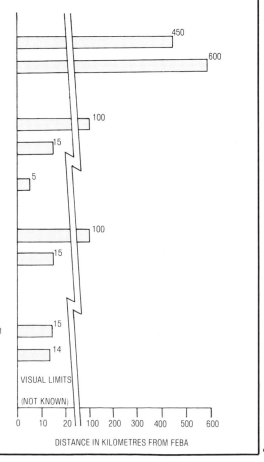

Effective range of Chinese reconnaissance means

	Distance in kilometres from FEBA
1 AIR RECONNAISSANCE	
A FIGHTER RECONNAISSANCE	450
B LIGHT BOMBER RECONNAISSANCE	600
2 PATROLS AND RAIDS	
A FROM ARMY RECONNAISSANCE BATTALION	100
B FROM DIVISION RESOURCES	15
3 OBSERVATION POSTS	5
4 MOTORISED RECONNAISSANCE	
A FROM ARMY RECONNAISSANCE BATTALION	100
B FROM DIVISION RESOURCES	15
5 ARTILLERY OBSERVATION	
A SURVEILLANCE AND WEAPON LOCATING RADAR	15
B SOUND RANGING	14
C FLASH SPOTTING	VISUAL LIMITS
6 ELECTRONIC INTERCEPT	(NOT KNOWN)

0 10 20 100 200 300 400 500 600

DISTANCE IN KILOMETRES FROM FEBA

China has thirty-five centuries of recorded history and it is natural that in that time her borders should have expanded and contracted in line with the successes and failures of the ruling dynasties. This history has been characterized by long periods of stability interspersed with short, but usually violent, periods of instability. The last period of stability was the Manchu reign which lasted from 1644 to 1911, although the Nineteenth Century was a time of increasingly rapid decline as the ever-weaker central government was challenged by the aggressive, ambitious, and frequently ruthless Europeans, aided towards the end of the century by the Russians and the Japanese. These people never attempted to colonise China itself, but they whittled away at the frontiers and wrung some humiliating concessions from the Manchus; this has left a legacy of mistrust and wounded pride which affects China's relations with other countries to this day
1. *One of the key areas of dispute is along the Ussuri river and*

forces declines as the terrain becomes more broken and the range at which targets can be acquired lessens. In Manchuria, therefore, the same terrain that favours tighter defensive formations also greatly lessens the effectiveness of PGM. Soviet ability to attack at night and along covered approaches, supported by smoke and perhaps other chemical munitions, would suggest a repetition of the successful Soviet offensive over the same ground against the Kwantung Army in August 1945.

Assuming the present overall force relationship on the Sino-Soviet border, it can be concluded that if the Chinese Army is successfully to resist attack it must be powerfully reinforced, re-equipped and assured of resupply by some allied power or combination of powers. The present size of the Chinese Army is not only irrelevant to solution of this problem, but probably is a serious detriment.

To receive and to use equipment on so large a scale would require a lengthy reorganization and retraining of Chinese forces weakened by decades of excessive involvement in political activity, internal security roles and the disruption of the country's educational structure during the "Cultural Revolution".

It is difficult to believe that if the Soviets consider a modernized China to be a mortal threat they would wait out such an interlude unless China's allies were willing to interpose their own forces along the northern border.

Footnotes

1. *The Military Balance 1978-1979*, The International Institute for Strategic Studies, London, 1978, p 56.
2. Ibid.
3. *Handbook of Chinese Military Forces*, US Defense Intelligence Agency, Washington, 1976.
4. Ibid, paragraph 2-53.

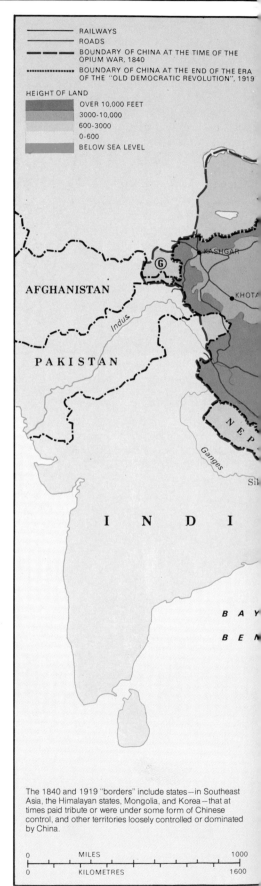

The 1840 and 1919 "borders" include states—in Southeast Asia, the Himalayan states, Mongolia, and Korea—that at times paid tribute or were under some form of Chinese control, and other territories loosely controlled or dominated by China.

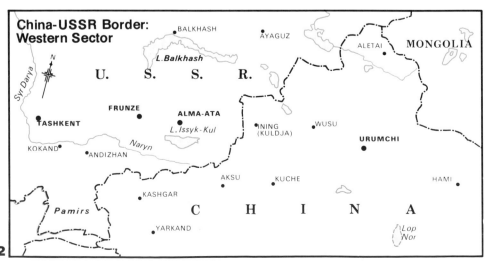

Source: US CIA Atlas

especially the large island of Hei-Hsia-Tzu at the confluence of the Ussuri and Amur rivers, which has been occupied by the Russians for many years following the Treaty of Aigun in 1858, although the Chinese have always claimed that it remained their property. As shown clearly on the map the crucial town of Khabarovsk with its key airfields would be seriously affected by a return of the islands to China.

2. Although attention has tended to focus on the Manchurian border, the north-western border with the USSR is also a potential "flashpoint", Chinese suzerainty once having extended as far as Lake Balkash. This border includes the five traditional land highways from Europe to the East and is strategically important to both countries. When preparing for the punitive expedition against Vietnam in 1978/79 the Chinese put more reinforcements into Sinkiang than into Manchuria.

3. Of the remaining areas in dispute the two most critical are Taiwan and India's north-east Sino-Indian border.

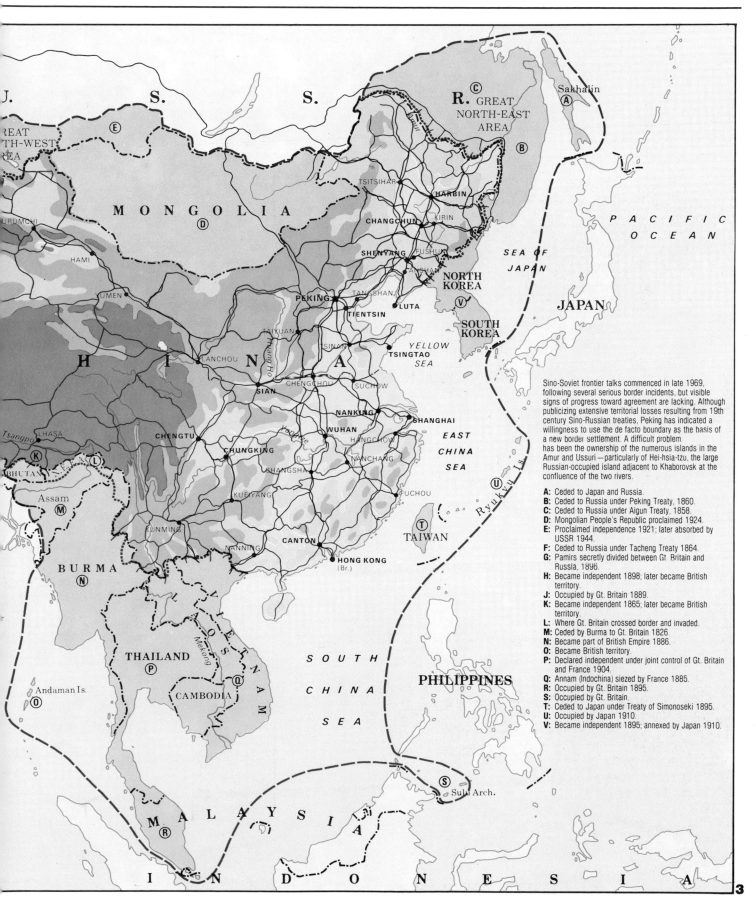

Sino-Soviet frontier talks commenced in late 1969, following several serious border incidents, but visible signs of progress toward agreement are lacking. Although publicizing extensive territorial losses resulting from 19th century Sino-Russian treaties, Peking has indicated a willingness to use the de facto boundary as the basis of a new border settlement. A difficult problem has been the ownership of the numerous islands in the Amur and Ussuri—particularly of Hei-hsia-tzu, the large Russian-occupied island adjacent to Khaborovsk at the confluence of the two rivers.

A: Ceded to Japan and Russia.
B: Ceded to Russia under Peking Treaty, 1860.
C: Ceded to Russia under Aigun Treaty, 1858.
D: Mongolian People's Republic proclaimed 1924.
E: Proclaimed independence 1921; later absorbed by USSR 1944.
F: Ceded to Russia under Tacheng Treaty 1864.
G: Pamirs secretly divided between Gt. Britain and Russia, 1896.
H: Became independent 1898; later became British territory.
J: Occupied by Gt. Britain 1889.
K: Became independent 1865; later became British territory.
L: Where Gt. Britain crossed border and invaded.
M: Ceded by Burma to Gt. Britain 1826.
N: Became part of British Empire 1886.
O: Became British territory.
P: Declared independent under joint control of Gt. Britain and France 1904.
Q: Annam (Indochina) siezed by France 1885.
R: Occupied by Gt. Britain 1895.
S: Occupied by Gt. Britain.
T: Ceded to Japan under Treaty of Simonoseki 1895.
U: Occupied by Japan 1910.
V: Became independent 1895; annexed by Japan 1910.

PRC interpretation of China's Territorial Losses

SHENYANG F-6bis (F-6B) Fantan-A

Artist's impressions of a new PRC aircraft, apparently based on the F-6, were first issued from China in 1977. A few weeks earlier the United States Secretary of Defense had said the "Fantan-A fighter bomber" was a major tactical type in the PRC naval air force. Both the name and designation are those allotted by the USA. At first it was thought Fantan was little more than an F-6 with nose radar. In late 1978 better photographs became available, showing that, though it

may use the propulsion system and most of the wing and tail of the F-6, the new aircraft is larger, has a totally redesigned fuselage, and is configured for the surface attack role. The cockpit has been moved forward about 2m (over 6ft), putting the unchanged type of ejection seat above the nose gear. Internal fuel capacity is increased, despite the fact that the space under the wing appears now to be a weapon bay. The engine inlet ducts are cut off on each side

instead of being continued to a common inlet at the nose. This has allowed the addition of a long conical nose which in many aircraft at present in use does not contain a radar. The PRC has sufficient information on several Russian and American radars to produce an effective installation which could be used in the air-to-surface and air-to-air roles. (About 15 years ago the PRC was flying F-6 development aircraft with R2L "High Fix B" MiG-21 radar.) In the

accompanying artwork the differences between the Fantan-A and the regular F-6 are noted wherever they appear to be externally obvious. But even this important aircraft is still imperfectly known in the West.

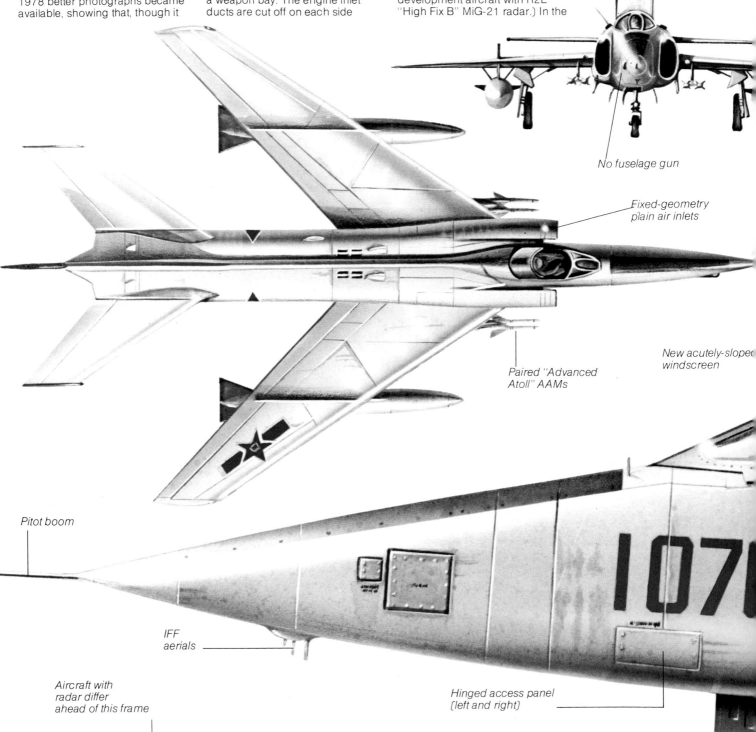

No fuselage gun

Fixed-geometry plain air inlets

New acutely-sloped windscreen

Paired "Advanced Atoll" AAMs

Pitot boom

IFF aerials

Aircraft with radar differ ahead of this frame

Hinged access panel (left and right)

Tandem both on r

Alternative noses

The first illustrations of Fantan-As showed a naval air force fighter with a radar (left). Though this continues to be seen, the clearest photographs in recent months depict a tactical model without radar (main drawing above). The difference appears to be confined to the nose ahead of a frame exactly in line with the start (left

side) or finish of the five-figure aircraft numeral. The no-radar Fantan has a nose pitot boom, angle-of-attack sensor, static ver IFF and what appears to be a ra inlet on the right side.

Text by Bill Gunston
Artwork by Martin Alton

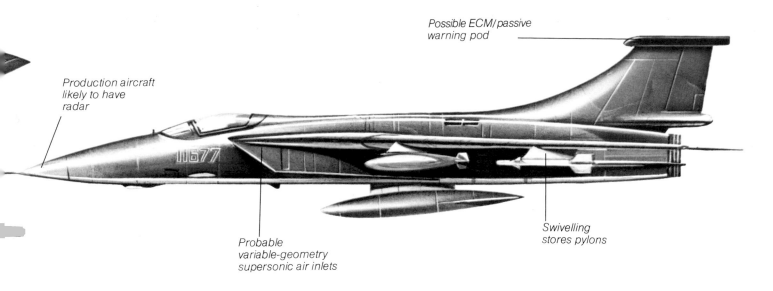

Possible ECM/passive warning pod

Production aircraft likely to have radar

Probable variable-geometry supersonic air inlets

Swivelling stores pylons

Tailerons

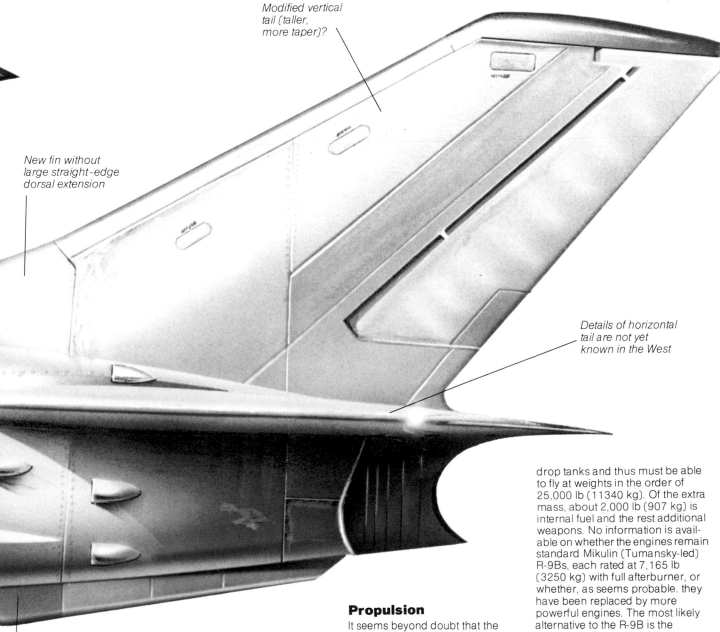

Modified vertical tail (taller, more taper)?

New fin without large straight-edge dorsal extension

Details of horizontal tail are not yet known in the West

Apparently different ventral fin, no separate tail bumper

Propulsion

It seems beyond doubt that the F-6bis in all versions has a much higher maximum weight than the F-6. The latter is normally cleared to 8700 kg (19,180 lb), but the Fantan-A has been illustrated with drop tanks and thus must be able to fly at weights in the order of 25,000 lb (11340 kg). Of the extra mass, about 2,000 lb (907 kg) is internal fuel and the rest additional weapons. No information is available on whether the engines remain standard Mikulin (Tumansky-led) R-9Bs, each rated at 7,165 lb (3250 kg) with full afterburner, or whether, as seems probable, they have been replaced by more powerful engines. The most likely alternative to the R-9B is the Tumansky R-11, of about 12,600 lb (5750 kg) thrust, used in early MiG-21s and previously built in the PRC. Other R-11 versions are rated up to 13,668 lb (6200 kg).

117

MISSILES OF THE PLA

CSA-1 This is the Soviet V750 series surface-to-air missile system called SA-2 Guideline by NATO. Very large numbers of this long-established SAM are believed to have been PRC-made.

AIRCRAFT OF THE PLA

B-5 The IL-28 Beagle light bomber, torpedo carrier and trainer was made in the PRC from the late 1950s, and it is estimated that 400 remain operational. Some belong to the naval air force.

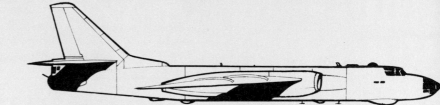

Be-6 Called Madge by NATO, this piston-engined flying boat remains the chief PRC maritime reconnaissance and ASW type. Features include retractable radome and rear MAD instead of a turret.

B-7? US designation of the PRC-built Tu-16 Badger is unknown. Manufacture of this large nuclear-capable bomber began at Shenyang in 1968, and over 80 are operational in this role.

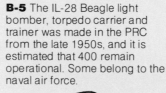

F-7 IN 1964-68 the PRC made a limited number of early-model MiG-21 fighters, without Soviet co-operation. This is an F-7 of the MiG-21F Fishbed C type. Some went to Albania and Tanzania.

F-4 The MiG-17 Fresco, in several versions, was the first combat aircraft made in the PRC, which itself designed the TF-4 trainer (upper view), a unique all-Chinese aircraft.

F-6 Most important PRC combat aircraft, the MiG-19 Farmer was built in the SF fighter/bomber and PF all-weather interceptor versions. The F-6 PF model has a unique Chinese radar nose.

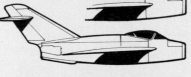

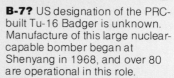

F-2 The MiG-15 is more important as a trainer (MiG-15UTI Midget), many hundreds of which were made in the PRC, some for export. Small numbers are still used as single-seat fighters.

Fong Shou No 2 Well over 5,000 of at least two versions of An-2 Colt multi-role transport have been made since 1958, with its 1,000 hp ASh-621R engine. Many have been exported.

IL-14 With the big four-turboprop IL-18 this remains a standard transport in the PRC air force, though neither was manufactured in China. The civil CAAC also uses both Ilyushins.

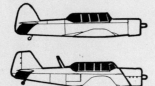

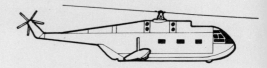

BT-6 Standard trainer is à PRC development of the Soviet Yak-18A Max (upper view), with large square-cut tail and many other changes.

H-5 This is the Mil Mi-4 Hound 14-seat helicopter, large numbers of which were made under licence at Shenyang. It is believed to be the only locally produced helicopter.

SA 321H Super Frelon At least 13 of these large multi-role helicopters have been supplied by France's Aérospatiale. They are used for transport and casevac missions linking remote centres.

Chinese SSMs (surface-to-surface missile) are almost completely unknown in the West, and these drawings represent the best consensus of opinion. **A,** CSS-X-4 full-range ICBM, said to be even bigger than Soviet SS-9 Scarp. **B,** CSS-3 ICBM (interim). **C,** CSS-2 IRBM, of up to 2,485 miles range. **D,** CSS-1 medium-range missile of early liquid-fuel design, in use since 1966. **E,** Later SLBM of general design like early Polaris.

CAA-1 So far the only air-to-air missile definitely identified in PRC use is the Soviet K-13A AA-2 Atoll, some versions of which are almost certainly manufactured in China.

SHIPS OF THE PLA–NAVY

Ming This code-name identifies the first class of conventional submarine to be designed in the PRC, to follow the Romeos after the break with the Soviet Union; only two of these six-TT boats were built.

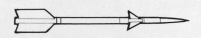

Han This modern nuclear submarine, with "spindle" (or "teardrop") hull, was begun at Luta about 1971 and went to sea in 1974; so far no more have been seen, suggesting prolonged problems.

Luta Significant in being PRC-designed, these destroyers owe a little to the Soviet Kotlin class; about six have been built, with more to follow, with progressively better weapons and ECM.

PLA INFANTRY WEAPONS

Type 56-1 (top right) No relation to the AK 56-1, this is one of the PRC models of the obsolete Soviet RPD (Degtyarev) squad light machine gun (7.62×39 mm); a version was also made in North Korea.

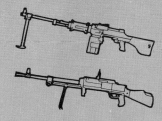

Type 56 This is the PRC-produced copy of the Soviet AK-47 (Kalashnikov), one of the most widely used weapons in the world; some have a folding spike bayonet, and the 56-1 has a folding stock.

Type 67 (bottom left) This important new PRC company LMG is an assemblage of features found in many other weapons, and is used by North Korea also; contrary to some reports it fires rimmed 7.62×54 mm.

Type 68 This important PRC-designed assault rifle uses any Communist 7.62×39 mm ammunition, and though it has a 15-round magazine can be adapted without difficulty to use the AK/AKM 30-round box.

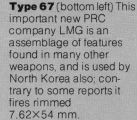

Type 64 This PRC-designed submachine-gun fires 7.62×25 mm ammunition and has an integral Maxim-type silencer; it has bolt mechanism resembling a PPS and a trigger group of the ZB-26 (LMG) type.

Type 65 PRC-designed, this 82 mm recoilless rifle was based on the 1950s-vintage Soviet B-10, but is much lighter (a mere 28.2 kg, 62 lb, compared with a B-10 weight of 72 kg, 159 lb).

Type 56 This carbine is a copy of the Soviet SKS (Simonov) semi-automatic weapon using the M-1943 cartridge of 7.62×39 mm size; late models have a spike bayonet which is not used on the SKS.

Type 54 The PRC made large numbers of 12.7 mm heavy machine guns of DShK-38 (Degtyarev) and DShKM Type 38-46 design, late production having a smoother barrel; some are used on AA single mounts.

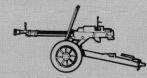

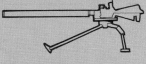

Type 59 This PRC AA gun of 100 mm calibre is a copy of the Soviet KS-19, and is similarly associated with Fan Song E radar; in the Warsaw Pact armies it is no longer in front-line service.

ARTILLERY OF THE PLA

SP howitzer US documents describe an AFV based on the M-1967 APC (amphibious with four wheels each side) mounts the Type 54 122mm howitzer; the first PRC SP gun.

BM-13 This is the Soviet designation for this multi-barrel 16×132 mm truck-mounted rocket launcher, used on ZIL-151 vehicles as an obsolescent training weapon in WP armies.

BM-14 Again, this is the Soviet designation for a mobile rocket system, the usual PRC model being BM-14-16 with 16 tubes of 140 mm calibre, mounted on a ZIL-151 or -157 truck.

Type 63-1 This appears to be standard 12-tube rocket launcher of PRC armies, with calibre of 107 mm; it has light-alloy tubes, reducing weight 300 lb (186 kg) compared to Type 63.

Type 54 This designation presumably indicates 1954 as the year this mass-produced Soviet 122 mm howitzer, the M-1938 (M-30), was first supplied to the PRC; many are still in use.

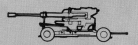

119

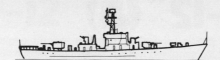

Kiangtung This PRC-designed frigate was the first to carry a SAM system, which may have been based on CSA-1 Guideline; the result was apparently not a success and only two were built.

Hainan These large patrol boats appear to be a bigger version of the Russian SO-I class, with two 76 mm guns as well as two twin 25 mm and simple AS weapons. Production appears to be complete.

Kiangnan This class of frigates was derived from the Riga, and at least five have been built since 1968; they have three 3.9 inch guns but (so far) lack SSMs, radar and modern AS weapons.

Gordi Unrelated to today's Krupny of this name, two ships of the former (pre-war) destroyer class were given to China in the mid-1950s. They were fitted with twin SSMs in 1971-74.

T-43 A batch of these ocean mine-sweepers was supplied by the Soviet Union in the mid-1950s, and 21 were then built in the PRC at Canton and, for a shorter period, at Wuchang.

Shanghai More than 375 of these 30-knot gunboats have been built in four versions, and many have been exported; there are various fits of 57, 37 and 25 mm guns, and a few have TT or 75 mm recoilless rifles.

Golf 1 A single example of this primitive three-missile submarine was built at Dairen (probably under Soviet licence) and commissioned in 1964. If it has missiles, these are Soviet Serbs.

Romeo Four of these pre-nuclear boats were supplied by the Soviet Union around 1960, and about 30 improved models have since been built in the PRC. They carry up to 36 mines and have eight TTs.

Whiskey PRC yards built about 21 pre-nuclear submarines apparently identical to the mass-produced Soviet type, with 20 torpedoes or 40 mines and a cruising range of 13,000 miles.

PLA SUPPORT VEHICLES

Type 76 (left) This anti-tank recoilless rifle is a second-generation derivative of the US M20, but the calibre remains 75 mm; usually mounted on two-wheel cart, with tow bar.

MTU Though the PRC probably still has many bridgelayers based on the T-34 chassis, this type based on the Soviet T-54 tank is believed to be the most important; it spans a 36 ft (11 m) gap.

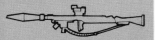

Type 69 PRC-made copy of the Soviet RPG-7 anti-tank launcher; has modified sights but no rear pistol grip.

Type 59 This PRC-designed artillery tractor is a tracked vehicle superficially very similar to the Soviet ATS-59 (but not necessarily a copy); no numerical data appear to be known yet.

AT-S Introduced in the early 1950s, this Soviet tracked artillery tractor is slightly less powerful than the Type 59 and may be used to carry radars and other special payloads.

KMM Treadway bridge, originally supplied by the Soviet Union, is carried in five 7 m spans on a ZIL-157 truck, and can be set up by a good crew to bridge a 115 ft (35 m) gap in 30 min.

TMM This is a truck-mounted scissors bridge, able to span a gap of up to 131 ft (40 m); it is usually mounted on the KrAZ-214 6×6 truck in Warsaw Pact armies, a 7-tonne payload vehicle.

KS18 This is the Soviet designation for the widely used 85 mm AA gun which was standard in North Vietnam in the SE Asia war; the PRC probably uses Fan Song E radar with this gun.

Type 59 This is the PRC-built copy of the Soviet M-1950 (S-60) 57 mm AA gun, the gun itself being similar to that of the M-1943 anti-tank weapon but on a different towed chassis, plus radar.

Type 55 This designation applies to the Soviet M-1939 towed AA gun of 37 mm calibre derived from the Bofors; the PRC model has been exported to several countries but is obsolescent.

Type 58 Soviet ZPU-2 twin anti-aircraft 14.5 mm (Vladimirov KPV) heavy machine guns are widely used as towed pieces throughout the PRC army, and some are mounted on APC chassis.

Type 55 This is the year-of-introduction designation of the Soviet M-1943 (ZIS-2) anti-tank gun of 57 mm calibre, which is considered obsolescent in Warsaw Pact armies.

152 mm howitzer No US designation exists for this PRC version of the Soviet M-1 M-1943 (D-1), probably used in China since the early 1950s but outclassed by the Type 66.

Type 66 Based on the Soviet D-20, this excellent 152 mm howitzer uses the same carriage (chassis) as the Type 60 122 mm gun and the Type 59-1 field gun; this gives 360° traverse.

Type 60 Again, the Soviet D-74 howitzer is known in the PRC by its year of introduction; a high-velocity 122 mm gun, it is widely used (but the Soviet 122 mm D-30 is apparently not).

Type 59-1 This 130 mm field gun is a PRC design closely resembling the Soviet M-46 (M-1946), but apparently with reduced range of 22 km instead of 27/31.

Type 55 Confusingly, the same year is used to identify the Soviet D-44 anti-tank and general-purpose gun of 85 mm calibre; this is possibly the most widely used gun in the PRC.

Kronshtadt Sometimes written Kronstadt, these post-war Soviet AS escorts (submarine chasers) have various guns and simple AS weapons; the Soviet Union supplied six and 14 were PRC-built.

Riga Not identical to Soviet frigates of this class, these four ships were built 25 years ago and updated from 1972 with twin SSMs (but still having no AS weapons except depth charges).

Kianghu This new class of frigate has the Kiangtung hull but two pairs of SSMs instead of the unsuccessful SAM system. Like many other PRC classes it is assumed to carry SS-N-2 Styx.

Komar (left) These 40-knot missile boats were supplied by USSR around 1964 and since built in modest numbers in the PRC.
Hoku (right) A development of the well-tried Komar, with a steel hull, pole mast and SSM boxes moved in towards the centreline.

Hola These missile boats are enlarged Osas, apparently of PRC design and still in production; they have three SSMs along each side but are not thought to carry any gun armament.

P6 (left) These are almost identical to the Soviet P-6 diesel torpedo boats, with two TT and speed of 43 knots. About 80 were built in the PRC. **Huchwan** (right) These diesel hydrofoils carry two TT and can exceed 50 knots. At least 70 were built at Shanghai.

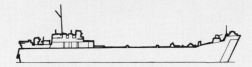

LST-1 First of a new class of locally designed LSTs, this series is replacing at least 16 former American LSTs and about 13 LSMs. There are also various wartime LSILs, LCUs and LCTs.

Osa About 40 of these missile boats have been built in PRC yards, following supply of a small batch of Osa I from the Soviet Union soon after 1960. They have two twin 25 mm guns.

Swatow (Left) Eighty or ninety were built of these 40-knot gunboats (based on Soviet P-6), they have four 37 mm guns, and two 12.7 mm, but no torpedo tubes. **Whampoa** gunboats (right) were derived from these (30 thought to be in use in 1972).

PLA AFVs

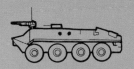

BTR-60 PRC designation of the locally built version(s) of this important 8×8 APC is unknown; most are based on the open-topped BTR-60P supplied by the Soviet Union in 1962.

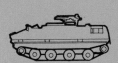

M-1967 (K-63) Apparently designed in the PRC, this 10-ton amphibious APC has only four road wheels on each side; it seats a crew of four and 10 troops, and has a 12.7 mm machine gun.

Type 56 This is the PRC-built version of the Soviet BTR-152 6×6; most seem to be APCs with an open top, but some have AA guns; command radio and other loads.

T-34 AA Not yet designated in the West, this is a recently disclosed T-34 chassis with twin 37 mm AA guns (80 rds/min per barrel, effective range 10,000 ft, 3000m) in a power turret.

Type 59 Around 1963 this went into production as the PRC main battle tank, the basis being the Soviet T-54B but without power traverse, stabilization of 100 mm gun or night IR sight.

SU-100 Derived from the SU-85 assault gun/tank killer, by fitting a 100 mm gun, still an old Soviet wartime AFV but serving in large numbers in the PRC.

T-34/85 Considerable numbers remain of the final (85 mm gun) version of the Soviet T-34, supreme tank of World War II; the PRC may have more still in use than the Warsaw Pact armies.

Type 62 Confusingly, this AFV is not a Soviet T-62 but a quite different light 21-tonner with an 85 mm gun. In rough terrain, as in southern China, it could be used as a main battle tank.

SU-76 Obsolete in Warsaw Pact armies, this thin-skinned tank destroyer has a 76.2 mm high-velocity gun with 60 rounds of four types; all in PRC use are believed to have been Russian-built.

Type 60 A light amphibious tank, use mainly for reconnaissance, this 18-ton AFV is an enlarged Soviet PT-76 with an 85 mm gun. The PRC also uses the PT-76 itself.

THE MODERNIZATION OF CHINA'S AIR FORCE

Bill Sweetman

The flight-line of a PLA Air Force fighter base, which demonstrates at last that the Shenyang F-6bis really does exist. Over the past five years this aircraft, formerly erroneously referred to as the F-9, has been the subject of more artists' drawings than almost any other type and it was only in 1978-79 that the PRC released photographs of it. The F-6bis (or F-6B, Fantan-A) demonstrates that in aeronautics, as in many other fields, China has the men and resources to produce modern equipment, albeit of a relatively unsophisticated nature. The IFF antenna under the nose of aircraft 10769 is noteworthy, and is almost certainly of Chinese design, while what appear to be weapons bay doors can be seen under 20136.

Despite plans to import combat aircraft, and the development of new and advanced indigenous designs, the PLA-Air Force needs radical modernization if it is to be able to make a significant contribution to the defence of China.

In sheer numbers, China's air arm is the third largest in the world, after those of the United States and the Soviet Union. It is, however, equipped almost entirely with aircraft of totally outmoded technology; even the smallest members of Nato or the Warsaw Pact have in general retired the contemporaries of such aircraft or are well on their way to doing so. China, for instance, is still thought to operate a handful of Tupolev Tu-4 Bull bombers, Soviet copies of the Boeing B-29 Superfortress; the only other operator of the ancient bomber is the US Confederate Air Force, a group of aircraft-preservation enthusiasts.

The most advanced first-line combat type operated by the Chinese air force is the F-8, the MiG-21F Fishbed C day fighter, and even this relatively unsophisticated aircraft — much inferior to later multi-role variants of the basic design — is in service only in limited numbers and does not appear to be in production in China. Apart from the MiG-21, however, China does not possess a single combat aircraft which was not flying in some form in the first half of the 1950s.

In fact, it is probably fair to say that the Air Force of the People's Liberation Army (AFPLA) and the Aviation of the People's Navy (APN) have not greatly increased in effectiveness since the late 1950s, when they were generally believed to constitute one of the world's most powerful air forces. Around 1960, the AFPLA was estimated to comprise some 3,000 fighters and tactical bombers; with the exception of the Tu-16 and the Shenyang F-9 (the latter a development of the MiG-19 rather than an all-new design), the force of 1960 included all the combat types in service in the late 1970s.

The retarded development of the Chinese air arm currently places severe limitations on China's ability to fight a conventional land war. Lacking, for example, all-weather intercepters or strike aircraft, the AFPLA would probably be unable to secure the ground forces against harassment from such types as Northrop F-5E Tigers (operated by many Western-aligned states on its periphery, and also apparently in service with Vietnam) or third-generation MiG-21s. Against such types as the MiG-23/27 Flogger or

2. *A group of women aircrew walk past an Ilyushin IL-14 (NATO Codename: Crate). As far as is known they are only permitted to serve in transport aircraft but judging by feminine progress in the West they will soon work their way into other fields as well!*

3. *Paratroops dropping from an Ilyushin IL-14 (NATO Codename: Crate), whose design dates from 1945-46. There are 4 parachute divisions in the PLA, centrally stationed in Wuhan MR, but their strategic value is limited by the lack of aircraft. It is now known that the Chinese aircraft industry is in production with a more advanced multi-role transport in the IL-14 class, which probably first flew with ASh-82 piston engines and is reported now also to be flying with turboprops of unknown type.*

1. China has frequently suffered from natural disasters and as with other air arms the PLA Air Force must join in relief work. It would be able to do this task much more effectively if it were to be equipped with modern transport aircraft with greater ranges and payloads.

2. There are at present approximately 400 airfields in China, the great majority of which are in the more densely populated eastern part of the country. This dearth of airfields explains why China wants to buy the BAe Harrier V/STOL aircraft, which is ideal in such a situation.

3. The Mil Mi-4 (NATO Codename: Hound) first appeared in 1951 and entered service in 1953, but it is still the most numerous helicopter in China.

4. The PLA-Air Force chain-of-command is based on the air districts, whose boundaries are identical with the Military Regions. The actual strength of each air district depends upon the threat facing it; thus, Shenyang, Peking, Nanching and Kwanchow Air Districts are stronger than the others. The major operational

Su-19 Fencer the AFPLA would probably be totally ineffective. The light ordnance loads and poor all-weather capability of such aircraft as the F-4/MiG-17 and F-6/MiG-19 would render any but clear-weather strikes totally ineffective, but such missions would be virtually suicidal against any form of concerted tactical surface-to-air defence.

The present poor state of the air arm is due to the Maoist doctrine that China would resist invasion by guerrilla warfare, in which aircraft play no part. It became clear following the take-over by the new Chinese regime that this policy had been abandoned, and that the military forces were to spear-head China's move to new technology and to greater industrialization. It follows that the most important aspect of Chinese air power is how much it can be expanded and modernized, given its present rather weak base.

Air power imported from Russia

The Maoist indifference to air power, despite its achievements in the 1939-45 war, may have originated in the successful revolutionary war of the Communist Chinese against the Nationalist Forces, in which air power was insignificant. Air power was an importation, introduced to China by its ally the Soviet Union following signature of a 30-year treaty of alliance and friendship in 1950. The AFPLA was then expanded with astonishing speed, with the aid of large forces of instructors and technicians from the Soviet Union. The Soviet Union's aim was to expand its power base in the region by creating a force which, although nominally independent, would rely on the Soviet Union for technical support and training.

By 1951 the Chinese-Soviet AFPLA was described by a United States estimate as "one of the largest air forces in the world". Even though this may have been an exaggeration, the AFPLA was already operating the advanced MiG-15 fighter and was engaged in air-defence operations in Korea. As might be expected considering the short time the Chinese air force had been in existence, the AFPLA pilots proved no match for their Ameri-

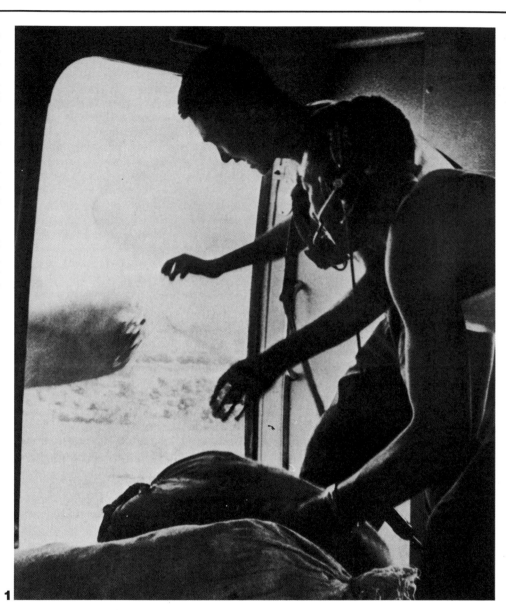

PRC AIRFIELDS (based on information from the US Defense Intelligence Agency)

Runway Length	Runway Surface*			Total
(in feet)	P	T	N	
14,000 and over	4			4
13,000–13,999	1			1
12,000–12,999	2			2
11,000–11,999	5	1		6
10,000–10,999	9			9
9,000– 9,999	11	2		13
8,000– 8,999	46	2		48
7,000– 7,999	85	7		92
6,000– 6,999	42	10	3	55
5,000– 5,999	10	16		26
4,000– 4,999	13	22	1	36
under 4,000	14	52	17	83
under construction				6
seaplane stations				2
	242	112	21	383

* P=Permanent; T=Temporary; N=Natural

formation is the air division, which comprises three regiments, each of three squadrons. It should be noted that the air defence units of the naval air arm come under the operational control of the PLA Air Force, but that the Navy retains control of its air units which operate out to sea in support of the fleet. The military region headquarters probably exerts some form of loose coordination over the air regions in peacetime and may, under certain circumstances, take command in war.

3

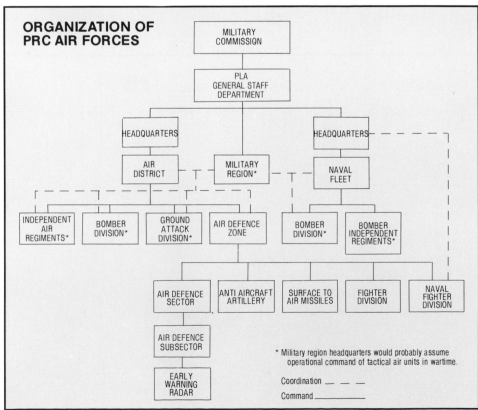

ORGANIZATION OF PRC AIR FORCES

MILITARY COMMISSION

PLA GENERAL STAFF DEPARTMENT

HEADQUARTERS — AIR DISTRICT — MILITARY REGION* — HEADQUARTERS — NAVAL FLEET

INDEPENDENT AIR REGIMENTS* — BOMBER DIVISION* — GROUND ATTACK DIVISION* — AIR DEFENCE ZONE — BOMBER DIVISION* — BOMBER INDEPENDENT REGIMENTS*

AIR DEFENCE SECTOR — ANTI AIRCRAFT ARTILLERY — SURFACE TO AIR MISSILES — FIGHTER DIVISION — NAVAL FIGHTER DIVISION

AIR DEFENCE SUBSECTOR

EARLY WARNING RADAR

* Military region headquarters would probably assume operational command of tactical air units in wartime.

Coordination _ _ _

Command _____

4

can opponents. The imbalance in pilot experience, together with the radar gunsight of the USAF F-86 Sabre—a refinement which the MiG-15 did not possess—largely accounted for the 10:1 advantage in "kills" recorded by the Sabres in Korea.

Expansion of the Chinese air force continued rapidly after the Korean war, and the service saw action against leaflet-dropping aircraft of the Nationalist Chinese forces, based on Taiwan, and in raids on Nationalist-held islands. There was, however, clearly a group within the Soviet military command urging caution in supplying military aid to China. Despite reports during the 1950s that delivery of atomic weapons and strategic bombers to China was imminent, the only long-range strike capability permitted to China was the force of 50 to 100 obsolete Tu-4s, delivered in 1953-54. Another sign of caution was that most of the training of Chinese personnel continued to be carried out in the Soviet Union itself, pilot recruits being trained *ab initio* at Tashkent, Kiev,

1. *Some six per cent, or over 50 million of the population of China, are from the "minority races", which range in size from the seven million Chuangs in Kwangsi province to only six hundred Hochihs living on the strategically critical Ussuri River. These two flying students represent two such groups: a Kazakh on the left and a Uighur on the right. Their flying clothing is World War II vintage and the model of their training aircraft is of much the same era—a Yakovlev Yak-18— but it would appear that the Chinese version has minor modifications.*
2. *". . . and there I was at 10,000 feet!" A pilot of the PLA Air Force illustrates a classic stern attack with the aid of a model.*
3. *Again, this picture shows the mixtures of nationalities that exist in the People's Republic, here seen learning the theory of aeronautics.*
4. *This picture was taken in the hey-day of the Maoist cult, and shows the political commissar running an impromptu political study session beside the tail of a*

MiG-15. All clutch their "little red books", while the pilots' flight manuals are faced with portraits of the great leader. Even the tail of the aircraft has not been exempted from the slogan writing, although whether it did anything to help it remain airborne is a different matter. Repeated breaks for political study may help Party control, but can do little for training in skills.

5. A fly-past at a training base, with old MiG-17s, actually the Chinese-built copy known as the Shenyang F-4.

1. Student pilots watch their comrades take to the skies. The minimum period of service in the PLA Air Force is four years, of which pilots spend two years in training. Primary flight training lasts six months and includes basic theory and meteorology.

2. These aircraft are Chinese-built versions of the Soviet Yakovlev Yak-18 (NATO Codename: Max). It has been modified by the Shenyang factory, with squared off wingtips and tail-fin. The Yak-18 first flew in the USSR in 1946 and has since been in wide service.

3. Students at an advanced flying school being instructed in fighter tactics. Instruction here lasts nine months, and follows nine months at intermediate level. Advanced training includes flight under difficult weather conditions, high altitude formation flying, instru-

ment training, and interception tactics. The use of aircraft models to illustrate the finer points of tactics—and especially aircraft attitudes and relationships one to another—is common to many air forces and does not indicate any deficiencies in the PLA Air Force.

Vladivostok and Novosibirsk. Technicians of all types were similarly trained within the Soviet Union. The intention was clearly to limit the ability of the Chinese air arm to remain effective without Soviet support.

Improvements in aircraft, airfields

The 1950s, however, still saw the progressive improvement of the Chinese air force. The AFPLA took delivery of the faster and more potent MiG-17 to supplement the MiG-15, and some supersonic MiG-19s were also delivered. The Ilyushin Il-28 light jet bomber was delivered to replace the piston-engined Tupolev Tu-2, and many ancillary types, including the Beriev Be-6 flying-boat and the Mil Mi-4 transport helicopter, were delivered. A new airfield-building programme proceeded in parallel with the deliveries of new equipment, augmenting the large number of bases built in 1944-45 by the US Army Air Force in Western and Central China. Intended for use in a final air offensive against Japan, the US-built bases were designed to support the B-29 bomber and were thus well equipped with long concrete runways.

A small-scale aircraft industry had fallen into the hands of the victorious Chinese Communists thanks to the Japanese, who had established various manufacturing and support facilities in Manchuria during the long-drawn-out war with Nationalist China. Some Japanese engineers were captured with the surrender of Japan in 1945, and work on small indigenous aircraft designs started in the early 1950s. Most of these fell into the utility and light transport category, and none seems to have been produced on a very large scale. Some licensed manufacture of small Soviet piston engines was also reported.

In 1957-58, apparently, production of the Soviet MiG-17 started at the Shenyang aircraft factory near Mukden. At a time when the transfer of new-technology equipment from the Soviet Union to China was slowing down, the Soviet decision to assist the production of combat aircraft in China seems anomalous. In part, the nature of Soviet

policy may have indicated internal rifts and changes in attitudes to China as ally or potential enemy, but it is also probably true that the Soviet Union took care to ensure that MiG-17 production could not be easily continued without Soviet assistance.

In the late 1950s there were reports that Chinese delegations had visited Switzerland and Sweden with a view to

acquiring aircraft technology from the neutral countries. Overtures to Sweden would presumably have concerned one of the Saab range of products, while FFA of Switzerland was at the time working on the P-16 strike fighter. An interesting feature of both the Saab designs and the P-16 was optimisation towards operations from short and basically equipped dispersal strips:

4. An instructor showing an advanced student the finer points of looping his Shenyang F-6. The standard of flying training is high, but the last time the PLA Air Force flew against a skilled enemy was in Korea in the early 1950s. There is no evidence that any members of the PLA Air Force were allowed to fly against the Americans during the Vietnam war and so actual combat experience will be confined to a few of the older pilots. Soviet pilots are, of course, equally lacking in recent combat experience.

also a feature of the British Harrier in which China was to express interest some 15 years later.

The Soviet Union was clearly more ready to supply the Chinese force with defensive systems than with offensive weapons which might be turned against the donor. Among the last items to be supplied to China before the first major breakdown of relations in the late 1950s were a number of MiG-19s, and the Chinese air-defence system was strengthened with the addition of V750VK SA-2 Guideline missiles (known as CSA-1 to Nato when in Chinese production and service) and MiG-21 intercepters. The supply of the latter may have been a gesture of conciliation on the part of the Soviet Union, and took place after the large-scale withdrawal of Soviet technical personnel from China in 1960.

The withdrawal of Soviet technical assistance had a crippling effect on production of combat aircraft, indicating that the Chinese still relied to a considerable extent on major imported components (possibly including turbine engines). The air defence system, on the other hand, remained operational, and there was no collapse of operational capability comparable to that which has followed the withdrawal of Soviet technical assistance in some other countries. With the continuing deterioration of relations with the Soviet Union, China embarked on a programme to achieve autonomy in the supply of such aircraft as it needed, given the low priority assigned to the air arm by Maoist military doctrine.

Production emphasis on interceptors

China's aim was to produce and rely on a nuclear deterrent as her defence against strategic attack. There was thus no great need for a defence system capable of coping with Soviet strategic bombers en masse. However, there was a requirement to prevent incursions into Chinese airspace by less well equipped neighbours or by tactical aircraft of the Soviet forces. In view of the large perimeter which the air force needed to defend, this role was probably best filled by a large force of relatively cheap and unsophisticated aircraft. Production effort, when output restarted in about 1964, was thus concentrated on the MiG-17 (F-4) and MiG-19 (F-6) together with the Klimov VK-1F engine of the MiG-17 and the Tumansky RD-9 of the MiG-19. Also put into production was the Ilyushin Il-28 light bomber, designated B-5 in Chinese service, which used the same engines as the MiG-17. All of these aircraft were based on examples originally supplied to China by the Soviet Union, and were put into production without Soviet assistance. The production of the B-5 and F-6 in particular was a remarkable achievement, akin to the Soviet Union's own copying of the Boeing B-29 at the end of the 1939-45 war. Also placed into production in the early 1960s were helicopters, light transport aircraft and trainers of Soviet design.

In the early 1960s the AFPLA still lacked any long-range bombers, with the exception of the now totally obsolete Tu-4 Bull. Production of the Tu-16 Badger bomber and its Mikulin AM-3 powerplant, however, started in the late 1960s. It is not known where

1. *An unusual line-up of three types of aircraft. The first three are Shenyang F-6s, the Chinese version of the Soviet MiG-19SF, with fully-powered slab elevators, three 30mm NR-30 guns and two RD-9 Klimov turbojets, each of 7,165lb thrust. The next five*

aircraft are Chinese versions of the MiG-19PF, with Izumrud (NATO Codename: Scan Odd) airborne interception radar in the inlet duct splitter and a ranging unit in the upper lip of the air intake. These improvements resulted in an increase in fuselage

length of 22in. (506cm). Finally, there are four Shenyang F-4s (tail of last just in picture), Chinese version of the MiG-17, specifically the -F sub-type (NATO Codename: Fresco C) with the same Izumrud radar and ranging unit as in the MiG-19PF, although

the resulting appearance is somewhat less elegant. From the numbers on the noses of the aircraft it would appear that they all belong to the same unit, which would seem to be a strange mixture in view of the differences in performance between the F-4

1

2

and F-6. The small bump on the tail filet of the -PF version is unusual and may house electronic equipment.

2. Two flights of Shenyang F-6s on patrol. These fine aircraft were considered obsolescent in the early 1960s, but have recently been reappraised, particularly as a result of reports emerging from Pakistan, which bought large numbers some years ago. The workmanship at the Shenyang factory is superb, while the aircraft's manoevrability is reckoned to be outstanding. Also, the hitting power of the three NR-30 30mm guns is devastating, and certainly much more effective than the Western 30mm cannon such as the British Aden and French DEFA.

3. Another fine shot of Shenyang F-6s. At the time of the Sino-Soviet split China had already taken delivery of some MiG-21s and had also started production of the type at Shenyang (some were exported to Albania). It is fascinating to speculate why they should have phased the MiG-21 out of production so quickly.

1. *Despite their lengthy training and skills as pilots these aircrew of the PLA Air Force cannot escape involvement in the "self-sufficiency" programme. Thus, while one of their Shenyang F-4s waits in the background these men tend their field of Choi Sam.*

2. *A woman student pilot climbs into the cockpit of her Yak-18 trainer. She will progress to train to fly piston-engine transports, but her chances of flying anything more modern or exciting are remote. Women receive the same pay as men in the PLA.*

China acquired the "pattern" for the Badger, but it may have been helped by Egypt during a strained period in Egyptian-Soviet relations. By the time Tu-16 production started the AFPLA was generally self-sufficient in technology and support, albeit at a low level compared with its neighbours and main potential adversaries. By the mid-1960s, the air defence system at least had gained a certain degree of competence, as evidenced by the shooting down in 1965 of two high-altitude Firebee reconnaissance drones of the USAF. However, overflights by USAF SR-71s continued with impunity until the US itself suspended them.

After 1965, however, there seemed to be little effort put into keeping the AFPLA comparable in effectiveness with other air forces. Although the manufacture of designs such as the F-6 might have been expected to lead to the development of indigenous designs, the only Chinese-developed combat aircraft was the F-6bis, an adaptation of the F-6. Some production of the MiG-21F appears to have been undertaken, and aircraft of this type, designated F-7, have been supplied to Tanzania and Albania. Together with Pakistan, these countries have been recipients of F-6s, and Albania may also have received B-5s. Because Chinese-built aircraft are ineffective by comparison with Western or Soviet types, however, China was not able to indulge in the same sort of "MiG diplomacy" as the Soviet Union, and

there was thus no political advantage to be gained from the existence of an aviation industry.

The present AFPLA is regarded primarily as an air-defence force by the US Department of Defense, and this is borne out by the limited role which the air arm played in the Sino-Vietnamese fighting in early 1979. On the Soviet pattern, there is also a land-based force under Naval command responsible for coastal defence and anti-shipping strike as well as the more normal naval duties of patrol and reconnaissance. It is smaller than the AFPLA, but is nevertheless quite large by world standards. The two forces, the AFPLA and the Aviation of the People's Navy (APN) exist in parallel.

Organization of the Chinese Air Force

The AFPLA is organised along the Soviet pattern, with squadrons of about 12 aircraft grouped into regiments of three squadrons operating the same aircraft type. Three regiments form a division, which will be assigned to a specific role: air defence, fighter-bomber, light bomber or long-range bomber. The division may operate one or more types. Following the Soviet model, the area of the country is divided into regional commands; there are reported to be 11 of these groupings.

The air-defence divisions operate the CSA-1 missiles—about 100 launchers are believed to be in service—together with most of the 80-100 F-7s (MiG-21s). The CSA-1 missile is the equivalent of the SA-2 Guideline, used extensively in Vietnam and the Middle East and reported to have reasonable effectiveness against medium-altitude targets. Its main operational function, however, has been to force enemy aircraft down to within range of anti-aircraft artillery (AAA); Soviet-supplied radar-guided AAA systems are presumably still in Chinese service, in the absence of any confirmed new surface-to-air missile system, such as a land-based version of that fitted to some Chinese warships. The F-7s are China's only Mach 2 combat aircraft, but carry no search radar (unlike later Soviet developments of the MiG-21) and an armament of a single cannon. It is not known whether China has successfully produced a version of the K-13A Atoll infra-red-homing air-to-air missile, but it is probable that this relatively simple task will have presented no insuperable problems to an industry which has put the more complex CSA-1 into production. In that event the K-13A copy might be expected to arm not only F-7s but air-defence F-6s as well: F-6s supplied to Pakistan are equipped to carry the very similar US Sidewinder missile.

Numerically the most important aircraft in the Chinese inventory is the F-6 (MiG-19) of which at least 1,500 are in service. The type is believed to

3. *A squad of student pilots being given a pre-flight briefing. There are some 170,000 men in the flying units of the PLA Air Force, of which approximately 10,000 are pilots. Most of those selected for pilot training have had some technical training at school.*

4. *This pilot climbing into the cockpit of his Shenyang F-6 is dressed in the standard flying outfit of the PLA Air Force. No G-suits have ever been seen, which must set a limit on the ability to get the most out of their aircraft in high speed turns in dogfights.*

1. *A flight of* Shenyang Sinshi-liyu Chaen-to Chi *(Shenyang Type 6 Fighter Aircraft or F-6) of the PLA-Navy Air Arm on patrol over the South China Sea. Their mission is to defend the coastline of the PRC against attack, and the only realistic threat is posed by the* Pacific Fleet of the Soviet Navy, *although the Republic of China in Taiwan cannot be entirely excluded. Fortunately for the PLA-Navy, the Soviet Pacific Fleet does not have any effective aircraft defences at the moment, although most Soviet ships possess surface-* *to-air missile systems. There are, however, two Kiev-class aircraft-carriers in service with the Soviet Navy, one of which deployed to the Indian Ocean in 1978/79. A third Kiev-class carrier is building in 1979 and there are reports of a very large ship under construction,* *which is most probably a nuclear-powered carrier. Such ships could provide air cover for an amphibious task-force in the Pacific area; while this would not present a threat to China as a whole, it would nevertheless cause serious concern.*

2. *A Shenyang F-6 interceptor, the Chinese version of the Soviet MiG-19PF, is prepared for a night sortie. These aircraft do not have air-to-air missiles and must depend upon their three 30mm NR-30 cannon. The Chinese air defence system depends upon* these aircraft, a relatively small number of CSA-1 surface-to-air missiles (Chinese version of the Soviet SA-2) and a thin and unsophisticated radar and control system. In this age of electronic warfare such a system might, in fact, stand a good chance of surviving, but it seems an excessive risk, especially in the face of aircraft such as Backfire, Fencer, Flogger and Blinder. As in so many other fields, to improve will cost money and there are so many competing demands, in both military and the civil fields, for the money available.

3. *There can be no doubts about the bravery, motivation and morale of these pilots of the PLA-Navy. The last combat experiece of any note was, however, in the Korean War and there will be very few veterans from that war still serving with the squadrons.*

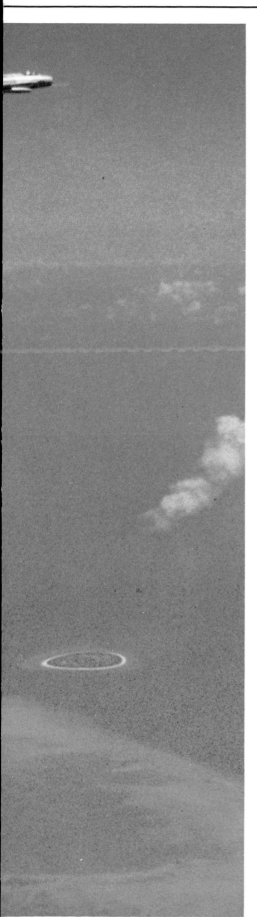

2

3

1. Scramble! A traditional air force scene as pilots rush to their fighters, the faithful ground crew waiting to help them into their ejector-seats. Such a line-up of fighters on an open apron should however be a thing of the past, as this begs for a pre-emptive strike

such as that practised by the Israeli Air Force on the Egyptians. Modern tactics demand that aircraft should at least be dispersed, and preferably be sheltered in hardened hangars as well. The aircraft are Shenyang F-6s, Chinese-built versions of the

Soviet MiG-19 (NATO codename: Farmer). This photo shows two of the three NR-30 30mm cannon on the aircraft in the foreground (the third is on the port side of the nosewheel well). The Pakistani Air Force has reported that the Chinese version is far better made

than the Soviet MiG-19.
2. A superb shot of the previously highly classified Shenyang F-6bis, a very much modified version of the Mig-19, designed and built in China. These two aircraft are taking part in an air show in October 1978, probably celebrat-

1

remain in large-scale production. Although unquestionably a veteran, having seen more than a quarter-century in operational service, the type has its merits. Its thrust/weight ratio is high compared to its Western contemporaries, and its small size contributes to its agility. It packs a heavy cannon armament, and its climb rate is excellent. Lack of warload capability is probably its worst weakness, and compared with Western aircraft now being supplied on a large scale (such as the Northrop F-5E) it is at a serious disadvantage due to its lack of an efficient search radar. Some of the Chinese F-6s are based on the limited all-weather MiG-19P, and these versions are presumably flown by intercepter squadrons. However, the performance of the 1950s-technology Izumrud radar installed in the intake lip and bullet of the F-6 probably permits only limited bad-weather interception.

A remarkable lacuna in Chinese defence capability appears to be the failure of Chinese technology to produce any form of geniuine air-to-air attack radar capable of all-weather interception, despite the fact that such radars have been standard equipment on Western fighters for a quarter of a

century. An indication that a need for such a system was perceived in the late 1960s was the appearance of the F-6bis fighter, codenamed Fantan A by Nato. This is a modification of the F-6 with a new forward fuselage, side intakes replacing the nose inlet of the F-6. Similar modifications have been applied to Western aircraft, experimentally or in production form, usually with the aim of installing a radar or some other operational equipment in the extended nose. It was therefore generally assumed that the F-6bis was designed as an all-weather derivative of the F-6, with a new Chinese-developed radar in the nose. However, none of the F-6bis seen in photographs released by the Chinese has been fitted with radar or any other form of equipment not found on the basic F-6. It has been widely reported that the new aircraft has been abandoned as a failure; this is not hard to believe, in view of the fact that the extra weight of the longer frontal fuselage probably penalised performance heavily by comparison with the basic F-6. The side intakes are of fixed configuration, and from their design it seems unlikely that the F-6bis can attain anything near the Mach 2 per-

formance mooted when it was first reported in the West; maximum speed is closer to the Mach 1.4 of the F-6. The F-6bis remains an enigma, developed to accommodate a radar which never appeared in production. About 50 of the type are reported to be in service.

After the F-6, the second most important aircraft in Chinese service is the even more venerable MiG-17 (F-4), of which 1,500 to 2,000 are reported to be in service with fighter bomber divisions. Together with F-6s and older F-2s (MiG-15s) the F-4 forms the backbone of the small coastal defence fighter force of the APN, which numbers about 500 single-seat combat aircraft in all. The basic design of the F-2 and the F-4 is almost as old as that of the Tu-4, the original MiG-15 having been strongly influenced by the wartime Focke-Wulf Ta183 project. With its heavy cannon armament, the F-4 is probably effective for ground attack in the hands of a skilled pilot, and combat experience in Vietnam showed that the type was a difficult target for some of the older and heavier US fighter such as the F-4 Phantom and F-105. Later Western combat aircraft such as the F-5E Tiger and F-16,

ing the 29th anniversary of the People's Republic of China. Of particular interest are the very large underwing pylons and the internal weapons bay, which is unique on modern jet fighter aircraft. Although based on the MiG-19 this aircraft is, in fact, such a redesign as to be virtually a new aircraft and appears to bear less relationship to its reported progenitor than does the Israeli Kfir to the Dassault Mirage, for example. The small missiles have been dropped from the weapons bay and are probably smoke bombs. It is possible that the Rolls-Royce Spey is being installed in the F-6bis.

3. A flight of Shenyang F-6 fighters on an interception mission. Like the F-6bis these are daylight-only, fair-weather fighters, and there is no doubt that the PLA Air Force urgently needs an all-weather fighter. The danger from Backfire, Fencer, and other Soviet interdictors is acute—as it is for Western Europe and NATO—and their chances of getting through would appear to be fairly good at the moment.

2

however, have been designed with the Vietnam experience in mind, and would probably have few problems in dealing with the Chinese F-4/MiG-17. A specifically Chinese development of the MiG-17 is a two-seat trainer version possibly designated F-5, with a canopy similar to that of the two-seat MiG-15UTI. Also in service—probably in decreasing numbers—is the MiG-15 or F-2. A few hundred of these aircraft are reported to remain in service with the AFPLA and APN.

None of the fighter types in service with the Chinese forces is capable of carrying a heavy weapons load. All of them are limited to two external hardpoints with the possible exception of the F-6, which may carry outer wing pylons for K-13A copies. (The F-6bis may also have an internal weapons bay (see fold-out and photo on page 122.) The main strike force available to the AFPLA consists of about 150 B-5s (Ilyushin Il-28) light bombers, a design dating from the early 1950s. Some Il-28s were supplied to China by the Soviet Union before the breakdown of relations in 1960, but the type is reported by US sources to have gone into production in China, possibly to make good attrition **3** in the force. The B-5 can carry a 6,000lb

China's only known surface-to-air missile is the CSA-1 shown here, which is a direct copy of the Soviet SA-2 (NATO Codename: Guideline) which was supplied to the PRC before the great split in 1960. In the background are Side Net and Fan Song radars. This weapons system is thinly deployed and the few hundred launchers are capable of the point defence of only a few key areas. A SAM system such as this is essential to force high-flying enemy aircraft down to low altitudes where the very widely deployed anti-aircraft guns can deal with them. This was the basis of the Vietnamese success, but a large number of SAMs are needed, and they do not seem to be available to the Chinese. This situation is typical of the unevenness of weapons development in China. On the one hand are the very successful ballistic missiles which have proved themselves repeatedly in satellite launches, and the nuclear weapons which have been developed in a single-minded concentration of effort and resources — and on the other are antiquated

and ineffective systems like CSA-1. The problem is, of course, one of priorities, and the PLA obviously does not have the money or resources available to develop all the systems it needs to meet all possible threats. The only answer is to take calculated risks, hoping that concentrating in some technological fields may make up for deficiencies in others. It is only in countries like the USSR that so much money and resources can be devoted to military budgets without the civil populace becoming restive.

1. *China is a land of extraordinary contrasts and this sturdy old tricycle appears, at first, to be just such an oddity standing beside a swept-wing jet fighter. Yet those who watch a Western airfield cannot fail to notice how everyone and everything moves on vehicles, even for the shortest journeys. Is it, therefore, such an anomaly that an armourer should move by muscle-power rather than waste petrol, a commodity which is bound to become increasingly scarce? Others may soon have to follow this example.*

bomb load and has at least some all-weather capability, but is certainly not capable of precision strikes except in clear weather. Its size and configuration rule out low-level manoeuvring, and its use against almost any type of modern defensive weapon system such as low-level surface-to-air missiles or radar-directed mobile AAA would be virtually suicidal. However, the Il-28 remains in production pending development of a new type with comparable strike capability. Also still in production is the Tu-16.

Training in China still appears to follow the pattern set by the Soviet Union for its own forces and those of its "satellites" in the 1950s, all training types being Shenyang-built versions of Soviet designs. Basic training is carried out on BT-6s (Yakovlev Yak-18) and recruits graduate to the faster Yak-11 (Chinese designation unknown) before proceeding to conversion trainers. Some Ilyushin Il-28Us are operated. The main transport type is the Antonov An-2 biplane, still in production for civil and military purposes; however, this single-engined 14-seater type can hardly be said to offer any strategic airlift capability. About 50 of the large Il-14s are reported to be in service, but again the military usefulness of the type is limited. Helicopters are used to some degree to augment the tactical airlift force. The Mil Mi-4 is probably in production as the H-5, but is outclassed in payload-range terms by later, turbine-powered helicopters. Thirteen Aerospatiale Super Frelon medium-lift helicopters have been supplied to China by France, but these form too small a force to be of any great military importance. Chinese use of airborne troops is thus likely to be limited, because the air force cannot supply any equipment heavier than light infantry weapons by air.

The only other type to serve in large numbers with the Chinese air arm is the Beriev Be-6 flying boat, operated by the APN. The examples of the type in service appear to have been supplied directly by the Soviet Union rather than being built in China; they are equipped with search radar in a retractable ventral "dustbin" radome and may carry magnetic anomaly detection (MAD) equipment. However, the effectiveness of so dated an aircraft against modern deep-running nuclear submarines is probably small.

On the whole, therefore, it appears that the equipment of the Chinese air arm is so outmoded in concept that sheer weight of numbers can no longer offset the technology gap. This problem is exacerbated by the vast periphery of the country, and the number of potentially hostile neighbours on its borders. This necessitates the dispersal of Chinese forces all along the periphery, because the short range of most of the serving types limits the area that can be defended from one base. The lack of any strategic airlift capability also suggests that it would be difficult if not impossible to transfer military units from one section of the frontier to another in time to deal with an emergency. Thus the air forces available to China on any one section of its periphery are probably limited to those stationed there.

As discussed above in the paragraphs dealing with the various types in service, the Chinese air force is likely to prove almost completely ineffective against any concerted air defence, whether Western- or Soviet-equipped. The balance has shifted markedly against the Chinese in the 1970s, with the supply of aircraft such as third-generation MiG-21s and Northrop Tigers to smaller air forces in the region, together with the increasing availability of short-range surface-to-air missile systems. On the other hand, China's sheer size and the absence of any large forces of strike aircraft in the Southeast Asian region make it relatively invulnerable to attack from that direction. The last point, however, does not apply to the Soviet Union. Although the bulk of Soviet Frontal Aviation (FA) tactical strike aircraft are based facing Nato forces in the west, the Soviet Union's rapid and growing transport fleet and the long range of the latest combat aircraft gives the Soviet Union a capability for long-range air reinforcement that China lacks. It is unlikely that China's air force could successfully protect the PLA from attack and interdiction by Soviet types such as the MiG-27 or Su-19.

The Chinese government seems well aware of the deficiencies of its air force, and is moving to correct them by direct imports of combat aircraft and by production of new, more advanced

2. A Shenyang F-4 (Chinese copy of the Soviet MiG-17) coming in on "finals" to land at a PLA Air Force base. The landing aids are rudimentary by Western standards and although probably sufficient would be ineffective in other conditions.

3. This commander would be able to exercise control over his aircraft in good visibility, but his airfield appears to be totally lacking in radar and advanced communications systems. This reinforces doubts about the PLA's "all-weather" defence system.

indigenous designs. In the former category, China is negotiating as these words are written for a large quantity of British Aerospace Harrier vertical/short-take-off-and-landing close-support fighters. Numbers of aircraft between 130 and 300 have been mentioned; it is likely that the lower figure represents an initial buy direct from the manufacturer, while the larger figure indicates a requirement for assembly or production of the aircraft in China.

China's long-standing interest in the V/Stol Harrier indicates that the AFPLA is convinced of the usefulness of such aircraft in the close-support role. The aircraft would presumably be deployed as a mobile force, capable of operating autonomously from semi-prepared strips near the battle area.

For this purpose it would be necessary to supply the force with some form of logistic support. Reported Chinese interest in the Lockheed C-130 Hercules —at present covered by a US embargo on the sale of military equipment to China—suggests that this aspect of Harrier operations is appreciated. The Harrier would give the AFPLA the capability to support PLA ground operations without exposing itself too dangerously to the counter-air strike potential of the Soviet Union.

Another aircraft type on which approaches have been made is the Lockheed P-3C Orion anti-submarine-warfare (ASW) aircraft. Like the C-130, this type is covered by the US ban, and is probably less likely to be released for export to China. However, a modern

ASW system is necessary if China is to be able to place some restraints on the operation of Soviet missile-launching submarines near its shores.

Chinese need to "Westernise" Air Force

Negotiations are also under way covering other weapon systems such as helicopter-launched anti-tank missiles (the Euromissile Hot is probably the leading candidate) and surface-to-air missile systems. Europe is probably the most likely supplier of such weapons to the Chinese, in view of the US restrictions on arms exports. The import of so many new systems will

These pictures epitomise the extraordinary position of the PLA-Air Force, whose capabilities range from nuclear bombs to "iron" bombs of very old design, and from sophisticated missiles to ancient biplanes and piston-engined transports based on the DC-3 (Dakota).

1. In an armed force where officers are accorded only the most minimal privileges the pilot is expected to help the ground-crew load his aircraft. This high-explosive bomb is of Soviet World War II design, but is manufactured in China in very considerable numbers.

2. In contrast is this atomic bomb explosion, with the characteristic mushroom cloud rising into the sky. From the size of the cloud this is one of the early 20 Kiloton (KT) weapons, which have now been replaced by the more powerful hydrogen bombs.

3. Development of the delivery means has not kept pace with that of the weapons; the PLA-Air Force's most modern bomber is a locally-manufactured copy of this Soviet Tupolev Tu-16 (NATO

Codename: Badger). Its chances of penetrating Soviet air defences are low.

4. Although it appears antiquated, the Antonov An-2 (NATO Codename: Colt) was designed after World War II. It is manufactured in China at Fong Chou and over 5,000 have been produced for use in paratroop and aircrew training, supply of remote places and general transport duties.

5. Even older than the An-2 is the Litvinov Li-2 (NATO Codename: Cab), which is based on the Douglas DC-3 and which was produced in the USSR before China began making copies. Ideally suited for use in under-developed areas it is likely to remain in service for many years.

6. The Chinese produced many hundreds of these bombers, which are straight copies of the Soviet Ilyushin IL-28 (NATO Codename: Beagle). The aircrews shown here are being trained in anti-tank tactics, with a Soviet T-62 as their potential target. These large, slow-flying aircraft would, however, be easy targets for the Soviet forward air defence systems.

1. In the early 1960s the only bomber possessed by the PLA Air Force was the Tupolev Tu-4 (NATO Codename: Bull), the Soviet-built copy of the American Boeing B-29. Then in the late 1960s the Chinese acquired the pattern for the Tupolev Tu-16 (NATO Codename: Badger) and it is estimated that some 60 have been built. The mainstay of the bomber force, however, is still this elderly aircraft, the Ilyushin Il-28, some 300 of which are in service with both the PLA Air Force and the air arm of the PLA Navy.

1

require a vast amount of training to be carried out by suppliers, and will inevitably lead to a period of partial Chinese dependence on the West before the Chinese could take over the operation of the force unaided. In order to make economic sense of acquiring such sophisticated systems, the Chinese will have to "Westernise" their air force. The operational philosophy will have to be altered to make more extensive use of a smaller number of more expensive aircraft and fewer, more extensively trained crews. Even if approval for all the imports which the Chinese are seeking were granted today, it would be at least the mid-1980s before the operational effectiveness of the air force would begin to improve as a result and the first Western-supplied systems became operational.

One large unknown quantity is the Chinese manufacturing industry. It is known that China is working on the design of an indigenous supersonic aircraft; when such a type will enter service, and how effective it will be, is very hard to tell. In late 1975 China signed an agreement with Rolls-Royce, with the British Government's approval, under which China acquired rights to manufacture the RB.168-25R Spey Mk 202 turbofan. A number of specimen engines have been delivered, and Chinese engineers have been trained in Britain. Rolls-Royce maintains technical supervision of the project. No firm details of the intended application of the Spey have emerged, but the variant being produced by China was designed for the specially modified Phantoms acquired by the Royal Air Force and Navy, and is thus suited to a Mach 2 combat aircraft.

Chinese designers at the Shenyang works have presumably had plenty of opportunity to examine the remains of US combat aircraft such as the Phantom and F-105 destroyed or forced down in Vietnam, and may also have examined captured US equipment after the final collapse of the South Vietnamese regime and before the breakdown of China's relationship with Hanoi. It is also reported that a MiG-23 Flogger was supplied to China by Egypt in return for overhaul work carried out on the engines of Egypt's MiG-21s; the Soviet fighter, powered by a Tumansky R-27 reheated turbofan very similar in size to the Spey, could be of crucial importance in providing the Chinese with the intake technology needed to extract maximum performance from the British engine. It is even possible that China's new fighter could be closely based on the MiG-23. Reports have applied the designations F-10 and F-12 to new Chinese developments, supporting suggestions that alternative delta-wing and swept-wing

2. *A class of student pilots stand in front of their Ilyushin Il-28U trainers. The Il-28 has now been in service for some thirty years and there is no sign of a replacement in Chinese service. With two centrifugal-flow Klimov VK-1 turbojets (copies of the Rolls-Royce Nene) they have a maximum speed of 559 mph and a service ceiling of 40,355ft. Maximum bomb-load is about 4,000lb and maximum range is 684 miles. A naval version capable of carrying torpedoes is also in service.*

3. *A pilot climbs into the cockpit of his IL-28, while a flight of the same type passes overhead. These would be useful should China become embroiled in a war with an unsophisticated enemy in South-east Asia, but their value against the USSR is questionable.*

4. *More IL-28s, this time preparing for a night operation. One of the unusual features of this design is the mixture of straight wings, with a highly swept tail unit. Also shown is the tail-gunners' position with its twin 23mm NR-23 cannon in a powered turret.*

designs are being evaluated. It is likely that the new type will be designed for the air-defence role, and clearly some radar and missile capability well in advance of anything previously produced in China will have to be incorporated if the new type is to be effective. Even with the aid of Western technology in these areas, it is hard to see a Chinese-designed supersonic fighter entering service before 1984-85.

In the near term, therefore, the restoration of Chinese air power to the comparative status it enjoyed in the 1950s must depend on the willingness of the West to supply material and know-how—both through training and licence agreements—and the ability of China to finance such massive imports and absorb such a quantum jump in technology.

147

CHINA'S NAVY: FOR COASTAL DEFENCE ONLY

Hugh Lyon

A fine picture of a squadron of Kiang Nan class frigates in line ahead being overtaken by Huch'uan class fast attack hydrofoils. Kiang Nan frigates were designed in China in the early 1960s and at least five were produced. Of 1600 tons full load displacement, they are armed with three 100mm guns in single turrets, six 37mm in twin mountings and four 12.7mm machine-guns. Anti-submarine equipment includes two MBU 1800, four depth-charge throwers and two depth-charge racks. They may also have a mine-laying capability. These are the first purely Chinese warships to emerge after the abrupt cessation of arms and equipment from the Soviet Union in 1960. The Huch'uan fast patrol hydrofoils were also designed and built in China.

China's Navy is a huge force in terms of numbers of vessels, but it is currently a coastal defence force, with few "blue-water" vessels and little offensive capability. It has a vital role in facing the increasing threat from the powerful Soviet Pacific Fleet now enjoying new operating bases in Southeast Asia.

1. Deeply rooted in the memories of the older generation are the once-dreaded "warlords" who held sway from the collapse of the Sun Yat-sen government to the success of Chiang Kai-shek in the mid-1920s. One such was Tu Hsi-kuei, a warlord in the coastal province of Fukien. Despite his splendid admiral's uniform his fleet is unlikely to have consisted of more than a few coastal vessels. Communist austerity appeared attractive after the depravities of the warlords and corruption of the Kuo Mintang.

The Chinese Navy is administered as an integral part of the People's Liberation Army (PLA), though for most practical purposes it operates as a semi-autonomous unit. Like the rest of the PLA it is generally efficient and well trained, but most of its equipment is unsophisticated and outdated. Numerically China is a major naval power, but she has little more than a coastal-defence navy. The bulk of the fleet comprises light missile and patrol boats, and there are few major surface vessels. The submarine force is the third largest in the world, but it is almost entirely composed of relatively small conventionally powered submarines, with less offensive power than their numbers would suggest. Similarly, the large Chinese Naval Air Force has few long range aircraft, and is mostly equipped with unsophisticated short range machines.

Development of modern Chinese Navy

China has a long naval tradition, going back about 2,000 years, but it was by no means continuous, with periods of expansion being followed by much longer periods of almost total neglect. The peak of China's naval power occurred in the early fifteenth century, when for the first and only time in China's history a series of large fleets made a number of voyages overseas. These were commanded by Admiral Cheng Ho, but they ceased abruptly in 1433, and were followed by four **1** centuries of neglect. This culminated in crushing defeats in the two Opium Wars in the 1840s and 1850s, which resulted in an attempt in the 1860s to set up a modern navy. (There were in fact three wars waged against China between 1842 and 1860). However, the French crushed the southern fleet in 1884 and the Japanese the northern fleet ten years later. A small coastal-defence fleet was built up in the first decade of this century, but this was sunk or taken over by the Japanese and by 1937 it had virtually ceased to exist.

After World War II the Americans and British rebuilt it from scratch round the ex-British 5,270 ton Cruiser Chung-King (formerly Aurora) and a number of ex-Japanese, British and

American World War II destroyers and escorts. At its peak the Nationalist fleet had a strength of over 40,000 men but by the time the Nationalists were finally overthrown in 1949 most of these ships and men had defected to the Communists. Although these ships were generally in poor condition, they formed the basis of the PLA fleet for the next five years, and some still remain in service as training ships.

Between 1950-1959 the Russians rebuilt and restructured the Chinese Navy. The first necessity was to train the crews and to build up the strength of the Chinese fleet. Over 2,500 Russian naval advisers were sent to

China, and in the mid-1950s four destroyers, thirteen submarines, twelve large patrol boats, two minesweepers and about fifty torpedo boats were transferred to the Chinese Navy. Most of these were built early in World War II, but, after rebuilding, the Gordi class destroyers are still in service today. In 1955 the Soviet rank system was adopted, though this was later abandoned after the expulsion of the Soviet advisers after 1960.

In 1949, the Chinese shipbuilding and ship repair industry was virtually defunct, and this was also rebuilt with Soviet help. Russian technicians were provided and Chinese shipbuilders

2. Chu Teh, one of the former principal Chinese military leaders, visiting a range-finder post at a coastal defence gun-site. The presence of the sailors at a land-based site is interesting, but is due to the fact that the PLA-Navy is responsible for coastal defences near its naval bases. The sailors are being assisted by members of the local People's Militia. While the army and air force have a common uniform for officers and fighters, the navy persists with the traditional international sailor's uniform, and even a special dress for officers.

3. A Whisky class submarine on patrol. These submarines were assembled in Chinese shipyards between 1956 and 1964 from kits of components supplied by the Soviet Union. The design shows German influence, although the value of the gun forward of the fin is doubtful, especially as it will generate very considerable noise when the boat is submerged. This class has six 21-inch torpedo tubes and a surface range of 13,000 miles at 8 knots. The W-class have played a vital role in training the submarine crews.

2

3

1. *A striking contrast as a flotilla of fast attack craft speed past a colony of Masked Boobies (Sula Dactylatra).*

2. *Hainan class fast attack craft on patrol. The crew are manning the MBU 1800 anti-submarine weapons, which are, in fact,* obsolescent. The PLA-Navy is well behind the other major navies in the development of anti-submarine detection devices and of the weapons needed to deal with a submarine once it has been found. This is a high technology area, which the Chinese may wish to avoid for financial reasons, but they are faced by a very considerable submarine force in the Soviet Pacific Fleet. The Soviets could deploy some 30 nuclear and 50 to 60 conventional submarines in Chinese waters and the chances of the PLA-Navy finding and dealing with them must be rated as very slim indeed.

3. *China possesses some 70 to 80 submarines. The first to enter service in any numbers were the Romeo class, one of which is shown here. The Soviets supplied a few in the early 1960s, after*

which the Chinese began to construct their own, modified slightly. These are being built at a rate of some six per year, with over fifty now in service. The boat shown here is actually in service with the Soviet Navy; the Chinese version is said to be slightly longer, with a greater displacement and two extra torpedo tubes. **4.** Another view of Romeo class submarines, this time of the Chinese version. The hull contours are very smooth, but the rails on top of the fin and the hatches in the foreground will give rise to considerable underwater noise, thus making them easy to detect by hostile anti-submarine forces. China also has one Soviet Golf class ballistic missile submarine and is also reported to have designed and built a nuclear boat of the so-called Han class. This was built in 1971-73 and went on trials in 1974. It is entirely within China's capabilities to design and build a nuclear submarine and at least one is already in service, possibly armed with solid-propellant nuclear missiles.

1. *The primary mission of the PLA Navy is the defence of the homeland against both a major seaborne invasion and against infiltration by small parties of spies or saboteurs. A key element in this surveillance task are some 66 patrol submarines.*

2. *A second element in this patrolling task is the relatively large force of fast attack craft, of which there are over 600 of various types. Fastest in the fleet are these* Huch'uan *class fast attack hydrofoils; 200 are in service and a further 10 are added every year.* **2**

1

programme. The Soviet Union no longer provided technical assistance, equipment or new designs, and there was no other country that China could turn to at that time to make up for this loss. It was particularly felt in the design and construction of sophisticated surface warships and submarines, and it resulted in the continued production of modified versions of existing, outdated ship types while the new designs were developed and put into service. In the circumstances the development of the *Luta* class guided missile destroyer and the *Han* nuclear attack submarine was a highly creditable achievement.

The situation was not made any easier by the political manoevrings that took place during the last years of Chairman Mao. The cultural revolution caused considerable dislocation, but even worse was the general cutback in the resources allocated to the PLA following the flight and death of Lin Piao. This hit hardest in 1972, but it continued until at least 1975. However, the Navy was more active operationally, capturing the Paracel islands from the South Vietnamese in a successful amphibious operation on January 19-20, 1974; in fact, the incident was perhaps seized upon by the Chinese Navy to prove its value to the State.

and designers were also trained in the Soviet Union. At first, warships were built from parts supplied by the Soviet Union, but the rebuilding of the shipbuilding industry proceeded very rapidly and the Chinese were soon able to build entire patrol craft and even submarines and frigates by themselves, though they still used Russian designs, weapons and electronics.

The Chinese navy was powerless to intervene to any serious extent in the Korean War, and the presence of the US Seventh Fleet and the strength of the Taiwan Navy effectively cut the Chinese Navy off from the South China Sea throughout the 1950s. Although the island of I-Chuanay was captured in 1958, the overwhelming American military presence effectively prevented China from taking Quemoy and Matsu in the same year. It was not until America disengaged from Southeast Asia and withdrew the US Seventh Fleet to the central Pacific in the early 1970s that China could conduct more than very limited naval operations in its own waters.

The widening rift between China and the Soviet Union in the early 1960s had caused severe dislocation to the Chinese Navy's fledgling re-equipment

3. More Huch'uan *on patrol. The PLA Navy never issues detailed statistics on the composition of the fleet and foreign voyages are never undertaken, so the precise strength of the force cannot be established. It is certain, that it is not a blue-water fleet.*

4. *P-6 type fast attack craft at speed. Wooden hulled craft, they were built prior to 1966 to a Soviet design. Armament is two 21 inch torpedo tubes and four 12.7mm machine-guns in two twin mountings. Some 70 are in service with the PLA-Navy.*

3

4

Navy's main role: defence of homeland

In keeping with the philosophy underlying the entire PLA, the primary role of the Chinese Navy is the defence of the homeland. From its inception the Navy has had to guard against the possibility of a major seaborne invasion, or of a large navy blockading its coasts. In addition, the long coastline with its many small islands has had to be patrolled continuously to prevent infiltration by small parties of spies or saboteurs. There has also been the need to escort merchant ships trading with foreign countries or along the Chinese coast in waters near Taiwan.

The Chinese have always denied that they have any desire to attempt to conquer Taiwan by force, and the absence of a large scale amphibious capability indicates that the Navy is not required to mount major invasions at present. However, they do possess the ability to land small numbers of troops in areas close to the Chinese mainland, and this has been done on several occasions, the last being the occupation of the Paracel Islands. In general the Chinese Navy is not offensively orientated. They lack experience in overseas deployment and they do not possess a fleet train, nor have they any recent history or experience of large-scale amphibious or combined operations.

The Navy's political role is likewise circumscribed. Chinese warships are not normally used to "show the flag". In addition to other types of aid, small numbers of unsophisticated patrol craft have been supplied to several third world countries and to Rumania, and naval advisers have also been provided, but the only country to have been given major warships is North Korea, which has received *Romeo* class submarines. The North Korean ship-building industry has also been given assistance to enable them to build their

155

CHINA'S NAVY: FOR COASTAL DEFENCE ONLY

1. *The crew of a twin 37mm mounting at action stations on board a Hai Kou class fast attack craft. In the foreground is a twin 25mm mounting.*

2. *Another in the series of political meetings which seem to be an inescapable part of Chinese life.*

3. *Sailors in their summer work uniform of striped shirt and blue trousers. Ashore they wear a blue version of the standard PLA uniform.*

4. *Shanghai class fast attack craft on patrol. These 155 ton vessels are constructed at a rate of about*

ten a year; some 340 are in service with the PLA Navy and many have been exported. They are armed with four 37mm twin guns in two mountings, and four 25 mm guns in two vertical mounts. Minerails can be fitted and some craft have been seen

with a recoilless rifle mounted on the foredeck. Eight depth-charges are also carried. These useful and numerous craft are capable of a top speed of 30 knots and are powered by diesel engines.

5. *A dashing spectacle as three P-6 class fast torpedo boats race*

along the coast. It is believed that 80 were built in the PRC and that some 70 remain in service. Armament consists of two twin 25mm guns fore and aft and two single 21in. torpedo tubes amidships. About 50 of the Swatow class motor gunboats, which were developed from the P-6, were also built in China from 1958. The Swatow class is armed with two twin-37mm fore and aft and two 12.7mm guns. Both classes are now being taken out of service. most of the earlier, smaller 18in. torpedo-armed P-4 class boats have already been discarded.

6. As with the soldiers and the airmen, so, too, do the sailors have to strive to achieve as a great a degree of self-sufficiency as possible. The succulent catch is "agar-agar", rich in calcium.

5

6

1. *A flotilla of Hainan class fast attack craft on patrol off the coast of China. Of 400 tons full load displacement these vessels were designed in China and are still being constructed at a rate of about four per year. This picture again shows the MBU-1800.*

2. *A sailor of the PLA-Navy stands guard on a radar station on one of the Hsisha islands in the South China Sea. The elaborate radar array belongs to a coastal defence set and is probably the equipment known by the Western codename of Cross Slot. This set operates in* the E/F bands (ie, 2-4 Gigaherz) and has an estimated range of 80km. Chinese radars observed to date tend to be either copies of Soviet equipment or relatively unsophisticated sets designed in China since the Sino-Soviet split. A country which can launch ICBMs and put satellites into orbit must, however, be fully capable of producing good radar and radio equipment, and China's electronic capability must not, therefore, be underestimated. Replacement of old equipment is a matter of priorities rather than capability.

own *Romeo* submarines, but this foreign aid in no way compares to the much larger involvement of the major powers in building up the navies of the third world.

Composition of the fleet

The main strength of the Chinese fleet lies in its submarines and small craft. In major surface vessels it is outclassed by most of the surrounding navies (see Table I). Only the Philippines, North Korea and Vietnam are significantly weaker. The Chinese have 10+ guided missile destroyers of the *Luta* and *Gordi* classes and 12+ reasonably modern frigates, half of which are also armed with surface-to-surface missiles (SSMs). A few old World War II escorts are still in service, but they appear to be employed mostly for training.

The old wartime Russian submarines have been discarded, and most of the 70 current patrol submarines are either Russian *Whiskey* or *Romeo* class medium range conventionally powered boats or Chinese developments of them. Only two of the considerably larger *Ming* class have so far been added to the fleet. The single *Han* class nuclear attack submarine is almost certainly primarily an experimental vessel, as is the *Golf* class SSB.

The most important light craft are the 100+ *Osa I*, *Komar* and *Hoku* class missile armed fast patrol boats, backed by the 200+ torpedo armed *Huch'uan*, P-6 and P-4 class boats. There are also some 35 large and over 430 small gun-armed patrol vessels. Exact numbers of any type of Chinese warship are impossible to acertain as they are not deployed overseas and no official figures are issued.

Most of the 50 or so landing ships of various kinds are used for commercial or auxiliary work, though most could still be used as landing ships in an emergency. Many of the 450+ landing craft are also used for other purposes than those for which they were designed. A large number of auxiliary vessels are used for minesweeping, but there are also 20+ Russian and Chinese built T-43 class ocean minesweepers.

The Chinese Navy operates about 10 survey ships of various kinds, but apart from a submarine depot ship, a few salvage tugs and about 20 coastal tankers there are virtually no major support vessels. There are, however, a number of habour support craft, and the Military Militia operate about 200 armed junks and motor launches.

These ships are divided between three fleets. Most of the major surface vessels and two squadrons of sub-

TABLE 1: THE PEOPLE'S LIBERATION ARMY-NAVY AND THE OTHER ASIAN NAVIES

	China	USSR Pacific Fleet[2]	Japan	Philipp-innes	North Korea	South Korea	Taiwan	Vietnam[4]
Submarines	75[1]	92[3]	14	0	15	0	2	0
Cruisers	0	8	0	0	0	0	0	0
Destroyers	11	28	31	0	0	7	22	0
Frigate	12	21	15	8	3	9	11	2
Corvettes/ Escorts	53	19	12	11	21	10	3	5
Missile-armed Patrol Boats	140+	35	0	0	18	8	2	2
Major Landing Ships	15	22	6	27	0	22	25	3

Notes: [1]Includes at least one nuclear. [2]Numbers in the Pacific fleet tend to fluctuate slightly. [3]Includes some 30 SSBNs. [4]Includes some ex-US ships captured from the South Vietnamese navy whose servicability is not known.

The strengths of the principal navies in Asia. The PLA Navy is a well-balanced force, although there is currently a slight weakness in heavier surface units. Much improvement is, however, required in the armament, especially in the fitting of missiles, and in the development of better radar and electronics. Also, the fleet is very much a coastal force and operations at any distance from the mainland could not currently be undertaken, particularly because there is no fleet train capable of sustaining any squadron at sea for any length of time. The major Asian-based naval force is the Soviet Pacific Fleet, which is numerically strong, well-equipped, well-armed, and also possesses an adequate fleet train. The Soviet SSBNs (nuclear-propelled boats with ballistic missile armament) pose a particularly serious threat to China and one which the PLA-Navy can at the moment do little to counter. Of the other powers in the area only the Japanese have a modern and effective navy. The other major naval force in the area is the United States 7th Fleet, with two carriers, 20 surface ships and some SSBNs.

3. The traditional heroes' return for a fast attack craft of the Shanghai class. The soldiers on the jetty are probably from a Regional Force unit and they are letting off the Chinese firecrackers which have been an integral part of celebrations and festivals for many centuries. The old belief was that the noise was necessary to alert the gods to the prayers and thanks that were being offered, but doubtless the Party has found a more prosaic explanation. Despite the welcome the crew are at battle stations, and fully alert.

4. The frigate Kuei Yang of the PLA-Navy. This is one of four ships of the Ch'eng Tu class, which are Soviet Riga class frigates built in China in 1956-57 from components supplied by the Soviet Union. With a 1600ton full-load displacement these ships have three 3.9in (100mm) guns in single mountings and four 37mm. All four were modified during refit in the early 1970s and had a twin SS-N-2 missile launcher installed in place of torpedo tubes. 50 mines can also be carried and are launched from stern rails.

marines are in the North Sea Fleet. This has its main base at Tsingtao and operates in the Yellow Sea, and comprises about 300 warships of all types. The East Sea fleet, with its headquarters at Shanghai, has about 600 warships, including one squadron of submarines; and the South Sea fleet, with its headquarters at Chan Chiang, has about 300 warships, most of which are light craft.

Major deficiencies in capabilities

The Chinese Navy is well trained and efficient, and it appears to be well led, but its ability to fulfil its primary role of defending the Chinese homeland is seriously impaired by major deficiencies in its equipment. In general its ships are well built and reliable, but even the ships that are at present under construction are being built to outdated designs, and their weapons and sensors are extremely unsophisticated by Western standards.

The major surface weapon is the SSM that equips the missile armed light craft and the frigates and destroyers. This is based on the Russian SSN-2 Styx, and although it retains its capability against unsophisticated vessels it has been outclassed by modern electronic counter-measures (ECM) and anti-SSM defences. However, the sheer numbers carried afloat by the Chinese Navy and in service

3

4

1. Gunners the world over have an insatiable instinct to polish their weapons and these smiling men of the PLA Navy are no exception. The carefully tended weapon is a 100mm (3.9in) gun mounted on a Ch'eng Tu class frigate. These are Soviet-designed Riga class ships, of which the Chinese assembled four in the mid-1950s. All were modified in the early 1970s to mount two SS-N-2 (Styx) launchers in place of the torpedo tubes. Note the simple radar arrays and the working-dress of the sailors.

2. The crew of a patrol craft receive political instruction from a visiting team. There are two elements in the Party control of the armed forces: political control of the command structure, and political education of all ranks. The first is achieved by having Political Commissars and Political Officers at all levels from the Ministry of National Defence down to battalion or ship level. These men share the command function with the military commander, a system which has obvious hazards. The commissar is responsible for

"political" matters such as security, personnel matters, discipline, ideological training and relations with the civil population. The predominance of commander or commissar tends to vary, depending to a certain extent on personalities, and also on the latest directions from Peking. The daily political sessions in every unit of the armed forces are an essential part of the programme to ensure their absolute loyalty to the Party, a policy which proved its worth in the Cultural Revolution.

3. A dramatic picture of gunners loading a twin-mounting. The primary task of the PLA Navy is coastal defence and its leadership has been instructed by the party to turn the nation's coastline into "a great wall of iron". Men for the navy are carefully selected, needing both good health and a sound political background. Their minimum period of service is five years, during which they can expect a fair amount of "sea-time", although really long voyages are seldom undertaken as yet. Naval pay is 10 per cent greater than the Army personnel's.

3

1. This organization table shows very clearly the difference in status between the Chinese armed forces and their Western counterparts. The overall body is the People's Liberation Army, which has a number of branches, two of which are the navy and the air force. These are thus equivalent to the artillery and the engineers, and are not separate services in their own right as are, say, the US Navy and the USAF. This explains why the Chinese use the titles "PLA Navy" and "PLA Air Force" to denote this subordinate status.

2. The scene on the bridge of a fast attack hydrofoil as signalmen use both radio and the traditional flag semaphore.

3. A gun crew on a Shanghai class fast patrol craft are instructed by a senior officer (cloth hat and spectacles).

with the PLA coastal defence batteries ashore mean that it might be possible to swamp even the most sophisticated vessel's defences. Even so, the range of the SSM is only about 20 miles (32 km) and the apparent lack of modern ECM on the Chinese warships makes them very vulnerable to hostile SSMs.

Chinese warships are also extremely vulnerable to air attack. Despite attempts to put a surface-to-air (SAM) system into service in the *Kiangtung* class frigate, the Chinese have no operational seaborne SAM, and although this deficiency is made up for to a certain extent by the presence of a large Naval Air Arm, it does mean that it would be difficult for Chinese warships to operate effectively out of range of land-based fighters.

The third major deficiency is in anti-submarine warfare (ASW). The Chinese possess hardly any ASW aircraft, and their ship-borne sensors and weapons are all obsolescent. Many surface vessels have only depth charges and even the more modern ships have nothing better than the MBU 1 800 ASW rocket launcher. The *Whiskey* and *Romeo* class submarines lack the submerged speed and endurance to be really effective ASW craft, particularly against nuclear submarines.

Like the surface vessels, the main strength of the Chinese submarines lies in numbers rather than individual effectiveness. Compared with Western submarines, they are relatively noisy and correspondingly easier to detect,

and they are armed only with conventional torpedoes. Their size also restricts them to operations in waters not too far distant from China.

Except for the frigates, the *Luta* class destroyers and the T-43 ocean minesweepers, the Chinese surface Navy lacks the capacity to operate on the open seas even in peacetime. The *Gordi* class destroyers are now due for retirement and are in any case notorious for their lack of seaworthiness. The effectiveness of the missile and torpedo armed light craft is severely reduced in a seaway and in any case they lack the range for anything other than local operations, and the same applies to almost all the landing craft.

In the absence of outside interference, the only offensive operation the Chinese Navy could undertake with some possibility of success, apart from purely local operations against the Korean or Vietnamese coats or the small offshore islands, would be the submarine blockade of Taiwan. The absence of a major amphibious capability or of sophisticated surface warships would make an attempted landing on Taiwan most unlikely. In the defensive role, the Chinese Navy could easily cope with attacks by Taiwan or South Korea, but it would sustain very heavy losses against the Soviet or United States navies, and would be unlikely to be able to prevent them from operating off the Chinese coast if either were to make a serious assault.

The Chinese have the capacity to

produce an operational submarine-launched ballistic missile (SLBM), but they have not as yet done so, though they are conducting research into solid fuel rockets. At present, therefore, the single *Golf* class SSB can only be employed operationally as a patrol submarine, and apart from the small number of obsolescent Tu-16 Badger aircraft operated by the Naval Air Arm, the Chinese Navy does not possess any strategic weapons.

Relationship between the Navy and Party

Because it is administered as an integral part of the PLA, the Chinese Navy is badly represented in the Government and in the higher command echelons. In 1977 there was only one Naval representative on the Politburo and only three full-time Naval members of the Party Central Committee (1 per cent compared to 30 per cent for the PLA as a whole). There were no Naval personnel on the council of the Ministry of National Defence and none in the General Staff Department (see Table 2). However, it does have representatives on the Ministry of National Defence's Scientific and Technological Commission, which supervises weapon research and development.

Because no official information has been released on it, the exact command structure and division of responsibilities

Table 2: CHINESE NAVY

```
                    ┌─────────────┐
                    │  POLITBURO  │
                    └──────┬──────┘
                  ┌────────┴─────────┐
                  │  PARTY CENTRAL   │
                  │    COMMITTEE     │
                  └────────┬─────────┘
            ┌──────────────┴──────────────┐
            │ MINISTRY OF NATIONAL DEFENCE │
            └──────────────┬──────────────┘
   ┌────────────┬──────────┴──────────────┬──────────────┐
┌──┴──────┐     │                   ┌──────┴──────────────┐
│TRAINING │     │                   │NATIONAL DEFENCE     │
│ESTABLISH│     │                   │SCIENTIFIC AND       │
│MENTS    │     │                   │TECHNICAL COMMISSION │
└─────────┘     │                   │AND OTHER RESEARCH   │
                │                   │AND PROCUREMENT      │
               PLA                  │ESTABLISHMENTS       │
                │                   └─────────────────────┘
   ┌────────────┼─────────────────────────┐
┌──┴──────┐  ┌──┴──────────┐        ┌──────┴──────┐
│GENERAL  │  │GENERAL STAFF│        │GENERAL      │
│LOGISTICS│  │DEPT         │        │POLITICAL    │
│DEPT.    │  │             │        │DEPT.        │
└─────────┘  └─────┬───────┘        └─────────────┘
              ┌────┴────┐
              │  NAVY   │
              └─────────┘
```

4. *The captain stands on the bridge of his fast attack craft, the uniform making his status quite clear.*
5. *A sailor operating a "Skin Head" radar, an I/J-band equipment giving surface target indication only.*
6. *The map shows the PLA-Navy's* three fleet commands, and major naval bases (HQs underlined). The North Sea Fleet protects Peking and the strategically critical north-east plains from attacks through the Yellow Sea and the Po Hai Gulf. The East Fleet defends the industrial Shanghai area and the contested Taiwan Strait. The South Sea Fleet guards commercial Canton and China's insular flank in the south. The Soviet Navy has many submarines and surface vessels based at Vladivostok and also uses base facilities in North Korea and the ex-US base at Cam Ranh Bay in Vietnam. China is becoming increasingly concerned at the spreading strength and influence of the Soviet Pacific Fleet. Further cause for alarm was the arrival at Vladivostok of the new 43,000 ton aircraft carrier Minsk, with VTOL aircraft aboard.

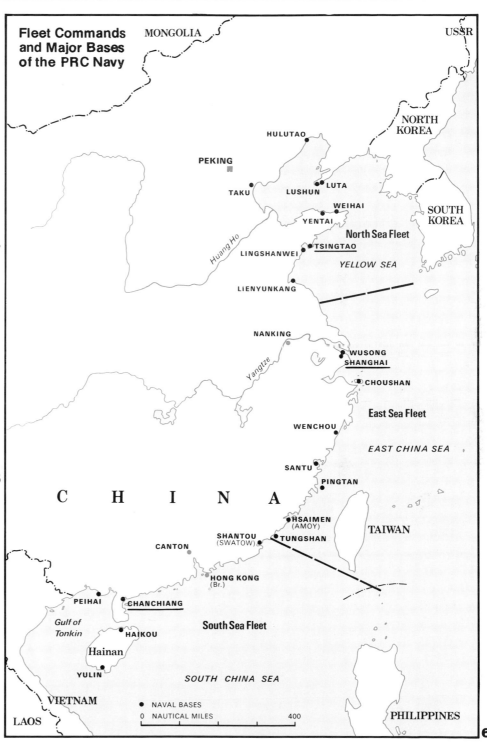

Fleet Commands and Major Bases of the PRC Navy

are difficult to ascertain. However, it is obvious that the Navy itself is highly decentralised. In peacetime, operational control seems to be vested in the Naval headquarters at Peking, but in wartime it devolves to the fleet commanders and the commanders of the military regions. The main function of the Peking naval headquarters appears to be the Navy's relationship with the Party and the rest of the PLA. The military regional commanders control the coastal defence batteries, and although the Naval Air Arm is permanently assigned to the Navy, it is administered as part of the Air Force. The Marines seem to be allocated to the Navy as necessary. For most practical purposes day-to-day command of the Chinese fleet is exercised by the three fleet commanders at Tsingtao, Shanghai and Chan Chiang.

In the Chinese Navy the Party, through its Commissars, has equal power to the military commanders. On board ship the military commander and the commissar share responsibility for command, although in combat the military commander has the final say in purely tactical matters. In general, the military commander is responsible for military training and tactics, while the Commissar is responsible for ideological training, security and non-combatant activities. However, the Commissar also has a responsibility for combat, and there is some overlap between the political and military command functions.

Rank structure and personnel training

The Chinese Navy has something over 200,000 officers and men. In the first instance, they enlist for five years, but there are considerable incentives to re-enlist at the end of this term. Officially, ranks of all kinds were eliminated after

CHINA'S NAVY: FOR COASTAL DEFENCE ONLY

1. The 10,000 ton freighter Fengqing was not only designed and built in China, but is constructed entirely of domestically produced materials.
2. A busy scene in Canton harbour. Although China's degree of economic self-sufficiency is high, there is still considerable overseas trade.
3. The engine controls on an ocean-going freighter. Chinese ships are efficient and reliable, but very few have been sold abroad so far. When the naval production is also taken into account it is obvious that the Chinese shipbuilding industry is doing well.
4. Fishing boats in harbour. The Chinese have always been great fishermen and for many centuries their junks have ventured far out into the oceans in search of fish. Today these modern deep-sea trawlers have made the romantic junk a thing of the past. The Soviet Union makes extensive use of vessels such as these for intelligence gathering (especially electronic intelligence), but there is no evidence that the Chinese have followed this practice.

3

4

1. *Nuclear fall-out wash-down drill being practised. Note the special suits and respirators, identical with those of the army.*
2. *The PLA Navy's minelaying capability is limited and there are some 40 minesweepers. The sailors' anxiety is understandable.*

3. *The PLA Navy has some 13 former United States landing craft (LSMs) and 15 tank landing ships (LSTs). There are also many smaller landing craft. It would be possible, therefore, to mount a limited amphibious operation against an island, but anything*

more ambitious against, say, Taiwan is out of the question in the foreseeable future. This craft is an LSM, supplied by the USA to the Nationalists and captured in 1949. The specially developed beach recovery tractor to the left of the ship is very interesting.

1

2

the departure of the Russian advisers, but in practice (apart from the Party Commissars) the Chinese Navy has a rank structure and specialist branches very similar to those of any other Navy. There is very little movement of personnel or ships within the fleets, and it seems to be common for men to spend many years in the same ship at the same base. Most officers and men are Party members. Many of the senior naval officers are still ex-Army men who transferred to the Navy after the Communist take-over in 1949, but these are gradually being replaced by men who have spent their entire career in the Navy.

The Navy has extensive training facilities. Many of these are situated in the area round Shanghai, including the officer training school at Tailien and the school of naval architecture. Basic training takes about six months, after which the better students are given more advanced training in the various

specialities. The junior officer's course takes about four years at the War College at Nanking, and the senior officer's course there takes about two-and-a-half years. Each fleet has its own facilities for continuation and combat training, but the South Sea fleet has less extensive facilities than the other two at present.

Shipbuilding and repair industry

China now has an extensive shipbuilding and ship-repair industry that is capable of building and maintaining warships up to the size of destroyers and submarines, as well as large merchant ships. About a quarter of the Chinese shipyards are in the region of Shanghai, including the largest, the Kiangun Yard. Other shipbuilding centres are Talien in the north and

Canton in the south. China is also capable of building its own warship machinery, weapons and sensors, and there are extensive research and design centres.

Considerable changes are now taking place in Chinese naval affairs. Since 1970 China has acquired its own merchant marine by purchasing about 300 ships of nearly 3 million tons GRT and by building another 100 ships of 1 million tons GRT; in the same period she has developed the Takang oilfield in the Pohai Gulf and the Yellow Sea. Offshore oil is also being sought in other places, including the South China Sea. This means that there is a much greater requirement for large surface ships capable of protecting the merchant fleet and the oil installations in all weathers at some distance offshore.

Closer relationship with the West

All this has coincided with the re-establishment of relations with the

United States and the possibility of purchasing Western military equipment. As a result China is actively seeking to make up for the deficiencies in her equipment, particularly in weapons systems and electronics. Her most urgent requirement is for modern SSM and SAM systems that will enable her warships to operate effectively against sophisticated ECM and render them less vulnerable to hostile air attack. China is also at present negotiating the purchase of examples of Western missile-armed patrol boats and other warships. The concurrent modernisation of her shipbuilding and electronics industry make it likely that she will only buy samples, and will adapt the Western technology to suit her own designs, although it is probable that she will licence-build Western designs until her own are ready. China has already received considerable help from the West, particularly from West Germany, in the development of her nuclear attack submarine, thereby easing its development.

Future emphasis on surface vessels

In the course of the next few years, the Chinese Navy is therefore likely to become an even more powerful force, with a greater emphasis on surface vessels such as frigates and destroyers, and with most of its deficiencies in equipment removed. However, even so, it is unlikely that it will be much more than a coastal defence force. China has relatively limited resources, and the Army and Air Force are likely to take the bulk of the money devoted to re-equipment. There is also little that can be done to make her submarine force less vulnerable, short of total re-equipment, and most of her ships are likely to be in service for many more years. However, it is conceivable that China might develop a submarine launched ballistic missile system during the next decade, to reduce the vulnerability of her deterrent forces. She already possesses the capability. What is not so certain is whether she would wish to divert the not inconsiderable resources needed to achieve an operational system from other, more immediately needed projects.

Colonel
William V. Kennedy
Armor, United States Army Reserve*

A Chinese CSA-1 surface-to-air missile is launched in a training exercise. Although it would be of value against an unsophisticated enemy, it is of 1950s design and would not be effective against an air attack by the principal potential enemy—the Soviet Union. Also, like so many other PLA weapons, it is purely defensive in nature. Indeed, it is very doubtful that the Chinese could conduct an operation requiring an advance of a major formce more than a hundred miles outside their borders. The top priority in the defence field is to buy time so that elderly equipment such as this can be replaced by modern, effective and reliable weapons systems, which will be able to operate throughout the 1980s and into the 1990s, and China is turning to the West for short-term help.

With the Soviet Union having drawn a noose around China, the West and Japan are set to provide military, technological and diplomatic assistance, but will this prove counter-productive in the long term, sowing the seeds for future conflicts?

1. *The turning point in the Viet Minh war against the French colonial army came in 1949 when the victorious Chinese People's Liberation Army moved up to the border with Indo-China. Supply routes were opened up and many training camps were established in the safety of Chinese territory. In 1953-54 the supplies provided by China were absolutely crucial to the great Viet Minh victory at Dien Bien Phu. Despite this support the Vietnamese turned on their former allies in the late 1970s with the troubles becoming really serious in 1977-78 when a campaign of deliberate harassment of the Chinese minority in Vietnam caused the Peking government to become increasingly involved in their welfare. Matters escalated rapidly and by the end of 1978 there was an increasing number of shooting and other incidents on the Sino-Vietnam border where once the talk was only of friendship and solidarity between fraternal Communist movements. This map shows the Chinese version of the provocation which led to their*

On the morning of February 17, 1979, China attacked Vietnam. It was the act of a nation driven to desperation by the noose Russia has been drawing tighter around China's neck for a decade.

During the ensuing weeks of the invasion, the arrival of Soviet Air Force transports at Hanoi, the assembly of Russian naval power offshore and reports of troop movements and civilian evacuation on the Sino-Soviet frontier made it apparent that this was no sideshow that the rest of the world could watch with equanimity, even though China had said from the outset that the attack would be limited to "teaching Vietnam a lesson".

In an interview with a group of visiting scholars as China was beginning its withdrawal from Vietnam, Chinese Foreign Minister Huang Hua said, "This is not the ending of a war. It is the beginning of a bigger war."[1]

On March 29, 1979, The New York Times reported that unnamed "Washington officials" had confirmed the arrival of Soviet warships at Cam Ranh Bay, the American-developed Vietnamese harbour long-coveted by the Soviets as the anchorage from which the Soviet Pacific Fleet could dominate the South China Coast.

What one high-ranking US official had called a "proxy war" between Vietnam and Cambodia[2] had become much less so as one of the "proxies" (Cambodia) was conquered and its sponsor (China) forced into direct combat with the conquerors, Vietnam.

The Chinese attack on Vietnam followed a brilliant five-month diplomatic *tour de force* by Chinese Deputy Premier Teng Hsiao-ping aimed at involving Japan and the United States in China's dispute with the Soviet Union.

In October, 1978, Teng had gone to Tokyo where he signed a Treaty of Peace and Friendship with Japan. China had insisted upon, and won, incorporation of a word — "hegemony" — that it publicly proclaimed to be an anti-Soviet epithet.

The Japanese Government proclaimed a continuing policy of "equidistance" between China and Russia. It even permitted delivery of a floating drydock that increased the sustained fighting power of the Soviet Pacific Fleet. But, in contrast, a flood of Japanese money, machinery and technology—including military technology—poured into China. Japanese financiers talked of credits to China in the neighbourhood of 20 to 30 billion dollars. No such flood moved toward development of Siberia.

China's attack on Vietnam followed by only two weeks a triumphal visit by Teng Hsiao-ping to the United States.

A handful of Western journalists, among them Harrison Salisbury, formerly of The New York Times, and this writer[3], had warned for several years that the Sino-Soviet conflict was heading toward a major military confrontation. Prevailing opinion in the West and Japan discounted the danger.

Although shaken by the dramatic events of February-March 1979, this opinion continued to prevail, based on the following assumptions:

That the issues at stake are primarily ideological and propagandistic and, therefore, could be resolved by a change of attitudes or personalities within the leadership in Peking and Moscow.

That China has succeeded in establishing a "finite" nuclear deterrent to any possible large-scale Soviet aggression.

That the Soviets would find themselves in an endless "people's war" if they were to attack China and eventually would be overwhelmed or forced to withdraw.

Far more than ideology is at stake in the clash between Russia and China. The advance by Russia into Asia during the past 300 years has been marked by repeated clashes with China, in almost all of which China has lost large tracts of territory that she claimed outright or by exercise of suzerainity over tributary tribes. The most serious of these losses occurred in the 19th century under treaties imposed by force or the threat of force on a faltering Manchu dynasty. These are what China now describes as the "unequal treaties".

The heart of the disputed territory is the Soviet Maritime Province lying between the Ussuri River and the Pacific. This is the anchor of Russian power in Asia. If it were to be lost, the Soviet Union would cease to be a

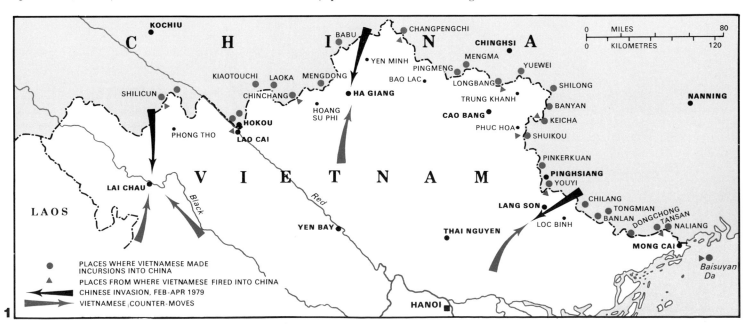

- ● PLACES WHERE VIETNAMESE MADE INCURSIONS INTO CHINA
- ▲ PLACES FROM WHERE VIETNAMESE FIRED INTO CHINA
- ➡ CHINESE INVASION, FEB-APR 1979
- ➡ VIETNAMESE COUNTER-MOVES

1979 "punitive" invasion; if it is correct it suggests that there was a carefully orchestrated campaign by the Vietnamese, with incidents taking place over a 500 mile front. China responded with public warnings and some very obvious troop movements, with two army corps being brought to the border from positions facing Taiwan and Hong Kong.
2. As the Chinese know only too well from training on their side of the border, the rugged and hilly terrain of north Vietnam is a logistician's nightmare, and in many parts only the traditional methods of human porters and pack-animals are of any value. These are hill tribesmen from Yunnan.
3. Deep in Vietnamese territory a soldier of the PLA stands guard over a captured supply dump as a T-59 moves towards the front.

Pacific power and its status as a world power would be greatly diminished.

Even the relatively minor border adjustments China has suggested as an interim solution pose a potential threat to Soviet control of the Maritime Province. For example, an island claimed by China opposite the Soviet Far Eastern city of Khabarovsk would place the vital Amur River bridge of the Trans-Siberian Railway—the lifeline of the Maritime Province—within range of Chinese medium artillery.

Russian fears that China will someday present its bill for the "unequal treaties", no matter what interim agreements are reached, are reinforced by the fact that the Russian population in the Maritime Province and elsewhere along the Sino-Soviet frontier is in decline while China moves steadily to develop and populate its northern marches.[4]

In January, 1976, the late Chou En-lai presented a long-term Economic Plan to the Fourth National People's Congress in Peking in which he set forth the goal of making China a great industrial nation by the year 2000. The Soviets are acutely aware of the fact that the resources necessary to enable China to achieve such a goal are in Siberia and that China has the manpower necessary to wrest those resources from a forbidding climate and terrain.

In its demand for border "adjustments" and its challenge for leadership of the Communist movement worldwide, China threatens the two most vital of all Soviet interests:

The territorial integrity of the Soviet Union.

The legitimacy of the Communist ruling group in Moscow.

The Soviet Union has responded by creating what amounts to a new army along the Sino-Soviet border. At least 40 divisions are deployed. Although many of them are considered to be at reduced strength, the Soviets have the airlift capacity to bring them to wartime strength and to reinforce them with airborne divisions from the central reserve, within a matter of hours. The Russian national investment represented by the China border deployment becomes even more significant when it is considered that it costs three times as much to maintain a division in the remote Asian borderlands than it does to maintain the same division in European Russia or Eastern Europe.

China's missile force: no strategic value?

The facts of the Soviet deployment in the East are well known. The significance of the deployment, however, is often downgraded or dismissed outright by the assumption that the Chinese have developed a nuclear deterrent to any large-scale Soviet attack. That assumption will not stand up under careful analysis.

Current evaluations[5], based on public statements by US Defense officials and unclassified publications of the US Defense Intelligence Agency, credit China with the following:

Two intercontinental ballistic missiles (ICBM) generally comparable to the US Titan and Soviet SS-9, with an estimated range of over 3,000 miles as yet unconfirmed by test flights.

15 to 20 liquid-fuelled intermediate range ballistic missiles (IRBM) with a range of up to 1,500 nautical miles.

50 to 100 liquid-fuelled medium range ballistic missiles (MRBM) with a range of up to 600 nautical miles.

An unknown number of nuclear weapons transportable by a mixture of obsolete Soviet and Chinese-designed aircraft.

The known warhead capacity of these weapons ranges from 20 kilotons (about the size of the weapons used in World War II) to four megatons, the size of the largest Chinese test to date.

Several questions must be asked about the Chinese ICBMs: Can it be assumed that both missiles will work to perfection? How good is the Chinese guidance system? Can it be assumed that both missiles will impact within the circular error probable (CEP) necessary to achieve the planned results? How good is the Chinese target data? Can the Soviet anti-ballistic missile system around Moscow cope with a one or two-missile attack? Since the loss of Moscow in 1812 and the abandonment of Moscow by the Soviet government in 1941 did not stop Russia from pressing the wars to final victory, would loss of Moscow to a successful ICBM attack produce different results?

Whether there are two Chinese ICBM's or 20, the probabilities of error and malfunction derived from US and Soviet tests of similar weapons indicate that China's chances of assured destruction of any Soviet target are small. Lack of testing experience, low probability of a satisfactory guidance system and lack of reconnaissance means to gather accurate target data make it doubtful that the Chinese can count on reaching the desired target areas with their missiles. The chances of a successful attack on Moscow are reduced further if any probability of success is ascribed to the Soviet ABM system.

The existence of the Chinese ICBMs does pose a threat to some unknown number of Russian (and Chinese) citizens wherever the Chinese missiles might come down. This could be numbered from the hundreds to the hundreds of thousands, with the lower end of the scale more probable considering the vastness of the Eurasian

1. A test launch of a Chinese missile by a unit of the "Second Artillery", the arm of the PLA responsible for the nuclear force. The missile is most probably that designated in the West as CSS-2, an Intermediate Range Ballistic Missile (IRBM) with a range of some 1,500 nautical miles. It is a single-stage weapon, reminiscent of the US Thor and the British Blue Streak. It is reported that 20 are in service. The next missile to be developed was the CSS-3, a limited-range ICBM, unofficially reported to have a range of some 4,000 miles (6,486km). There is, however, no evidence that CSS-3 has ever been deployed, possibly because the PLA have concentrated their efforts on the CSSX-4, a true ICBM, with a range of some 8,000 miles (12,875km). It is known that the Soviets have recently rearranged their anti-ballistic missile (ABM) defences around Moscow to counter an attack from China, and it may be that the CSSX-4 prompted such a move. Whereas earlier Chinese strategic missiles have been liquid fuelled it is probable that the

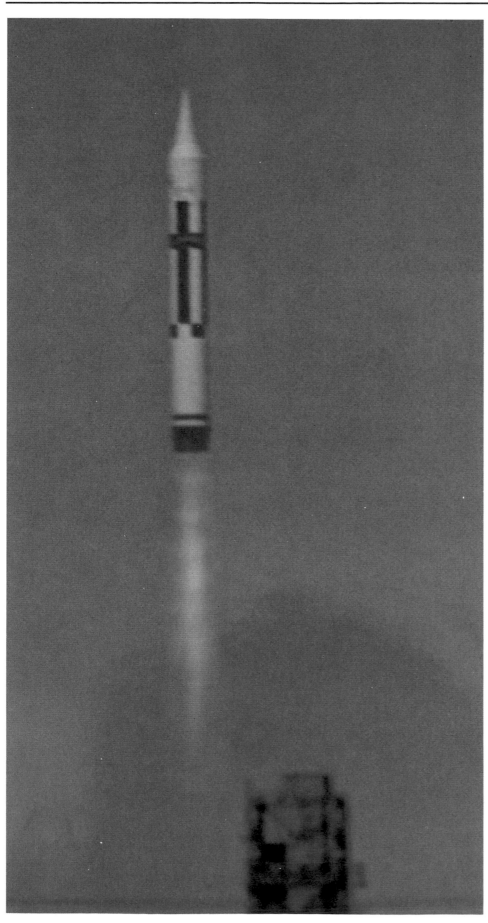

CSSX-4 uses solid fuel, following the changes in other countries.
2. Officers of the PLA observe the explosion of a Chinese nuclear weapon. The massive size of the fireball suggests a warhead in the 1 to 3 Megaton (1 megaton = 1 million tons of TNT equivalent) range. The nuclear explosion raises the temperature to some 10,000,000 °C and the enormous pressures which result give rise to this incandescent sphere (the fireball) which climbs rapidly to produce the typical mushroom cloud. Some 35 per cent of the energy released by the explosion is radiated by the fireball in the form of intense heat, which vaporises materials very close to "ground zero" and which can cause burns to human tissue, the severity of which depends upon the distance. Possession of nuclear weapons has radically altered the strategic balance between China and the Soviet Union, because the Soviets cannot rule out the early use of such weapons by the Chinese to counter their deficiencies in conventional weapons.

1. The achievements of the People's Republic of China in developing its own nuclear weapons and space programme are quite remarkable when the paucity of industrial and technical resources are taken into account. The table shows the development of the programme starting with a very rudimentary atomic device in 1964 and moving inexorably towards the first "hydrogen" or thermonuclear device in June 1967. In such a programme there are bound to be problems and it will be noted that there have been several at least partial failures.

2. Development of the delivery means has proceeded in parallel with the warheads. The aged Tupolev Tu-16 is still in service and has dropped nuclear weapons in a number of tests, but its ability to penetrate Soviet air space is to be doubted. It could, however, be used to deliver nuclear weapons against less well defended countries in Asia, such as India, although this seems to be an unlikely requirement. The missile programme has proceeded steadily, but the

CHINA'S NUCLEAR TESTING PROGRAMME

Year	Date	Estimated Yield	Type of Explosion	Delivery Means	Remarks
1964	16 Oct	20 KT	Ground	Tower-mounted	'Primitive' implosion device using Uranium-235 (U-235)
1965	14 May	20-40 KT	Air	Tu-4 bomber	Fission device: U-235.
	9 May	200-300 KT	Air	Tu-16 bomber	Fission device: U-235 with some thermonuclear material.
1966	27 Oct	20-30 KT	Ground	Missile (Soviet SS-4)	Fission device: U-235
	28 Dec	300-500 KT	Ground	Tower-mounted	Fission device: U-235 with some thermonuclear material.
1967	17 Jun	3 MT	Air	Tu-16	Thermonuclear device: fission-fusion-fission type using U-235.
	24 Dec	20-25 KT	Air	Tu-16	Thermonuclear device. Not publicly reported by PRC and may have been at least a partial failure.
1968	27 Dec	3 MT	Air	Tu-16	Thermonuclear device: U-235 with some plutonium.
1969	22 Sep	20-25 KT	Underground	—	Fission device.
	29 Sep	3 MT	Air	Tu-16	Thermonuclear device: possibly first test for CSS-2 warhead.
1970	14 Oct	3 MT	Air	Tu-16	Thermonuclear device, not publicly reported by PRC.
1971	18 Nov	20 KT	Ground	Tower-mounted	Thermonuclear device: U-235 with some plutonium.
1972	7 Jan	Less than 20 KT	Air	Not known	Thermonuclear device: U-235 with some plutonium. Reported to have been a partial failure.
	18 Mar	20-200 KT	Air	Not known	Possibly a trigger device, but reported to have been partial failure.
1973	27 Jun	2 MT+	Air	Tu-16	Thermonuclear device.
1974	17 Jun	2 MT+	Air		Thermonuclear device.
1975	27 Oct		Underground	—	
1976	25 Jan		Ground		
	26 Sep		Air		
	17 Oct		Underground	—	
	17 Nov	4 MT			Thermonuclear device.
1977	17 Sep	Less than 20 KT	Air		
1978	15 Mar	20 KT	Air		

1

CHINA'S STRATEGIC NUCLEAR ARSENAL

Weapon System	Nuclear Warhead	Range (Nautical Miles)	Development Started	Entered Service	Nos. in Service 1979	Remarks
Tupolev Tu-16 (Badger)	1 MT	2000	1960	1968	60	Although possessing long range and accuracy, would be unlikely to penetrate Soviet air defence system.
CSS-1 MRBM	20 KT	600-700	1959/60	1966	30-40	Design based on USSR SS-4.50 in service in late 1960s, rising to 100 by 1975. Now being phased out.
CSS-2 IRBM	1 MT	1500-1750	1960/61	1971	15-20	First Chinese thermonuclear weapon, but has only served in limited numbers. Design believed to have been based on Soviet SS-5.
CSS-3 Limited Range ICBM	3 MT	3000-3500	1967	1978	10 (Est)	This system seems to have been developed as a safeguard against possible failure of CSS-4. For the first time it has brought most of European USSR within range, including, possibly, Moscow.
CSS-4 Full Range ICBM	4 MT	8000	1969/70	1980/82	—	In the same class as US Titan and Soviet SS-9. Still launched from hardened silo, a method now very vulnerable to the very accurate Soviet warheads.
CSSN-2 SLBM	1 MT	1000	Late '60s	Early '80s	—	To maintain the credibility of their deterrent the Chinese must develop a SLBM; they already have a nuclear submarine, but with conventional weapons.

2

CHINA'S SPACE PROGRAMME

Date of Launch	Launcher Designation	Payload (kg)	Period (minutes)	Perigee (km)	Apogee (km)	Inclination to Equator	Remarks
24 Apr 70	China-1	173	114	439	2384	68.5	Launched by a modified CSS-2 rocket the Chinese satellite was the heaviest first for any nation (USSR Sputnik-1 84kg, USA Explorer-1 14kg. Broadcast "The East is Red" to let the world know that China was in the "space race".
3 Mar 71	China-2	221	106	266	1826	69.9	Again launched by a modified CSS-2.
26 Jul 75	China-3	—	90.98	184	461	69.02	Launched by a modified CSS-3 this may well have been China's first photographic satellite. It returned to earth after 50 days.
26 Nov 75	China-4	2700-4500	91.09	170	479	62.59	Almost certainly a photographic mission; a data capsule returned to earth after six days, but a "large object" remained in orbit for a further 27 days. Believed to have monitored Soviet military activities on Sino-Soviet border.
16 Dec 75	China-5	2700-4500	90.1	188	385	69.0	This may well have been another photographic mission. The USSR is known to be planning interceptor satellites to deal with these Chinese devices.
30 Aug 76	China-6	2000	107.5	194	2030	69.0	Believed to have been China's first electronic "ferret".
7 Dec 76	China-7	1200	89	163	489	50.0	Another photographic mission; part of the payload was recovered.
26 Jan 78	China-8	3600	90.9	161	479	57.03	A reconnaissance satellite. First section of 2400kg was recovered on 30 Jan 78 and the balance on 7 Feb 78.

Sources: IISS "The Military Balance"; IISS "Strategic Survey"; SIPRI Yearbooks; SIPRI "Outer Space- Battlefield of the Future?"; Gelber "Nuclear Weapons and Chinese Policy"; Far Eastern Economic Review. Keesings Contemporary Archives.

3

Chinese must be already reviewing their fixed silo policy, and they will undoubtedly be forced to follow the lead of other nuclear powers and develop nuclear submarines and sub-marine launched ballistic missiles. They already possess one Han-

class nuclear submarine, although it does not seem to be fitted for missiles and could well be an experimental boat to develop the technology.
3. Arising from the missile programme for the nuclear force has been the ability to start a

space programme. This has proceeded at a steady pace and dogs and mice have already been launched into sub-orbital trajectories. "Aviation Week" reports that thought is being given to a manned programme.
4. This picture of a Soviet SS-9

Scarp intercontinental missile shows the approximate size and shape of the Chinese CSS-4, which is in the same class and is reported to have a similar performance. SS-9 is 118ft long, and 10ft 2in in diameter, and has a range of some 7,500 miles.

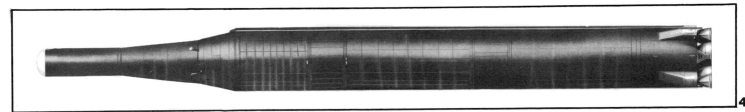

geography and the relatively low population density along most of the likely trajectories.

If the Soviets decide that the threat posed by China to their vital interests requires a military solution, would they be willing to sacrifice those interests because of a fear that the Chinese ICBMs might kill some large (or small) number of Soviet (or Chinese) citizens?

The 150 or so smaller Chinese missiles pose a more convincing threat to the Soviet Union in that some might be delivered successfully against the Trans-Siberian Railway and Soviet Asian cities. Here again questions of reliability and accuracy must be raised. Also, there is a question of survivability.

The operational history of liquid-fuelled missiles indicates that not all of the Chinese IRBMs and MRBMs will get off the launcher without accident. Some unknown number of additional missiles will fail on the way to their targets. Guidance systems become an increasingly critical matter as the size of the target and the size of the warhead decrease. The chances, therefore, of cutting the Trans-Siberian Railway and keeping it cut for more than a few hours or a few days by this means are very small. Since the smaller Chinese missiles must be fired from launching areas relatively close to the Soviet border, the chances that they will be identified and targeted by the Soviets in advance of the attack are good. If it is assumed that the Chinese have no intention of attacking the Soviets, least of all with nuclear weapons, then it must be assumed that the Chinese nuclear weapons would be used only after the Soviets had struck at preplanned targets such as launching sites and communications centres. The remaining Chinese communications systems would have to coordinate the missile counterattack in the face of the most elaborate electronic warfare system in the world.

It can be concluded, therefore, that in a strategic sense the Chinese

nuclear arsenal has little military value. It threatens one or several of the Soviet cities in Siberia and there is some remote possibility of a successful ICBM strike against an urban target in European Russia. Again, however, the question must be asked whether possible civilian casualties would deter the Soviet government from what it considered to be a necessary course of action. If so, it would be the first time in Soviet, or Russian, history that a decision was made on that basis.

A Chinese attempt to deliver nuclear weapons by aircraft would have even lower prospects of success. As Bill Sweetman has made clear in an earlier chapter, the PLA Air Force is no match for Soviet air power. Lacking modern electronic countermeasures, Chinese aircraft would find it difficult to penetrate Soviet air defences. Chinese airfields would be among the pre-planned Soviet targets, particularly in the immediate border region. Chinese aircraft approaching from more distant bases would be susceptible to identification and engagement by Soviet air defences while still over Chinese territory. The possibility remains that low-level penetrators could escape detection long enough to carry out a suicide mission against one or more Soviet cities. The probabilities imposed, however, by Soviet air superiority and surface-to-air Soviet missile defences would require that China be prepared to assign a large number of aircraft and a large number of its limited nuclear weapons to such a role with the near certainty that almost all would be lost before a meaningful target could be struck.

A Chinese decision to use its relatively small store of nuclear weapons in what would be essentially a terroristic mode would invite Russian retaliation against Chinese cities with disproportionate results, to say the least. Would the Chinese risk destruction on so large a scale when the benefits to China would be, at best, a transitory emotional satisfaction?

If the Chinese were to decide that provoking a strategic nuclear exchange with the Soviets is not in their best interests, they might elect to use their nuclear arsenal in a battlefield mode in the hope that the Soviets would confine themselves to the same level.

Assuming, once again, a Soviet attack on China, what could the Chinese hope to gain? The terrain of most of the Sino-Soviet border, the armoured and mechanized nature of the Soviet forces and the limited armoured protection available to the Chinese would provide the Soviets with an inherent advantage in nuclear and chemical warfare.

Deployed armoured and mechanized forces are tough targets, even for nuclear weapons. To assure knocking out an armour-protected manoeuvre battalion it would be necessary to destroy at least one third of the unit, and that would require a weapon several times the "nominal" (20 kiloton) size. Since the Soviet units would be on the move under air superiority it would be difficult for the Chinese to locate, identify and retain worthwhile targets. Here again, disruption of Chinese launch points and communications by pre-emptive Soviet attack and electronic warfare would be a major factor. If the Soviets elected to move at night the chances of the Chinese being able to launch a successful counter-attack would be further reduced.

Under the best of circumstances, the Chinese do not have the means to deliver accurately enough nuclear weapons of sufficient size to halt the Russian formations now in place along the Sino-Soviet frontier, much less the forces that could be brought from Central Asia and European Russia. In return, China would trigger a Soviet nuclear and chemical counterattack that would destroy all Chinese armed forces in the forward combat zone.

In either the strategic or the tactical mode, therefore, the potential advantage to the Soviets is so great that they probably would welcome Chinese first

THE PERCEIVED THREAT TO CHINA'S FUTURE

1. The Soviet Union has some 40-45 army divisions in the four eastern Military Districts and in Mongolia, six of which are tank divisions, at least one airborne and the remainder motor-rifle. The major concentrations are in the Komsomolsk-Khabarovsk-Vladi- vostok area, and on the start-lines of the approach routes for any invasion of China. A few divisions are stationed in the hinterland, but they are difficult to resupply and there is no major strategic role for them. Each Military District includes a Tactical Air Army. Until only a few years ago the equip- ment of these forces in the Far East was obsolescent and the manning level of the units held at some 50 to 75 per cent of the war figure. Recently this has begun to change; manpower is well up and the equipment is much improved. These Antonov An-12 (NATO Codename: Cub) tactical trans- ports give the airborne division at Khabarovsk the capability of penetrating deep into Chinese territory in support of an invasion. **2.** The Soviet Long-Range Air Force has now deployed at least

1

2

3

4

five Tupolev Tu-26 (NATO Codename: Backfire) bombers to an airfield in eastern Siberia. This impressive aircraft is reported to be capable of an unrefuelled radius of action of about 2,500 miles on a Hi-Lo-Hi mission, while in-flight refuelling or carrying stand-off missiles would add significantly to this.

3. Equally elusive would be the Sukhoi Su-19 (NATO Codename: Fencer). Coming in low at supersonic speeds it would be virtually invulnerable.

4. On the ground, too, the Soviets enjoy much greater mobility than all except the few tank divisions in the PLA order-of-battle. These T-62 tanks and BTR-60 wheeled armoured personnel carriers currently predominate in the Far East, but the more modern T-72 tank and BMP are now issued.

5. The map shows very clearly the great vulnerability of parts of northern China. Manchuria includes many important mineral resources and manufacturing centres. Inner Mongolia and Sinkiang also have great resources but are difficult to defend.

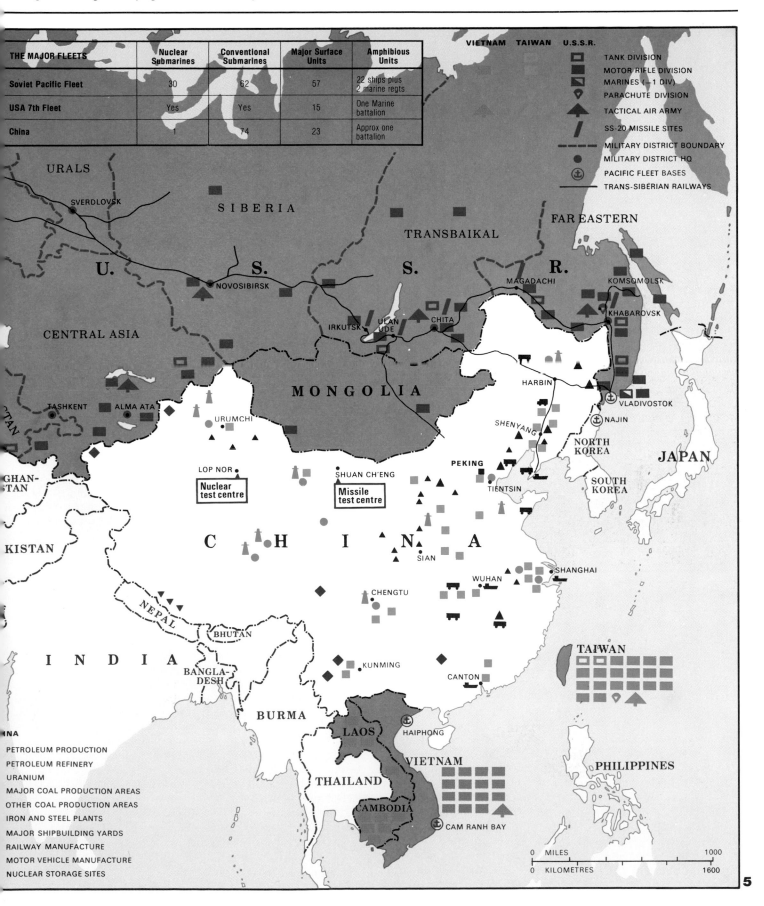

THE MAJOR FLEETS	Nuclear Submarines	Conventional Submarines	Major Surface Units	Amphibious Units
Soviet Pacific Fleet	30	62	57	22 ships plus 2 marine regts
USA 7th Fleet	Yes	Yes	15	One Marine battalion
China	1	74	23	Approx one battalion

U.S.S.R.
- ☐ TANK DIVISION
- ▥ MOTOR RIFLE DIVISION
- ◩ MARINES (=1 DIV)
- ⬖ PARACHUTE DIVISION
- ▲ TACTICAL AIR ARMY
- ◢ SS-20 MISSILE SITES
- – – – MILITARY DISTRICT BOUNDARY
- ● MILITARY DISTRICT HQ
- ⚓ PACIFIC FLEET BASES
- —— TRANS-SIBERIAN RAILWAYS

PETROLEUM PRODUCTION
PETROLEUM REFINERY
URANIUM
MAJOR COAL PRODUCTION AREAS
OTHER COAL PRODUCTION AREAS
IRON AND STEEL PLANTS
MAJOR SHIPBUILDING YARDS
RAILWAY MANUFACTURE
MOTOR VEHICLE MANUFACTURE
NUCLEAR STORAGE SITES

Nuclear test centre

Missile test centre

Location of Soviet military units estimated with advice from Professor John Erickson, Edinburgh University.

1. The spearhead of any Soviet invasion of China will be the T-72 tank. This new vehicle is armed with a 125mm smooth-bore gun firing armour piercing, fin-stabilised, discarding sabot (APFSDS) rounds which will easily penetrate the armour of the Chinese T-59 and T-62 tanks, and from outside the maximum range of the Chinese tank guns. Thus, any mass attack by PLA tanks (as shown on pages 85 and 98-99) would be decimated before reaching the Soviet positions. Further, the Soviet T-72 is made of a new type of armour which will be impervious to the 100mm main gun of the Chinese T-59 except at very close range. Early issues of the T-72 were to Soviet forces facing NATO, but they are now being supplied to the forces in the Far Eastern areas and it is a very urgent requirement for the PLA to find some means of countering it, as described on pages 180-181.
2. Yet another problem for the PLA: a typical battery of Soviet SS-1 Scud-A tactical missiles which presents a threat to which

use of nuclear weapons, considering the political advantages gained by placing the opprobrium for first use on the Chinese.

The ability to use their nuclear firepower freely would give the Soviets additional advantages, both strategic and tactical. Availability of nuclear weapons coupled with superior Soviet reconnaissance systems would make it possible to substitute surveillance and firepower for large ground formations along most of the border from Sinkiang to eastern Mongolia. In the areas, principally Manchuria, where the Chinese have developed extensive fortifications, nuclear weapons would speed the Russian breakthrough and reduce Soviet casualties. The area of China that the Soviets could control without direct ground attack or occupation would be expanded. China's ability to concentrate and sustain the forces needed to counterattack would be pre-empted. In general, the conditions would exist for a negotiated peace by which China would be stripped of a nuclear capability and condemned to permanent inferiority.

Soviet perception of the Chinese threat

If China's nuclear "deterrent" is largely a figment of Western imagination, what of the assumption that Soviet invaders must inevitably be drawn into a prolonged and unwinnable "people's war"? That supposition turns on the question of likely Soviet political objectives.

To protect its teritorial integrity at any given time in history, the Russian state has sought to create a buffer of weak, non-Russian territories between itself and major opponents. As the Russian population expanded, the core state grew and a new system of non-Russian buffers was created. At present, potentially threatening major powers border the USSR directly only in the Bering Strait and on the frontier with China.

Periodically, some Soviet writer or official laments the sale of Alaska to the United States and the direct contact this created with a power that, in the short term, is considered to be the most dangerous potential foe but which is considered in the light of the Vietnam debacle to be in a state of moral decay. By far the greater Soviet concern is with the mortal, long-term threat it perceives from China. These fears are all the greater because the Russian population is no longer expanding to fill the great voids of territory. Instead, in the Soviet Far East, the Russian population is in decline. Throughout the Soviet Union the population growth of the non-Russian peoples exceeds that of the Russians. As China's huge population moves closer to the frontier by means of forced migrations from Central China and land reclamation and development, both the USSR and Mongolia grow increasingly apprehensive. No interim political arrangement can dispel that fear.

The Russian and Soviet empire has moved steadily toward occupation of the line marked out by General Alexei Kuropatkin in 1916; that is, from the Khan Tengri Mountain in the Tien Shan range to Vladivostok. Control of Mongolia attained approximately 50 per cent of the Kuropatkin Line. Political and economic pressures in the 1930s and 1940s almost gave the Soviets control over Sinkiang and Northern Manchuria. For a time after World War II, the Soviets reoccupied the old Russian naval base at Port Arthur on Manchuria's Liaotung Peninsula.

Kuropatkin's concern over Sinkiang stemmed from a fear that a modernized China could strike west and north through the Dzungarian Basin to cut the Russian Empire in half. The present-day nightmare of the Soviet Union is that a China allied with the United States and Japan could make this threat a reality. Indeed, only six months after the Sino-Soviet border clashes of 1969 made a China-US alliance a possibility, an article by then Lt. Col. David E. Palmer in the US Army's journal, Armor, portrayed such an attack in graphic detail[6]. Control over Sinkiang and the adjoining Kansu Corridor would place the Soviets in the best possible position to block the sort of attack Kuropatkin and Palmer have described.

Soviet control over Northern Manchuria would cripple China economically by depriving her of the oil fields and industry basic to attainment of Chou En-lai's goal of a great modern

2

society by the year 2000. These gains combined would make it impossible for China to sustain a challenge to Soviet ideological leadership of the Communist movement.

Without occupation of Peking or of any of the larger Chinese cities a Soviet advance to the line described by General Kuropatkin would give the Soviets control over the needed buffer region and political control over a much larger region—amounting to a position of domination of the entire Eurasian landmass.

Most important, for the reasons discussed in my earlier chapter, the Soviet military advance would have stopped short of the point at which the "people's war" doctrine could come into play. It would then be possible for the Soviets to turn their attention to Europe or the Middle East without fear of a major threat from the East.

The longer the Soviets wait and the more successful China becomes in developing its northern frontiers the more difficult a Soviet attack will become.

From all the preceding chapters dealing with the current state of the Chinese military forces, it is apparent

1

the PLA currently has no answer; it has no surface-to-surface tactical missiles of its own for counter-battery missions, while its ground-attack aircraft would be unlikely to be able to penetrate far enough into Soviet rear areas to reach targets such as this. Even

elderly missiles such as the Scud-A can therefore be deployed by the Soviets to face the PLA and as more modern SSMs are deployed so the threat will increase.
3. For immediate battlefield support the Soviet Far East forces still deploy numbers of these

elderly, but still effective FROG-3 unguided artillery missiles (FROG is anacronym for Free Rocket Over Ground). They have a nuclear, conventional (and possibly chemical) warhead of 992lb (450kg) and a range of about 25 miles.

Russian demands for a favoured position in Sinkiang and Manchuria. That has happened often enough in the past to be a source of worry to any Chinese leadership that seeks to stand up to the Russians.

This analysis of the military relationship supports Professor Hinton's conclusion that China must rely on diplomatic means to right the balance. Teng Hsiao-ping conceded as much in his statement in March, 1979, that, "If the Russians decide to come there is nothing we can do about it."

Japan is the key to world power balance

China seems to have recognized that the true prize in the modern version of what Rudyard Kipling called the "Great Game" in Asia is Japan. A Soviet victory in Manchuria and North China, by which the Soviet Pacific Fleet returned to Port Arthur and perhaps Tsingtao would put Japan in a desperate strategic situation. She lacks the military power, as yet, to defend against a Russian attack and she perceives American power in the Pacific and Asia to have declined to a point where it is doubtful that the United States could respond in time by any means short of a strategic nuclear attack. Such a war probably would be worse for Japan than surrender or "neutralization" under Soviet influence.

If the Soviets were to move against China and, at the same time, to demand that Japan accept the status of an Asian Finland, it is possible that Japan would have no choice but to demand departure of residual (but what are beginning to be perceived as ineffectual) US forces from their bases in Japan and accept a drastic limitation on her own Self-Defence Forces. In that event, the balance of power would **3** have changed not only in Asia but in the world.

The pattern of Chinese diplomacy throughout the late 1970s indicates that China sees this equation more clearly than any of the other principal actors, save, perhaps, the Soviets.

To the dismay of the Japanese Communist Party and the Left-Wing Socialists, China has urged Japan to build up its military forces. While still

that China lacks the means to defeat a Soviet attack before the Soviets attain the decisive strategic objective represented by the Kuropatkin Line. So long, therefore, as the Soviets are able to retain their present degree of military superiority in Asia, China will be in danger of being reduced to the status of a Soviet vassal, if not by direct military

attack then by the political and economic pressures that can be generated by the threat of such an attack. The most serious danger here is that some internal Chinese faction anxious to transfer defence expenditures to economic development might attempt to resolve the strategic problem, at least temporarily, by giving in to

1. *The Soviet T-64 and T-72 tanks — whose armour could probably defeat any tank or anti-tank gun the PLA has — is the main land threat. To counter this, Chinese military missions have been scouring the West for anti-tank weapons, and in May 1979 it* *was reported that the American Fairchild-Republic company had held informal talks on the possibility of the sale of A-10 Thunderbolt II aircraft. This large and rugged close-air support aircraft has been specifically designed for anti-tank missions* *and is armed with six AGM-65 Maverick missiles and a GAU-8/A 30mm Gatling-type gun.* **2.** *Although it has developed its own intermediate- and medium-range ballistic missiles, China has made little progress in the tactical missile field. This has aggravated* *the weaknesses in their anti-tank defences and urgent measures have had to be taken to purchase from abroad. One of the first orders to be announced was a £350million deal with France for the supply of Milan and HOT anti-tank missiles and Crotale anti-*

saying, in public, that it supports withdrawal of US forces from South Korea, China has made it known by every possible private means that it hopes to see American land combat forces as well as naval and air forces kept in Korea. Chinese military officers believe that the US 2nd Infantry Division in Korea is the tip of an American spear aimed at the flank of a possible Soviet advance into Manchuria and, therefore, a deterrent to a Soviet attack. Remembered well is the fact that a Japanese army moving from almost the same positions now occupied by the 2nd Infantry Division struck the Russian Army in the flank during the Russo-Japanese War of 1904-05 and defeated the first major Soviet effort to detach Manchuria from China. In this, China is following its ancient strategy of "using barbarians to fight barbarians".

Japan and the West buying time for China

In public statements, China often has urged the United States to rebuild its Air Force and Navy in the Pacific and Asia. During his visits to Japan and the United States in the Autumn of 1978, Teng Hsiao-ping proposed an outright China-US-Japan alliance against the USSR.

What can China hope to achieve by this bizarre reorientation of its foreign policy? Japanese journalists visiting Peking have been told that China hopes to use its new ties with Japan and the West to buy time until China can rectify the present military imbalance along the Soviet frontier. China's prospects of achieving such a goal depend, first and foremost, on avoidance of any more self-imposed economic disasters on the scale of the 1958-59 "Great Leap Forward" or the sort of socio-political turmoil that went on almost continuously from 1966 to 1977.

In the estimate of foreign oil company executives and engineers who have visited China in recent years, the Chinese industrial complex extending from Manchuria south to Shanghai has the same potential for an economic "takeoff" that Japanese industry had in the 1950s. If this is the case, China may be within striking distance of Chou En-lai's goal — attainment of great

power status by the year 2000. At that point the political and economic strategic power balance would begin to turn against the Soviet Union. How soon China could catch up in a military sense would depend upon what advances in military technology the USSR would make in the meantime. It is conceivable that China never would be able to catch up if forced to rely on its own resources. Large-scale help from Japan, the United States and Western Europe could change that situation dramatically.

Can the Soviet Union stake its presence in Asia and its future as a world power on the chance that China never will catch up, or that continued

political instability in Peking will enable the Soviets at some point to detach Sinkiang and Manchuria by subversion or political manoeuvre?

The reluctance of the Soviets to take decisive military action against China — even when deliberately baited by China as during the 1979 Chinese invasion of Vietnam — suggests that, so far, "wait and see" has prevailed over "action now" in the counsels of the Kremlin.

Working against prolonged Soviet delay are two major factors:
The slowing and possible decline in overall Russian population growth.
The danger that a crisis in Europe, the Middle East or within the Soviet Union itself might force a withdrawal of forces from the Chinese frontier and create a situation in which China could regain control over Mongolia, or directly threaten the Maritime Province. Just such an occurrence, in 1941, forced the Soviets to give up when they almost had complete control of Sinkiang. All of Siberia was detached from Moscow's control during the Russian

aircraft missiles.

3. Another serious problem is the lack of modern anti-submarine detection and attack capability. There is a strong need for an effective ASW aircraft such as this Lockheed P-3C Orion.

4. One of the top priorities in any Soviet invasion would be the destruction of the PLA-Air Force's airfields, all of which will have been carefully plotted by satellites. The Chinese have not yet begun any programme for hardening aircraft dispersal sites and the attrition is therefore likely to be high. The best answer to this is the British Aerospace Harrier whose unique capability fully meets the Chinese requirement. In its ground attack role it will be of great value, while its newly-appreciated counter-air capability will be a bonus.

long as China chooses to combine the ethnocentrism of its traditional "middle kingdom" attitudes with an ideology of world revolution its war machine will be regarded by all of its neighbours as a threat to their national independence. Freed from fear of Soviet invasion, China could dominate all of Southeast Asia and challenge India. Key observers in Japan[7] see such a development as a threat to Japan's vast economic interests in that region. Therein lies the potential for renewed Sino-Japanese and Sino-Indian rivalry and eventual hostility.

Short-term solutions to China's present military inferiority *vis a vis* the Soviet Union, therefore, contain the seeds of future troubles that could exceed those the short-term "solutions" are designed to prevent. There is a need for consultation among the United States, Japan and the leaders of military technology in Western Europe to work out a common policy that will protect China's legitimate interests, but not turn her loose in the world as a military monster.

Footnotes

1. Reported by a participant in the visit, Prof. Michael Y. M. Kau of Brown University, at the 31st Annual Meeting, Association for Asian Studies, Los Angeles, Calif., March 31, 1979.
2. Zbigniew Brezezinski, US Presidential Adviser on National Security Affairs, "Indochina Conflict Seen as 'Proxy War'", by Bernard Gwertzman, The New York *Times*, January 9, 1978, p A3.
3. *War Between Russia and China?*, by Harrison Salisbury, "Will the Soviets Attack China?", *America*, May 15, 1976; "The Dragon and the Bear: Asian Perceptions of a Sino-Soviet War", *America*, September 24, 1977.
4. Russian apprehensions relative to the "unequal treaties" issue are further reinforced by the example of the Vietnam experience. As reported by Nayan Chanda in the March 16, 1979 *Far Eastern Economic Review*, China continues to regard the border with Vietnam as subject to change because it is based on "unequal treaties" imposed by France in 1887 and 1895. These remain "unequal" in Chinese eyes even though the Chinese and Vietnamese Communist governments agreed during negotiations in 1957-58, according to the Vietnamese, "to maintain the status quo of the frontier left by history". It is just such an interim solution that the Chinese have proposed to the Russians.
5. Principally that contained in "Chinese Strategic Missiles," Jane's Weapon Systems 1978, pp. 4-5.
6. "The Eighth Road to Moscow," *Armor*, November-December 1969, pp 51-55.
7. Interviews with senior foreign affairs and military editors of The Mainichi Shimbun and The Asahi Shimbun, Tokyo, 1975-78.

Revolution and Civil War, 1917-22.

In public, China's leaders continue to voice the belief that they will be permitted the time in which to catch up. In private, China's military leadership is more pessimistic. China's actions in the diplomatic sphere reflect pessimism rather than optimism. The gamble in Vietnam, as Professor Hinton has stated earlier, may have been taken "in the hope of galvanizing the United States and others into taking a strong anti-Soviet stand". China succeeded in devastating Vietnam's border provinces, but the end result was that the Soviet noose grew tighter with the arrival of Russian warships in Cam Ranh Bay.

Japan and the West can hasten the day when China will be a match and more than a match for Soviet military power in Asia. But, in so doing, they will heighten Russian fears and possibly trigger the very attack they seek to avert. The United States, in cooperation with its allies, possesses the power to protect China against attack while discouraging her from a military buildup that would divert resources from social and economic development and, in the long term, possibly threaten Japan and the United States.

During his visit to Southeast Asia in 1978, Teng Hsiao-ping avoided any commitment to withdraw support from pro-Peking Communist insurgents. So

INDEX

PICTURE CREDITS

The publishers would like to thank wholeheartedly all the organizations, agencies, companies and the many individuals who have scoured their collections and so helped us to illustrate this book in the best manner possible.

Most of the photographs published in this book were obtained with the help of the People's Republic of China Military, Naval and Air Attache in London, and by Hsinhua New China News Agency, and by other Chinese sources. Other photographs were supplied by the following (page number followed by picture number on that page):

Eugene Kolesnik: 10-11, 40/1, 152/2, 153/3, 164/1, 165/3.
US Govt: 21/3, 21/5, 24/1, 31/3, 32/1, 32/2, 32/3, 36-37, 43/2, 44/1, 44/2, 44/3, 52/2, 52/3, 53/4, 55/3, 58/1, 59/2, 61/7, 167/4.
US Naval Institute: 38/1, 150/1, 151/3, 154/1, 159/4. **MacClancy Press:** 27/3, 42/1. **British Dept. of Trade:** 63/3. **Novosti:** 144/3, 176/1, 176/3, 176/4, 178/2, 179/3. **Interconnair:** 172/1. **Swedish Government:** 176/2. **International Defence Review:** 179/1. **Fairchild Republic:** 180/1. **MBB:** 180/2. **Lockheed:** 181/3. **British Ministry of Defence:** 181/4.

PRINTED IN BELGIUM BY
proost
INTERNATIONAL BOOK PRODUCTION